Computer Supported Cooperative Work

Springer

London
Berlin
Heidelberg
New York
Barcelona
Hong Kong
Milan
Paris
Singapore
Tokyo

Also in this series

Elayne Coakes, Dianne Willis and
Raymond Lloyd-Jones (Eds)

The New SocioTech

Graffiti on the Long Wall

Westminster Business School, University of Westminster, 35 Marylebone Road, London NW1 5LS, UK

Diane Willis, BSc, MA, PGCE, AMBCS
Information and Communication Technology Section, Doncaster College, Waterdale, Doncaster DN1 3EX, UK

Raymond Lloyd-Jones, MA, FIPD, CMC
Careers Plus - Gyrfâu a Mwy, St David's Building, Daniel Owen Square, Mold, Flintshire CH7 1DD, UK

Series Editors
Dan Diaper, PhD, MBCS
Head, Department of Computing,
School of Design, Engineering and Computing, Bournemouth University, Talbot Campus, Fern Barrow, Poole, Dorset BH12 5BB, UK

Colston Sanger
Shottersley Research Limited, Little Shottersley, Farnham Lane, Haslemere, Surrey GU27 1HA, UK

ISBN 1-85233-040-6 Springer-Verlag London Berlin Heidelberg

British Library Cataloguing in Publication Data
The new SocioTech : graffiti on the long wall. – (Computer
  supported cooperative work)
  1. Organizational change 2. Technology – Social aspects
  I. Coakes, Elayne II. Willis, Dianne III. Lloyd-Jones, Raymond
  658.4'06
ISBN 1852330406

Library of Congress Cataloging-in-Publication Data
The new Sociotech : graffiti on the long wall / Elayne Coakes, Dianne Willis, and
  Raymond Lloyd-Jones (eds.).
     p. cm. – (Computer supported cooperative work)
  ISBN 1-85233-040-6 (alk. paper)
  1. Information technology-Social aspects. I. Coakes, Elayne, 1950- II. Willis, Dianne,
  1952- III. Lloyd-Jones, Raymond, 1949- IV. Series.
  T58.5 N49 2000
  303.48'34-dc21
                                                                    99-050084

Typesetting by EXPO Holdings, Malaysia
Printed and bound at The Athenæum Press Ltd., Gateshead, Tyne & Wear
34/3830-543210 Printed on acid-free paper SPIN 10680519

Contents

List of Contributors

Manju K. Ahuja
Information and Management Sciences, College of Business, Florida
State University
Tallahassee, FL 32306-110, UK
mahuja@cob.fsu.edu

Eliat Aram
University of Hertfordshire, College Lane, Hatfield, Herts AL10 9AB,
UK
Cm-centre@herts.ac.uk

Stefan Berndes
Lehrstuhl Technikphilosophie Fakultat 1, Brandenburgische
Technische Universitat, Cottbus, Postfach 101344, 03013 Cottbus,
Germany
Berndes@tu-cottbus.de

Steve Clarke
The University of Luton, Department of Systems and Operations
Management, Park Square, Luton, LU1 3JU, UK
Steve.Clarke@Luton.ac.uk

Elayne Coakes
Westminster Business School, University of Westminster, 35
Marylebone Road, London NW1 8LS, UK
Coakese@wmin.ac.uk

Tony Cornford
Department of Information Systems, London School of Economics,
Houghton Street, London, WC2A 2AE, UK
t.cornford@lse.ac.uk

Andrew Dillon
HCI Lab, SLIS, 10th and Jordan, Indiana University, Bloomington IN
47405, USA
adillon@indiana.edu

Frans M. van Eijnatten
Institute for Business Engineering and Technology Application,
Faculty of Technology Management, Eindhoven University of
Technology, TUE/TM, Pav.U10-T&A, P.O.-Box 513, 5600MB
Eindhoven, The Netherlands
F.M.v.Eijnatten@tm.tue.nl

Kay Fielden
Institute of Information and Mathematical Sciences, Massey
University at Albany, Private Bag 102 904, NSMC Auckland,
New Zealand
k.fielden@massey.ac.nz

Richard T. Grenci
University Of Virginia, Mcintire School Of Commerce,
Charlottesville, VA 22903, USA
Grenci@Virginia.edu

E.C. Lieke Hoogerwerf
Nijmegen Business School, Faculty of Policy Sciences, Catholic
University of Nijmegen, KUN/FBW, Thomas van Aquinostraat 1,
P.O.-Box 9108, 6500 HK Nijmegen, The Netherlands
L.Hoogerwerf@bw.kun.nl

Brian Hopkins
University of East Anglia, Norwich NR4 7TJ, UK
j.b.hopkins@anglia.ac.uk

Annette Karseras
The SOLAR Centre, Nene – University College, Moulton Park,
Northampton,
NN2 7AL, UK
annette.karseras@northampton.ac.uk

C. Bruce Kavan
University of North Florida, College of Business Administration,
4567 St Johns Bluff Road South, Jacksonville FL 32224-2645, USA
Bkavan@unf.edu

Frank Land
flandlse@aol.com

Brian Lehaney
The University of Luton, Department of Systems and Operations
Management, Park Square, Luton, LU1 3JU, UK
Brian.Lehaney@Luton.ac.uk

Angela Lin
Department of Information Systems, London School of Economics,
Houghton Street, London, WC2A 2AE, UK

Raymond Lloyd-Jones
Careers Plus – Gyrfâu a Mwy, St David's Building, Daniel Owen
Square, Mold, Flintshire, CH7 1DD, UK
admin@careersplus.co.uk

Uwe Lünstroth
Lehrstuhl Technikphilosophie Fakultat 1, Brandenburgische
Technische Universitat, Cottbus, Postfach 101344, 03013 Cottbus,
Germany

Enid Mumford
Em@enid.u-net.com

Bjørn Erik Munkvold
Agder College, Department of Information Systems, Postuttak,
4604 Kristiansand, Norway
Bjorn.E.Munkvold@hia.no

John Nicholls
John.nicholls@comlab.ox.ac.uk

Markku I. Nurminen
University of Turku, Department of computer Science,
Lemminkaisenkatu 14 A
20520 Turku, Finland
Nurminen@cs.utu.fi

Margaret T. O'Hara
East Carolina University, Greenville NC, USA
mohara@mindspring.com

Sajda Qureshi
Department of Information and Decision Sciences, Rotterdam School
of Management
Erasmus University Rotterdam, Burg. Oudlaan 50, PO Box 1738,
The Netherlands
squreshi@fac.fbk.eur.nl

David Sutton
System Six Ltd, PO Box 107, Macclesfield, Cheshire, SK11 9SX, UK
Scsutton@systemsix.co.uk

David Tuffley
School of Computing and IT, Griffith University, Nathan, Qld 4111,
Australia
d.tuffley@cit.gu.edu.au

Antti K. Tuomisto
University of Turku, Department of computer Science,
Lemminkaisenkatu 14 A, 20520 Turku, Finland
Atuomist@cs.utu.fi

Doug Vogel
Department of Information Systems, City University of Hong Kong,
Tat Chee Avenue, Hong Kong
isdoug@is.cityu.edu.hk

Leoni Warne
DSTO C3 research Centre, Department of Defence Act 2601,
Australia
Leoni.warne@dsto.defence.gov.au

Richard T. Watson
The University of Georgia, College of Business Administration,
Brooks Hall, Athens GA 31602, USA
rwatson@uga.edu

Dianne Willis
Information and Communication Technology Section, Doncaster
College, Waterdale, Doncaster, South Yorkshire, DN1 3EX, UK
Bd.willis@zetnet.co.uk

Foreword

The beginning of the new millennium is a time to celebrate two more anniversaries. The year 2001 will mark the 50th anniversary of the publication by Trist and Bamforth of an account of the historic study and analysis of the National Coal Board's attempt to introduce long wall mining technology to the UK's coal mines. The study was the precursor to what became known as the socio-technical approach to industrial change and organisation. Although the value of the socio-technical approach received widespread recognition, and many derivative approaches were developed, the actual application of these in organisations has been limited.

The second 50th anniversary falling in 2001 is that of the world's first computer application, the use of by J. Lyons, the British food and catering company, of their LEO computer to a business problem: the valuation of the output of their many bakeries. In those 50 years information technology has transformed the way organisations administer and carry out their work. Despite the undoubted impact of the use of information technology, there is a widespread feeling that too many new systems fail or at least fail to deliver the expected benefits.

These two anniversaries make it opportune to review where we are today in relation to the ideas and values formulated by the pioneers 50 years ago, and how these ideas have impinged and affected the major enabler of change today, the application of information technology. This book, edited by Elayne Coakes, Dianne Willis and Raymond Lloyd-Jones under the auspices of the British Computer Society's Socio-technical Group, has contributors from many countries. It tries to answer some of the questions: How far have the ideas and definitions of the pioneers been accepted as part of the common language related to organisational change? To what extent have those ideas and methodologies been modified in the light of experience and of alternative world views? How far have the ideas, methods and values been assimilated by other methods, such as BPR or TQM? How relevant are the original ideas and their derivatives applicable to the changing world of global economics in a networked world? Are there new ideas related to those of the socio-technical concepts of the pioneers now being proclaimed and will they overcome the problems of acceptance faced by the older approaches?

The book takes on the concepts developed half a century ago when the analysts of the Tavistock Institute searched for reasons why the new long wall technology failed to deliver the hoped-for productivity gains. In doing so it delivers far more than mere graffiti on the long wall.

This book is dedicated to the pioneers both of 50 years ago who recognised the possibilities of information technology to change the world of the organisation, and those who developed this idea that organisational change and values were linked – that effective change required that human values should be regarded as a vital ingredient in the change process.

Frank Land
Ivybridge, September 1999

Part 1
Tracing the Foundations

Chapter **1**

Graffiti on the Long Wall: A SocioTechnical Conversation

Elayne Coakes, Dianne Willis and Raymond Lloyd-Jones

During one of our many editing meetings we decided to record a conversation which would form our introduction to the book. What follows is a transcript of our conversation which we believe is in keeping with the spirit of what is discussed in the following chapters.

E = Elayne
R = Raymond
D = Dianne

E: Why "Graffiti on the Long Wall"?

R: Well, I think it's partly linked to the fact that we tried to convey a new perspectives on something that has been around for half a century. Perhaps more importantly it reflects the diversity, freshness andquestioning in the various chapters we have received from around the world.

E: And the "Long Wall" in the title refers to the original coal mining studies of the 1940s which led to the development of the sociotechnical approach to work and organisation. A key element of the Long Wall method was, of course, autonomous work groups using technology in an effective way.

R: Yes, and it's been important to us not to lose sight of these fundamental aspects or principles. But at the same time we've become conscious of new approaches that did not call themselves sociotechnical yet clearly embodied these principles.

E: So the "Graffiti on the Long Wall" was a way of describing in a metaphor, the enduring and robust roots of the principles whilst showing the new ideas overlaid.

R: New things to say about these enduring ideas and principles in a lively and sometimes novel way.

E: But what about the "The New SocioTech"?

D: Or Socio-technology as it is more usually called – is it important that we discuss the form of the word, whether it's hyphenated, or the different acronyms that it has? Does that make any difference to the subject? Is perhaps the way it is expressed a product of different cultures? Do different cultures

3

perceive sociotech in a different way and have a slightly different acronym or way of expressing sociotechnical ideas?

E: I think one of the most interesting things to emerge is that the concept of sociotechnical seems to be a lot broader than the history, and the historical definition, would imply. I think the book and the chapters that have been submitted for the book show that the concept is very relevant now but is not necessarily what people understand, and that's why perhaps some say that sociotechnical is no more. They're not seeing the "the sociotechnical" in the current way in which people are working and yet our authors show it's there. Look at the chapters by Mumford, Clarke and Lehaney, Eijnatten, and Sutton who are re-interpreting the traditional views in the light of current society.

R: I wonder if that's because we focused on the "the sociotechnical" in the area of computer systems rather than more traditional views. One traditional sociotechnical setting is in manufacturing, in a manual labour, product context rather than the so-called information age, information economy, information society. Is it perhaps that?

D: I don't know. Manufacturing industries are in decline and it is the information-based industries that are expanding now. So if sociotech is going to move forward and be important it has to be part of those new systems.

E: But it is inherently part of those systems. It's just that there has been an expectation or an understanding that it is related to the manufacturing base.

R: And not, maybe, something that is more oriented towards the age of information and communications technology.

E: The chapter by Munkfold shows this quite clearly when he looks at business process re-engineering and change processes. He looks at organisational change processes and says, "But this is the same as sociotech by another name, the elements are still there". It's just that we've called them something else. We're still using the same principles in many cases even though this may not be widely acknowledged.

R: Yes, that's an interesting point. Coming back to Dianne's question, does it matter what we call it? I think there's still a lingering question where chapters use these different terms. It may be due to different cultures or the ways authors have been immersed in sociotechnical ideas, thinking or practices. But it may also be some lack of clarity about what we mean by sociotechnical. For example, one of the issues in my mind is this use of the word "systems". Sometimes it's used in a general sense when talking about something which is all-encompassing, and others when referring to an information system which is a very specific type of system. So that's just one element of where I think perhaps this book will promote debate and discussion to create a clearer and a more modern understanding of sociotechnical.

E: I think books in the past and currently as well, are very unclear on definitions of terms. There is a great deal of confusion in books as to what is a system, what's information, what's a computer information system. And there are "Americanisms" and "Englishisms" and definitions and arguments as to what these things might mean. And I think the whole area is rife with these differences in terminology.

R: Of course, but does it matter?

D: The authors seem to be using the different terms in a fairly similar way in the book. Although they're calling sociotechnical by different names, I think they mean the same thing. S-T, STS, STST are all sociotechnical aspects of a particular organisation or a particular concern that they're looking at.

R: Oh, right, yes. To me, it's a fascinating part of the subject because there are these different ways of expressing and thinking of it. But is that not a bit of a hindrance to getting the whole idea of sociotechnical to reach a wider audience or to make it more receptive? And is that one of the barriers, where people say, well what is this sociotech? Is it a design methodology, is it a way of describing the way you go about a project? Is it just a philosophy? Sutton's chapter raises that question very explicitly and it's put forward in some other chapters too.

E: I think it is a problem in the way that you can't have a guru for sociotech because people don't understand it, in the way you have the guru Michael Hammer for BPR. It was easy for him to write about BPR and explain it in a very short article, and say, this is what BPR is about and I can show you. You can't say that so clearly for sociotech and it's therefore less easy to put it over.

R: Do you think so? I would argue just the opposite because there's a long history of sociotech. It's been going for 50 years or so. There's a lot been written about it and there are lots of case studies and examples, though not necessarily in the area of CSCW. Grenci and Munkvold suggest that BPR was a very thinly veiled way of selling computer technology which totally ignored the social, people and organisational aspects initially.

D: I also think that BPR is easier to dismiss because it is such a narrow, condensed, tight thing and it doesn't work very well. Whereas sociotech is so broad and it spreads into so many different areas. I think it's a much more important concept.

E: It's a much more all-encompassing concept. It's becoming more apparent that it's needed when one looks at virtual organisations that are now supported by information and communications technology. The semi-autonomous work group seems to be the way in which virtual organisations are developing. This kind of organisational model demands a perspective that asks questions like: "how do people work together, how do people organise themselves, how can technology support this?" The chapters by Aram, Qureshi, Ahuja, Karseras and Nurminen all support that view.

D: And look at where it's successful and where it's less successful.

E: And how technology can support different work types and different cultures … there's at least two of the chapters which discuss the attitudes of work such as the chapter by Berndes looking at attitudes in Germany, and Warne's work with the Australian Defence Force.

R: Yes, that's interesting. It comes across as a much more integrated or holistic overall approach than perhaps is conveyed by the name, which still tends to characterise it as social and technical.

E: Yes, it implies a dichotomy that in fact isn't there.

R: Exactly. So again we've raised this question about terminology. Should we try and call it something else? It's difficult to call something which has got roots and a tradition by another name. Curiously a lot of authors responded to our Call for Contributions to the book even though sociotechnical terms didn't appear in some of their earlier drafts. They understand it but don't use the terms. On the other hand, a lot of people seem to be using the term but don't actually have the understanding to apply a holistic approach. In practice we seem to end up either ignoring the practical realities, saying "it's got to be very human oriented" or being totally driven in a functionalist, instrumental way by technology. I think that sociotechnical is still being cast largely in technological terms.

D: No, I think it's probably become more unclear because we've got an international perspective and these people are seeing it differently in different countries. We unfortunately haven't got many Asian or African experiences, which I think would have helped to give us a global picture of what sociotech is. I think they've gone a long way in their interpretation. I do wonder if countries where sociotechnical hasn't got such defined roots, like Australia and New Zealand, then perhaps their interpretation is much looser because they're more removed from it.

E: It has very strong roots in Europe of course and we see this quite clearly from the participative design schools that come out of Scandinavia in particular, and participative design and sociotechnical have very close links. Yet it's easier to talk about participative design and to understand what you mean by it than to talk about sociotechnical. The chapters by Dillon, Fielden and Tuffley all illustrate this.

R: It's also easier to talk about it than actually do it in practice. I think there's still a lot to explore within the principles of sociotech. How the actual underlying principles are enacted in organisations or in the design of a social system or a technical system is elusive I think. For example, what do we mean by design? Is it something you can actually say (a), (b), (c), (d) and then implement in stages? In practice it's much more of an emergent process not something which is a step change from one phase to another, from one activity to another. It is a swirl of activities which are all linked in a very dynamic way.

D: I think John Nicholls makes a very interesting point talking about design saying, we know who designed our knives and forks. We know who designed all sorts of things. We've no idea who's designed the software we use. Does that mean it's less important? Are people less skilled? Is it just something that no-one's interested in or would we all like to know who designed what we're using? Then we might just be able to say to them, this doesn't work.

E: Put a name to the face.

D: Rather than being faceless, should we have names? Should we know who's responsible?

E: One would have thought that if people were truly proud of their work that they had designed, they would wish to be associated with it in the way that architects are associated with their buildings and painters are associated with their paintings and so on. If computer software engineers are truly proud of their design then why shouldn't they wish to be associated with it? The fact that they don't wish to be associated makes one question whether they are proud of their work, whether they feel their work is designed and does the job that it was required to do.

R: That's a really interesting question because if we're not just talking about a bit of technology but about the intertwining of human, organisational, technical and other facets, then might a manager feel proud of the organisation he or she has helped to create? What is the bottom line? When is this going to get done? How are we going to organise? Very necessary considerations which are driven by time and resource constraints. Richard Grenci addresses this aspect by clearly linking sociotechnical ideas with the economic dimension which managers are concerned with.

E: What's also interesting is that very rarely have people looked at the way in which people are working and designed the organisation around that with the supporting technology. It tends to be, here's the organisation, we'll set up this chart, we'll set up this hierarchy. Here's the networking infrastructure, the technology infrastructure, now get down to it and work. And people work round what is existing rather than building technology into the way in which people work.

D: Don't you think to some extent the intranet is an example of that? Where people are actually building things to assist their work on top of the existing network topologies? It's something else they're putting in.

E: I think there are emerging technologies, the intranet being one of them, and some of these virtual communities that are being supported by e-mail are others. And the way in which we've actually created the book has been a way of using technology on top of anything else and making it fit our needs.

D: As far as the book is concerned, without the enabling technology, we wouldn't really have been able to get the international aspect in the timeframe that we had. From that point of view it's been excellent. But it hasn't all been plain sailing, has it?

E: There have been some interesting highlights!

R: I suppose it's been driven by our wanting to be proud of something at a very high level.

E: It's also important that one of the things that I particularly wanted to show was that sociotech didn't need to be revived, it actually was there and actively being used but that perhaps people weren't recognising it and that it is more pervasive than just the West Europeans with their participative designs and democratic trade unions that seem to have driven it. It's there in other countries and is being used, but perhaps is not recognised under the same terminology.

R: I agree with that. I spent a lot of the early part of my career in a part of an organisation which was providing technological means of communication to enable people to get on with their work. The emphasis there was always on the work first and what people had to do, and the technology was then driven by that. This particular organisation had the resources and all the capabilities to be able to do that. I've grown up with that emphasis, technology purely as an enabler and something to help you...just like a knife and fork that you mentioned earlier enables you to eat in a more efficient way than with your fingers. But eating is primarily what you want to do. I then moved on to a company which basically integrated technological things. This gave me a completely new perspective because there it was very much, we have the technology, how can we fit it to your organisation? In fact I first learnt the term sociotechnical whilst being with that company. But the first name I came into contact with was CSCW. I went along to the inaugural meeting because the flier talked about people trying to work and communicate across distance which I've grown up with. It was only after that I heard the term sociotechnical. It's been fascinating to come to a name from something which I've lived with for many years and strongly believe in. Throughout much of my career there seemed to be an implicit requirement to be "technical". You got rewarded for being technical and it's only in the nineties that I've come to realise that technical can mean lots of different things. Chapters like the one by Hopkins that talk about education are actually addressing that issue. If we're perpetuating a view of sociotech which is rooted largely in the technical, if people are being awarded degrees for courses which pay lip service to a holistic approach, then aren't we encouraging people to think it's valuable? This again brings us back to meaning and terms.

Elayne, how have you come to this book?

E: Well I guess I came to computing from social science anyway so my views on computing were always coloured by the fact that I always thought of technology as a tool to help me in what I wanted to do. I was never into computer science. I only wanted to know how computers could help me do what I wanted to do. Here's the job I need to do, what can I use to help me do this job better? Here's the way I want to work. And I also have a very ethical and moral standpoint based on my own personal beliefs that we should determine our own lives. That includes in the workplace and the way in which we work as well as any other aspects of our life. So participative design and sociotechnical has always appealed on these ethical issues. I'm also very interested in looking at things holistically (again this comes from my background) and knowledge management, an area that I am currently investigating and researching. I see that they're very closely linked to sociotechnical because what I see is an emergent culture where technology is being used by semi-autonomous workgroups and developed to work the way they wish to work and it's become very much the enabler of these new ways of disseminating knowledge and increasing knowledge. We are constantly battling with the technologists who want to put it all into large databases and call it knowledge. And there is the same dichotomy there between computer scientists and information systems people, that is and that is not the reality. Knowledge is emergent, knowledge is implicit. You cannot always make it explicit. And technology is there as something that can support and be utilised. We see people making technology work the way they want it to work, deliberately or unconsciously. Right from the first computer system that was ever put into place, people changed it if they were unhappy with the way in which it worked. Either they didn't use it at all, or they used it for a different purpose. Now people still do the same except perhaps with less malice than before.

R: The social motive in organisations is groups of people working together. So you're saying that the driving force should be, does the technology match what they need to support what they're trying to do? And working in groups, by implication, requires people to talk to each other as much as anything. Whether it's using e-mail, the telephone, some other technology or even face to face, it still involves talking. Everything involves talking to each other. It's a dialogue, it's a conversation – ongoing, and dynamic. The technology to support these dialogues/conversations/ongoing exchanges of information and communication requires an approach which is very different from engineering. It requires a new metaphor and I think that comes back to this term sociotechnical. One of the challenges may be to re-cast it and perhaps this book will help in some small way to say, look, there are different hues to this thing called sociotechnology and it's a much broader thing. Sociotechnology still tends to be seen as a means to an end. But in a group there are lots of different ends, and there's all kinds of dynamic organisational things which are often not being addressed.

E: I think the other issue, and it's something that Grenci brought out, is "where is the bottom line?" Because we don't think about it in bottom line terms. We're thinking about it in ethical terms. I think we come back to why did BPR take off? BPR took off because there was a bottom line that organisational owners could say, here I'm going to make more profit, save money, save costs etc., etc. It appealed because there was a bottom line. In sociotechnical, it is very much more difficult to prove this bottom line and that's why so very often sociotechnical consultations have worked, and worked extremely well in organisations but have not been repeated because, although they saw that they worked at the time, they looked at the costs again and said, well I can't see a profit – the accountant mentality came in. It might have worked and everyone might have been very happy but that's not what I can count.

Where did you come from into sociotech, Dianne?

D: Like you Elayne, I came from a sociological background and my experience has always been that there's never been the technology available to be the tool that I wanted. I was always very interested in the actual technology of computing, the bits and the building and the putting of stuff together. I've worked for public sector organisations and the experience there has always been that technology and spending on technology was last on the list. You could never get hold of the technology you wanted. It was almost very much the opposite experience to yours Raymond, where you'd always had the technology to support it. My experience hasn't really changed because, even now I'm in the education world, I still find it an uphill battle to get the tools that I actually want. I'm very interested in international projects and working across boundaries and across cultures. I've always wanted something like e-mail to enable me to talk to people, discuss things, exchange ideas and it's only recently that I've had this facility. So I've always felt that the technology's been lacking rather than the technology's been driving where I've been. That's due to my own particular experiences obviously. I thought the book was an ideal opportunity to just sort of test this out and see if people can work collaboratively over a distance, different time zones. The material that we've had has come from a wide range of sources and, from that point of view, the book to me has been a great success in that it has enabled this to happen and I've finally been able to achieve one of my real aims in life which is to work on something internationally in a collaborative way. So, the sociotechnical angle? I think I probably come at it slightly differently because I've always had this negative experience where the technology's not there when I want it. It's always been the other way round, it's been people trying to get the technology to support the way in which they work. I could never actually define the boundaries of sociotech myself, because I could see all sorts of ways in which it could develop and be part of working life and I could never quite work out which little square was sociotech and I've been really pleased by the book to discover that other people don't see it as a defined but as a very wide-ranging and pervasive thing.

R: That's interesting.

E: Yes, the way that we set out to do the book has been a sociotechnical way in that we started by having three editors who live at three very distant points of the United Kingdom and whose major means of communication had to be technical because of lifestyles and lack of opportunities to meet in the flesh.

D: Even the telephone. It's not that easy with the way we work, we work evenings and it's not even that easy to ring up people to talk to them.

E: So we've had to support the editorial process very much through an e-mail system. The way we garnered our authors was through an international electronic mailing list. The vast majority came from a call into the blue. Hey, anybody out there interested?

R: Yes. And that was the Call for Contributions. Because we spent quite a lot of effort on producing it we were able to convey this idea that we weren't just after chapters containing the term sociotechnical as long as other people could recognise the elements. I think it's been an interesting collaborative exercise as well. But perhaps more important than that is the approach. We've tried to encourage people to take a much broader view and not to say we want (a) on this topic, (b) on this topic…to make it very structured. We've tried to enable the book to emerge. We keep reminding ourselves that, even over something like the title of the book, we want it to be drawn from what's in the book rather than being firm on the title and then fitting things to that title.

D: The development I would really like to see from here now is that the contributors can all be in contact with each other and build up a relationship/knowledge base and then sort of ripple it out so that they can involve people that they know who are interested in the subject.

E: I would like this now to become a virtual community, a virtual sociotechnical community and perhaps, from here, the authors and their colleagues can set up some kind of mechanism of exchanging information. Hopefully, if we get a conference going next year, that will be a start to send maybe articles, maybe discussions and actually make the working group that we work with in Britain communicate and link with other organisations externally. And also, it will help to clarify in a lot of people's minds that, although they call sociotech different things, it is the same principles they are looking at.

R: I come back to this thinking about this moving on thing.

D: But the moving on I think is part of the way that it's actually used, rather than changing the original idea.

E: Yes, the ethical principles, the moral principles are still there. They are the grounding, the heart. It's where we come from… How we change it, is very much the debate for how organisations might work.

R: Yes, at least we are offering this as a way of thinking about how they're going to use the technology to serve their needs. I agree with you, Elayne, that work needs must ultimately be grounded in not just the organisational needs, but in the needs of individuals as part of their own lives. I think that's a balance that's gone away, certainly in the last ten or fifteen years where work seems to be the centre of things and society is increasingly complex. I think sociotechnical offers a way of encompassing or even just recognising that we're not in a simple world, if we ever were in a simple world. Look at the chapter by Lin and Cornford for instance.

D: O'Hara talks about there being almost no alpha level change left. It's all far more complicated than that. We've progressed beyond the simple automation stage and we're now into looking at complex change.

R: And it's not predictable any more. Technology as we all seem to agree is an enabler. It's a way of helping you to do things, it's not the thing that should structure what has to be done.

E: Yes, first decide what you want to do and how you want to do it and then decide whether technology would help you in any way, shape or form.

D: Even with our reasonably successful story with the technology, we have little instances where we've trusted the technology to work and it hasn't. And it's not notified us it hasn't either. Some of the reviews didn't actually get to the authors, they went as attachments and never arrived. So, where are they?

E: The interesting way in which different e-mail systems fail to communicate with each other. Where you send something as an attachment from one e-mail system, it arrives at the other e-mail system then pulls the attachment in and then opens it up, but opens it up as garbage.

D: I have some experience of this. You try to decode it and it says it can't and then what do you do? You've got a load of gibberish, but it's meaningful to the person who's sent it you and you really need to look at it so where do you go from there? Was it Dillon who said, how do I cope in a Mac environment? I send it, it doesn't bounce and I presume it's arrived. And then they say, we haven't heard from you. What's happening.

E: And of course there are the issues about who reads their e-mail and how often. Why should we assume that people will read e-mails? It goes all the way back to the Call for Contributions doesn't it? Sending it that way requires people to read their e-mail regularly to pick it up by the deadline date.

R: But there is an assumption, a great assumption, that somebody will read it. To me communication is the acknowledgement.

D: The other issue I have is that we don't really know how many people are out there that really would like to contribute to this book that we never reached, that we never made any form of contact with at all.

R: That's a really good point, yes.

D: And maybe the book itself will help to generate interest with those people.

R: Exactly, and the forthcoming conference would be a beautiful follow-up because having done this using electronic means it would produce perhaps a new dimension of sociotechnical thinking. It would be a much richer environment to explore some of the issues that have been raised in the book. A lot of the lingering questions that surround it. For example, even if it's not called sociotechnical, are the principles useful to people in practice? Are they used? How are they used? Do they help to create better work situations, happier people, better social outcomes? And that, to me, is the most important thing and I think the conference would allow that.

D: We still won't reach everybody that we want to reach. We need to explore what other options we have.

R: That's true. But even if we reach another thirty people, or however many, that's a small step forward.

D: And I believe that the other really good thing about the book is it has got a lot of contentious issues in it. It's got points for debate that people can actually take away and consider and apply to their own organisations. And that in itself should generate more interest in the sociotechnical field.

R: Yes, let's hope so.

Chapter **2**

Tracing the Roots: The Influence of Socio-Technical Principles on Modern Organisational Change Practices

Bjørn Erik Munkvold

2.1 Introduction

The principles of socio-technical thinking have had a major impact on the practice related to the design of organisations and their technology for the last fifty years. The importance of mutual alignment of the social and technical systems in organisations, structuring of work in self-autonomous teams and participation of stakeholder groups in change activities is well acknowledged. However, relatively few organisational change projects today are run under the "socio-technical flag". Instead, new concepts and methodologies are being used as guiding principles for organisational change activities and the development of information systems. More commonly used labels for organisational change projects today are business process reengineering (BPR) and total quality management (TQM). Similarly, activities related to the design and development of information systems are now conducted under the headings of software engineering or participatory design.

In trying to answer these questions, this chapter compares the basic principles of some of the modern methodologies related to organisational design and the development and implementation of information systems (IS) with socio-technical principles and methodologies. This

> Does this mean that the socio-technical approach has become outdated and is now replaced by new methodologies that provide better guidelines for organisational change? Or, are these methodologies merely modern applications of the socio-technical principles?

comparison serves to illustrate how socio-technical principles can be seen as a foundation for much of the current practice related to organisational change and information systems development. The essential conclusion of this chapter is that those dealing with organisational change could benefit from returning to the socio-technical principles as the "roots" for their current practice and that these principles still have a lot to offer, especially as they relate to the implementation of change activities including empowerment and involvement of stakeholders.

The next section presents a broad overview of key principles of the socio-technical perspective as a basis for comparison with other methodologies. The subsequent section compares the socio-technical principles with two other methodologies related to organisational design, that is, BPR and TQM. This is followed by a similar comparison with current methodologies for IS development and implementation. The final section presents conclusions and implications and outlines further challenges and possibilities related to the application of socio-technical principles.

2.2 Socio-Technical Principles and Methodologies

As one of the most dominant paradigms for organisational design, the basic principles of socio-technical systems (STS) thinking today are "universally known". STS is often thought of as a unified concept with the focus on joint optimisation of the social and technical system and empowerment of workers as key tenets. However, as with any theory or paradigm, socio-technical systems thinking has undergone a major development since its origin in the 1950s and the early coal mine studies of the Tavistock Institute and the Norwegian industrial democracy project (Emery and Trist, 1960; Mumford, 1985). Eijnatten (1993) provides a comprehensive account of the development of the socio-technical perspective. He identifies different stages in this process and discusses how several variants of the perspectives have evolved in different areas of the world, for example in North America, Scandinavia, the United Kingdom and the Netherlands. These directions vary both in terms of scope and methods applied. As a result, the socio-technical perspective can now be characterised as a "pluralistic fabric" (Eijnatten, 1993).

However, rather than focusing on the variations of this perspective, I will only focus on some of the key principles of STS as a basis for comparison with other methodologies (see Table 2.1).

The goal according to the socio-technical perspective is to obtain joint optimisation of the technical and social systems in an organisation (Mumford, 1985). The social system comprises the attributes of people (attitudes, skills, values, etc.), the relationships among people, reward systems and authority structures, while the technical system includes the processes, tasks and technology needed to perform the organisation's operations (Bostrom and Heinen, 1977a). Optimisation of one of these systems at the expense of the other will only result in sub-optimal solutions. Thus, all organisational design processes should also focus on the quality of work life (QWL) of the employees. To achieve this goal, the socio-technical perspective puts a strong emphasis on participation by different stakeholders in the design process. It is believed that

Table 2.1. Key principles in STS

Joint optimisation of technical and social system

Quality of work life (QWL)

Participation

Semi-autonomous work groups

decisions regarding the specification of work are best made by those who actually perform the tasks. In accordance with this, semi-autonomous work groups are a central form of organisational unit in this perspective.

There are several different methodologies associated with the STS principles. Variance is a critical concept in STS analysis, referring to any deviation in a work process from some standard or norm which will affect the system performance or output.

An example of a socio-technical systems change model is that presented by Pasmore (1988). This is introduced as a methodology for socio-technical systems redesign consisting of nine major steps:

1. Define scope of system to be redesigned.
2. Determine environmental demands.
3. Create vision statement.
4. Educate organisational members.
5. Create change structure.
6. Conduct socio-technical analysis.
7. Formulate redesign proposals.
8. Implement recommended changes.
9. Evaluate changes/redesign.

This model assumes that the target system is already in existence and is being redesigned. Redesign situations are here seen to require greater preparation than new designs. However, the same steps could also be followed in new design processes. The model assumes the existence of a consultant who acts as a third party to labour-management discussions. The model is based upon a high involvement change strategy. The education of organisational members initiated in Step 4 continues throughout the process.

Related to the development of information systems the first applications of the socio-technical principles can be dated to the early 1970s. Bostrom and Heinen (1977a, 1977b) argue for the use of the STS perspective as a basis for more successful design of information systems. This involves making the systems designers' frames of reference explicit and focusing more on the inter-relationship between social and technical system, in the effort of arriving at a jointly optimised design. Their approach includes the following three stages:

1. *Strategic design process* – making the goals and responsibility of the project explicit (user focus);
2. *Socio-technical system design process* – joint consideration of technical system requirements and social system requirements;
3. *Ongoing management process (action research process)* – constant monitoring of the new system to see if it is meeting its goal, with necessary adjustments being made.

The last stage shows the implementation process as an iterative process, as new design is expected to indicate a need for further redesign.

The most influential work related to the use of STS principles in information systems development is that of Enid Mumford at the Manchester Business School. She has developed a methodology for systems development that represents an operationalisation of the STS principles, termed ETHICS (Effective Technical and Human Implementation of Computer Systems) (see Mumford, 1983a). This method consists of six steps, as follows (Hirschheim and Klein, 1994):

1. Essential systems analysis.
2. Socio-technical systems design.
3. Setting out alternative solutions.
4. Setting out compatible solutions.
5. Ranking socio-technical solutions.
6. Preparing a detailed work design.

ETHICS specifies the formation of two design teams focusing on the technical and social design. A facilitator is used for overcoming possible obstacles related to lack of trust, conflicts of interest, time pressures and stress, low morale, effects of authority, and communication gaps (Mumford, 1983a). Although focusing strongly on participation, ETHICS does not seek to increase the quality of work life at the expense of economic efficiency. Rather it seeks to achieve joint optimisation, building on the notion that increased QWL will also lead to increased quality and efficiency (Hirschheim & Klein, 1994).

Socio-technical systems design has been criticised on several aspects. First, the emphasis on balance and consensus has been seen to ignore the political conflicts in organisations (Bjerknes and Bratteteig, 1995). Also, it has been argued that the participative design specified according to this perspective will only function when employee numbers are small (Winfield, 1991).

Even though the importance of the socio-technical perspective is widely acknowledged, statements such as "the ghost of sociotechnical thinking is still with us" (Winfield, 1991) seem to indicate that STS has been buried in the "methodological graveyard". In this sense, the strong historic roots of the socio-technical perspective may actually work against

> Some critics maintain that the socio-technical approach has been "hijacked by conventional forces" and thus lost its status as a radical counterface to the Taylorist orthodoxy (Winfield, 1991).

itself. The socio-technical term has a certain "ancient ring" to it – who would hire a STS consultant today when there are BPR experts and TQM gurus available? There is also a frequent misconception that this perspective applies only to manufacturing processes, despite the many examples of how it has been applied successfully in white-collar work (Mumford, 1985, Eijnatten, 1993).

In the following sections it is argued that it is time to brush the (coal) dust off the STS perspective, and that its principles actually are very much alive through their influence on current methodologies.

2.3 Organisational Design

The last two decades have brought about an increasing focus on organisational change as a result of a set of changes in the operating environments of organisations: increasing global competition; deregulation of markets; increasing customer selectivity on price, quality and service; environmental protection issues; and rapid technological development, for example, the integration of information and telecommunication technologies (Scott-Morton, 1991). Based on this, it is argued that organisations need to restructure, to become more flexible and adaptive to these changing conditions. A plethora of new organisational forms has been suggested, such as virtual organisations and dynamic networks. However, a closer inspection of the different concepts reveals that there are some key characteristics common to these new forms (Munkvold, 1998):

- focus on business processes instead of the traditional functional organisation;
- focus on team organisation;
- decentralised decision-making;
- information technology as an important enabler of the new organisational forms.

The traditional hierarchical organisational structure is considered to be too rigid for today's dynamic environments and therefore needs to be replaced by a flatter structure built around business processes. Cross-functional teams are considered to be the most important organisational unit. Also implied is a decentralisation of decision-making and semi-autonomous teams. Information technology (IT) is regarded as an important enabler of these new organisational forms by supporting co-ordination and collaboration across geographical and organisational boundaries. Thus, rapid development in information and telecommunications technology plays a dual role in this restructuring, being both a factor contributing to the need for organisational change and an enabler of the new forms. Baskerville and Smithson (1995) argue that the frenzy related to these new terms sometimes results in too much emphasis on the role of IT in this organisational transformation, and a corresponding lack of focus on other important organisational factors such as power and authority structure.

The socio-technical perspective is seldom discussed explicitly in the literature on new organisational forms. Instead, new concepts and methodologies are presented. In the following sections, business process reengineering and total quality management are addressed in terms of their relationship to STS principles. These two methodologies have been dominating the area of organisational change over the last decade and are still considered as important methodologies for designing organisations for the next century (Bjørn-Andersen and Chatfield, 1996).

2.3.1 Business Process Re-engineering

Since its origin in 1990, BPR has become a dominating methodology for organisational design and continues to have considerable impact on practice. A business process is usually defined as "a set of logically related tasks performed to achieve a defined business outcome" (Davenport and Short, 1990, p. 12). reengineering is defined as "the fundamental rethinking and radical redesign of business processes to achieve dramatic improvements in critical contemporary measures of performance, such as cost, quality, service and speed" (Hammer and Champy, 1993, p. 32). The key principles for BPR are summarised in Table 2.2.

The concept of radical change is the most unique element of BPR. The new work processes are envisioned to be performed by cross-functional teams, thus empowering the process workers (Hammer and Champy, 1993). However, the extent to which empowerment is really compatible with other elements in the BPR methodology, such as strong leadership and top-down orientation, is the subject of much discussion (Jones, 1994). Finally, although there are examples of BPR projects being conducted without the introduction and use of some form of IT support, IT is usually regarded as an important enabler for realising redesigned business processes (for example through the use of workflow technologies).

In the following discussion BPR is treated as a single concept based on the principles listed in Table 2.2. A BPR approach is typically presented as comprising the following steps (Manganelli and Klein, 1994):

- *Preparation* – recognising the need, training the reengineering team, planning the change;
- *Identification* – mapping organisation and resources, process modelling, prioritising processes;
- *Vision* – measuring process performance, identifying improvement opportunities, defining required changes;
- *Solution (technical design and social design)* – designing the new processes, defining the need for technical and social resources;
- *Transformation* – implementing the process design, realising the process vision.

Built on a powerful rhetoric, BPR has been embraced by managers as a radically new perspective that breaks away from existing paradigms. However,

Table 2.2. Key principles in BPR

Process modelling
Radical change
Cross-functional, self-managed teams
Empowerment of workers
IT as process support

several authors have pointed out that BPR is really a synthesis of several existing concepts, such as management science, the quality movement and STS (!)

These roots are seldom acknowledged with the result that some of the important lessons from past experience seem to be lost.

Mumford (1995b) makes a strong point of this in her review of the Hammer and Champy "BPR bible", pointing to the many similarities between STS and BPR, and questioning why this is not acknowledged by the inventors of BPR. She concludes by stating that: "This book is an interesting if dangerous read. Managers persuaded by it to embark on the fundamental redesign of their organisations would be well advised to read the socio-technical literature as well, and with great care. This has a more powerful humanistic value position, a better theoretical base and a more precise methodology. Even more importantly, it has nearly fifty years of experience behind it." (p. 117).

"Part of the problem with re-engineering as it is classically understood is that it ignores much of what we have previously learned about the value of participative work design, at least for the details of a business process" (Davenport and Stoddard, 1994).

Comparing the steps in the BPR process as presented above with the socio-technical redesign process presented in the previous section, reveals striking similarity with the focus on (re)design of business processes, use of semi-autonomous teams, and empowerment. However, there are also differences between the approaches. While BPR advocates radical change, STS prescribes continuous change through monitoring external events. It is argued that the radical change approach in BPR actually may be a risky endeavour for an organisation, if this is taken to mean that one should completely substitute existing, well established practices by new, unfamiliar systems (Mumford, 1995b).

"Using BPR for organisational restructuring is like getting a haircut by setting your hair on fire, and putting out the fire by using a Hammer!" (King, 1995).

Although team building and empowerment is stated as a goal in the BPR perspective, this is to support business goals, rather than to improve the quality of work life (Mumford, 1995b). Argyris (1998) argues that while reengineering has led to improvements in performance, it has failed to produce the number of highly motivated employees needed to ensure consistently high-performing organisations.

A reengineering project in the Norwegian telecommunications company Telenor (formerly Norwegian Telecom) can serve to illustrate this point. To prepare for the deregulation of the European telecommunications market in 1998, the company underwent a major reengineering effort initiated in 1993. Under the term Project 98 (P98), a series of projects were conducted resulting in a restructuring of the company's operations into a set of key business processes. External consultants played a strong role by providing the methodology for process design. Although these methods are trademarked and presented as something "special" they can be seen as standard BPR approaches, comprising the following major steps: Process Visioning, As Is Description, To Be Design, Piloting, Implementation.

The initial stage of this project included interviews with 400 representatives from selected areas in the organisation. Together with the consultants, these representatives conducted two-hour brainstorming sessions, mapping strengths and weaknesses related to the existing organisation. The results from these sessions were made available in various meeting places, for comments from other employees. Thus, the project was presented as a bottom-up process with emphasis on the participation by "ordinary employees". However, all major decisions regarding the project were made by top management entirely and the reengineering effort focused solely on economic measures. Job enrichment or quality of work life was never part of the agenda.

As a result of the restructuring, over 4700 workers (so far, the process still continues) out of 18 000 became redundant. To handle this, Telenor introduced what was termed by the CEO as "the largest social experiment in Norway": the creation of a new, temporary division staffed by these surplus workers. Named "Telenor Nye Muligheter" (Telenor New Opportunities), this division originally was marketed as a golden opportunity for employees to get a "fresh start" through obtaining funding for developing new business ideas or taking further education. Although for some employees this became a positive experience (for example, this author received funding for his doctorate through this programme), most employees experienced this as a "transit camp" before finding a new position. An evaluation of the restructuring process conducted shows a large degree of discontent with the process, especially related to the information provided from their management and there have been several instances of psychological problems among the employees after the restructuring.

BPR in Practice? Dilbert © 1995 United Feature Syndicate, Inc.

It is easy to see how the conduct of this process conflicts with the principles of socio-technical design. Being run mainly as a top-down process, the employees in this organisation did not have real influence on decisions related to their work. This case also illustrates the question of how to facilitate participation in a large, distributed organisation. As stated by one of the project co-ordinators, "there is no way we could have invited all 18 000 employees to the drawing board".

However, while this may be true for the overall design, when it comes to specifying the detailed content of the new work processes it is recommended that this should include those impacted by the change (Davenport and Stoddard, 1994).

In general, the implementation of BPR has been found to have some major problems. For example, Hammer and Champy (1993) state that 70 per cent of reengineering efforts fail. A study by Grover *et al.* (1995) identifying and rating problems related to BPR implementation also found change management to be the key challenge in BPR projects. The BPR methodology has been criticised for being weak on the implementation side. This weakness is also supported by the Telenor case.

2.3.2 Total Quality Management

Total Quality Management can be traced back to the period after the Second World War and the work conducted in Japan by the quality "gurus", Deming, Juran and Ishikawa (Hackman and Wageman, 1995). However, it is only during the last decade that this principle really has gained significant acceptance among managers in Europe and the US. Key issues according to this principle are summarised in Table 2.3 (Hackman and Wageman, 1995; Bank 1992).

The TQM methodology focuses on establishing a system for obtaining quality in all customer-related processes. The notion of a customer is both internal and external. Since the quality of products and services is most dependent on the processes by which they are designed and produced, the primary focus is on these work processes (Bank, 1992). Cross-functional teams are central, being responsible for identifying and solving quality problems. Implied is a focus on involvement and empowerment with these teams being, to some extent self-managing.

Compared to BPR, the role of IT in TQM is more limited, the nature of change defined being characterised as focusing on learning and continuous improvement.

BPR and TQM have often been presented as irreconcilable perspectives. However, it can been argued that these should be seen as complementary approaches, where BPR activities are followed by periods of continuous improvement, followed by new reengineering efforts, and so on (Hammer, 1996; Kelada, 1996).

Table 2.3. Key principles in TQM

Customer focus
Focus on work processes
Use of cross-functional teams
Employee involvement
Self management
Analysis of variability
Benchmarking
Learning and continuous improvement

Several of the tenets in TQM can be seen as similar to STS principles, including the focus on work processes, use of autonomous, cross-functional teams, and the focus on employee involvement. However, the focus on empowerment in TQM can be seen to contrast with the strong focus on top-down implementation, leading to questions about the nature of this empowerment (Argyris, 1998; Hackman and Wageman, 1995).

2.3.3 Summary

Several similarities have been identified between key principles for organisational design in the STS perspective, and those in BPR and TQM. The main conclusions from this comparison can be summarised as follows:

- all three methodologies have a primary focus on work processes in the organisational analysis;
- cross-functional teams are the basic organisational units in the new organisational design;
- the change strategy applied differs, radical change is a key element in BPR, while both STS and TQM focus on continuous improvement.

All three perspectives emphasise employee involvement, although to a different extent. It is argued here that only the STS approach involves real empowerment of the workers, through its explicit focus on increasing the quality of work life, and establishing democratic work processes where employees have direct control over their work.

2.4 IS Development and Implementation

The development and implementation of information systems can be seen as a special form of organisational change activity. The mutual relationship between organisations and information technology makes this process socio-technical "by nature". However, as with the organisational change projects, few IS development projects today are explicitly related to the socio-technical perspective. A brief overview of current methodologies for IS development and implementation that have some links to the socio-technical perspective is provided below.

2.4.1 Systems Development Methodologies

IS development methodologies are largely dominated by a functionalist perspective; that is, how to produce functionally correct and efficient user requirements, as a basis for system specifications (Hirschheim and Klein, 1994). They argue that the modest success of this approach calls for a revised perspective based on neohumanist values. While the neohumanistic perspective will also include the aims specified in the functionalist perspective, in addition it introduces an emancipatory ideal placing strong value on quality of life and personal freedom. The ETHICS method described previously is the existing methodology that best meets these ideals. Hirschheim and Klein therefore suggest further development of this model through increased focus on self-reflection and improved methods for realising technical design objectives.

A strong influence from the socio-technical perspective can be found in the different forms of participatory design (PD) methodologies in Scandinavia. Bjerknes and Bratteteig (1995) provide a detailed historic account of the development of these methodologies. They identify several different directions, stemming from the trade union projects in the 1960s.

An example of a recent methodological development that has clear links to the socio-technical perspective is the MUST method for participatory design (MUST is a Danish acronym for theories of and methods for design activities), developed by researchers at Roskilde University in Denmark (Kensing, Simonsen and Bødker, 1998). This method is based on six principles:

1. Participation.
2. Close links to project management.
3. Design as a communication process.
4. Combining ethnography and intervention.
5. Co-development of IT, work organisation and users' qualifications.
6. Sustainability.

Further, the overall design process is constituted by five main activities: (a) project establishment; (b) strategic analysis; (c) in-depth analysis of selected work domains; (d) developing visions of the overall change; and (e) anchoring the visions.

The method is presented as different from other participatory design approaches in that it also includes management issues in relation to design processes in an organisational context, and also considers the relations between a design project and an organisation's business and IT strategies. The relationship of this model with the socio-technical approach is explicitly acknowledged by the developers of this method, especially related to the co-development of IT and work organisation (principle 5 above), and the inclusion of management issues in a participatory approach.

2.4.2 IS Implementation

The importance of the implementation process for successful use of the technology is well acknowledged. The key ingredient for this is the mutual alignment between technology and the adopting social system. For example, Leonard-Barton (1988) argues that technology implementation requires adaptive response in the form of "adaptive cycles", where the technology and/or the organisation are refined to reduce "misalignments", that is, mismatches between the technology and the organisation. Still, few IS implementation projects today make explicit the use of socio-technical principles at the implementation stage, such as that prescribed by Bostrom and Heinen (1977a) or the ETHICS method.

However, the STS perspective is also used as an analytic tool for understanding the technology implementation process. One example is the analysis of the implementation of a group support system in the World Bank in 1996. Here the apparent success of this implementation is ascribed to the "unusual degree of socio-technical balance", involving close collaboration between the organisational development department and the information technology department throughout the implementation process. The use of process and technical facilitators was found to be a critical element in the World Bank's socio-technical infrastructure (Bikson and Eveland, 1996).

2.5 Conclusion and Implications

This chapter has provided a brief discussion on the influence of socio-technical principles on current methodologies for organisational design and IS development. The conclusion from this discussion can be summarised by the following arguments:

- Modern management methodologies like BPR and TQM comprise several elements that build on socio-technical principles, such as the focus on business processes and the use of cross-functional, self-autonomous teams as basic organisational units.

- Many characteristics of the so-called new organisational forms can be seen as the implementation of socio-technical principles supported by new types of IT. However, excepting some participatory design methodologies, the inheritance from STS is seldom acknowledged explicitly.

- Current change practices like BPR often fall short when it comes to implementing the required changes.

- This can often be ascribed to a lack of focus on empowerment of employees, quality of work life and stakeholder involvement in these methodologies. These aspects are given strong emphasis in STS. It is therefore argued that the socio-technical perspective should regain its status as an important change methodology that constitutes a useful alternative to other methods.

2.5.1 Future Challenges and Possibilities

As described previously, the socio-technical perspective has been criticised both regarding its content and methods. Several authors have argued in favour

Pava (1986) suggests that STS design should be seen to offer "a way of viewing phenomena from a different angle, of enabling self-designed improvements to match organisations with their technology in a dynamic environment" (p. 219).

of revitalising the socio-technical perspective. The new organisational forms discussed in this paper imply changes in the forms of work. Flexible work arrangements such as virtual teamwork, telecommuting, inter-organisational teamwork and "hotelling" are now being implemented on an increasing scale. This results in increased worker responsibility and altered social relations in the workplace. Socio-technical principles can play an important role in the design of these new organisational forms – for example, in the process of developing the new routines and roles related to these work arrangements – as the questions related to the need for new reward policies and new roles for management related to virtual, self-autonomous teams and teleworking, are largely left unsolved by other methodologies.

Several of these organisational changes are enabled by emerging technologies, such as groupware and the Internet. These technologies can also be seen as important tools for increasing participation in the new organisational arrangements (Bjernknes and Bratteteig, 1995). The Telenor case illustrates some of the problems related to participation in restructuring projects in large, distributed organisations. By using technologies like videoconferencing, group support systems and electronic bulletin boards, it is possible to increase participation from members throughout the organisation. Even more important is the possibility for using this technology to create a dialogue among members at various levels of the organisation. This can also be transferred to broader contexts at the societal level. There are already examples of how new communication media like the Internet and the World Wide Web are being used by local government for supporting democracy, by making information available to the public and opening issues for comments and debate ("teledemocracy").

2.5.2 Challenge to Socio-technical Design

As new organisational forms develop, the principles and methodologies also have to be adapted and developed further.

Only through this can the socio-technical perspective regain and maintain its status as a change methodology that also applies to organisations in the next century. This can prove to be an important element in the development of sustainable organisational structures that meet both economic and social challenges in the future society.

Acknowledgements

I am grateful to Deepak Khazanchi for performing "variance control" on my English.

Part 2
The Writing on the Wall

Chapter **3**

*Technology and Freedom: A Socio-Technical Approach**

Enid Mumford

History is being made at the speed of light
Inside today's computers
Shaping our collective destiny
No records are kept
I am trying to save some of that experience
To ask where it may lead.

(Jacques Vallee, 1981)

3.1 Technical Progress

A paper which discusses technology and freedom must begin by defining its terms. Technology can be described as both an artefact and a process. It consists of tools that help men and women extend their abilities and knowledge, but it is also the generic knowledge and skill required to design a specific product or process. It covers both scientific discovery and industrial applications and, to be effective, it must include the flow of ideas between industry and the academic community. It must also be introduced and used in a manner that fits with the needs and hopes of society.

> Today, the development of computer technology proceeds at breakneck speed and the impact of technology spreads with frightening rapidity

Alvin Toffler tells us we must now actively move towards the telecommunity – the substitution of communication for transportation. In this brave new third wave world we will not suffer the hazards of constant travelling and we will never be lonely. Our friends, and enemies, will be with us at the touch of a button, or the wave of a finger or even the sending out of a thought wave. Everything we want to know will be immediately to hand and arrive in a variety of forms and, assisted by our computers, we will be able to be great artists, writers and poets, without the need for natural ability. (Toffler, 1980)

---

* This chapter is a shortened version of "Technology and Freedom: Hope or Reality", *Information Services and Use* 15 (1995), pp. 3–24, reproduced with kind permission by IOS Press, Amsterdam.

But will we be free? Will we enjoy life, will it give us what we want? Let us try and define this vague concept of "freedom". If we wish to have more of it then we must know what it is we are seeking and we must recognise that freedom can be defined in different ways. What is freedom to North Americans and Europeans may have no meaning for people who live in other parts of the world. For the poor and oppressed, freedom is not being hungry and not being killed. It is freedom "from" not freedom "for".

3.2 Ideas on Freedom

In America and Europe freedom has always been an important issue and something that liberal groups have striven to increase, but it has had many different meanings. In 1776 the American Declaration of Independence proclaimed the need for political equality and political freedom. In the preamble to the Constitution it declared that the people institute their government in order to:

> "form a more perfect union, establish justice, insure domestic tranquility, provide for the common defence, promote the general welfare, and secure the blessings of Liberty to ourselves and to posterity"

In Germany, at the same time, the philosopher Immanuel Kant saw freedom as conforming to moral law. Only good behaviour was free behaviour. A man was free when his ideal self determined his behaviour. And the State had an important part to play. If the State imposed laws that regulated society in a beneficial way, then the State was assisting freedom.

Another 18th century German philosopher, Georg W.F. Hegel, had a broader definition of freedom. He saw freedom as associated with harmony. One became free when one did something good or beneficial with another person. He believed that freedom is only possible when we act rationally and when others support and benefit from our actions. Hegel also thought that the State had an important part to play. Its collective interest must harmonise with the interests of individuals and individuals must be conscious of this harmony. He believed that the harmony of beneficial social interest helped the individual to grow and develop in a positive way. (Woodward, 1980)

Yet another German, Francis Lieber, emigrated to the United States in 1827 and became influential in liberal thinking. He saw freedom as social development. People were social beings, therefore they should fulfil their individual and social natures through being good members of society. Men and women must try to cultivate, develop and expand all their powers and endowments. Lieber, too, was interested in the role of the State in assisting freedom. He saw the nation state as the highest form of social life, while government was a natural extension of the family and a positive good. This was the promise of American life and something for which citizens must actively work. America was the centre of liberal change, and universal progress would follow from what America achieved (Ross, 1991).

As the 19th century progressed these ideas were developed by John Stuart Mill in England and by John Dewey in America. Dewey equated democracy with freedom and saw it as the ideal form of social organisation – one in which the individual and society blended easily with each other. But Dewey widened the sphere of freedom believing that democracy must play a role in industry as well as in civil and political life. Like his predecessors the emphasis was on goodness and harmony. Men and women must think and make choices, but these choices must be for the good of all. In making morally correct choices the individual grew in knowledge and virtue and gained the respect of others.

In the 20th century there have been many definitions of freedom. Liberal individualism has tended to see freedom as an absence of constraints. It sees the welfare of society, and even the welfare of its most deprived members, as being served by the pursuit of individual self interest and by the efficiency of a free market. In England this was the dominant set of values of the Thatcher government for ten years.

After the Second World War a number of individuals who had assisted in providing therapeutic services for released prisoners of war, and other war-damaged veterans, came together and formed the Tavistock Institute in London. Their aim was to apply notions of freedom to industry by replacing the many routine and soul-destroying tasks of mass production with opportunities for personal growth and job satisfaction. They saw freedom as the capacity for choice and its exercise, the absence of constraining conditions and the availability of means. It meant equal opportunity for self-development in association with one's fellows, enabling conditions and the encouragement and motivation to take this route (Galston, 1991). Self-development involved the creation of new capacities and the enrichment of existing ones – in other words, a general enhancement in the quality of individual, group and organisational life (Gould, 1988).

We are still striving to achieve these objectives while recognising that their realisation requires some generally agreed values. For example, an acceptance of a work ethic which requires personal independence to be associated with the desire to do a job well, and a restriction on untrammelled self-indulgence so that the needs of the group are in harmony with the needs of the individual. But the future is a hopeful one. As industry moves increasingly into flatter hierarchies, multi-skilling, personal responsibility and employee involvement, today's answer must be the optimistic "perhaps they are attainable".

3.3 Computers, Freedom and Work

In the 1960s no-one knew what the impact of computer technology on offices would be and the great fear was that it would cause unemployment. There was a belief, fostered by the media, that the speed and efficiency of these new machines would be so great that large numbers of women and some men would lose their jobs. In fact, it was a considerable time before this prophecy came true. The early machines were so unreliable and so difficult to program that many business organisations found they were employing more, rather than less, labour as programmers and operators were added to their staff.

Some new and unpleasant female jobs now appeared on the scene. One was punch operating. Large numbers of women were required to punch the cards or papertape that provided input to the new computers. This job, while extremely boring, required considerable accuracy and so provided a new mani-festation of a job hardly fit for humans. While shop floor assembly jobs had always been dull and demanding, at least the women doing them had been able to talk to each other across the moving line. The new computer work was both monotonous and required concentration. To add insult to injury, as the tech-nology developed women found that the speed at which they worked was being recorded by their own machines. Too slow a pace meant loss of pay or even dismissal.

Generally, then, for women if not for men, these early computer associated jobs reduced rather than increased freedom. Work that in its manual form had a degree of interest, and might require some problem solving and decision taking, became routinised and also segmented. Instead of being responsible for a sequence of activities, women were limited to preparing input for the com-puter or correcting errors in its output. The fear of a loss of the freedom to work because of redundancy also became stronger in offices employing large numbers of female staff. In time, computers did increasingly displace clerks although for a while, in both America and Europe, growing economies meant that new jobs could replace the old.

Two factors led to the routinisation and segmentation of clerical jobs. First, the primitive nature of early computer systems encouraged technical designers to focus on the needs of the computer and ignore the needs of people. An information systems specialist, Harold Sackman, explained the ideology of the technical systems analysts of the time.

"Early computers were virtually one of a kind, very expensive to build and operate. Computer time was far more expensive than human time. Under these constraints, it was essential that computer efficiency came first, with people last. Technical matters turned computer professionals on; human matters turned them off. Users were troublesome petitioners somewhere at the end of the line who had to be satisfied with what they got." *(Sackman, 1974).*

While the new computer specialists were not concerned about people, the influence of Taylorism was still to be found in Work Study and Organisation and Methods departments. Here the philosophy was one of breaking work down into a series of simple and repetitive tasks, each task being undertaken by a different individual. The logic behind this was that it increased production and saved money. Clerks on simple clerical jobs received low pay and were easily replaceable if they left the firm. Computers provided a new vehicle for this philosophy by their ability to handle complex numerical transactions, leaving the human being with the simple, routine tasks.

Worried by this extension of routine work into the clerical area and the increased dominance of machines in offices the author, assisted by a group of like-minded friends and associates, persuaded the British Computer Society to agree to the creation of a new group concerned with computers and quality of work issues. This led to the creation of the Socio-technical Working Party which, in its early days, reported to the BCS Human–Computer Interaction Group whose principal interest was ergonomics. The Socio-technical Working Party has now become the Socio-technical Group and is actively extending its influence through the recruitment of new members and the provision of lectures and publications on the humanisation of work in situations where computers are in use (Mumford, 1995a).

But the old philosophy, in certain areas, continues to the present day. Some technologists still try to remove the human being from the systems they design, even when it has been demonstrated that a person can perform a complex task better than the machine. Some monotonous data input jobs still remain, many a response to telephone input, and a number of British companies have been sued by female employees for repetitive strain injury. But both the culture and the technology are changing. Modem technology requires an intelligent, skilled workforce and the principles of Taylorism are losing their strength. It has always been possible to offer employees either freedom or constraint. Today the business advantages of flexibility and freedom are increasingly being recognised and accepted.

3.4 Information, Technology and Freedom

Can a humanistic use of information technology assist in creating an environment for greater personal freedom in our political, economic, social and cultural lives? Can technology assist self-development by providing opportunities to develop new capacities and enrich existing ones? Can it help us improve the quality of the activities we undertake? In other words is technology a progressive or a conservative force? (Gouldner, 1976).

Technology is usually acquired to meet a need or a problem. It is then implemented and finally it is used. All of these activities can play a part in increasing society's freedoms. If carefully selected and designed, information systems can support the human being in work, in social interaction and in the workings of democracy. They can greatly change organisational life and improve the processes of communication. Organisations which suffer from the illegitimate use of authority and power, from tunnel vision, from the restriction of knowledge, and from dysfunctional organisational cultures can be improved by ensuring that knowledge is shared, that norms and values are known, discussed and agreed by everyone affected by them and that creative ideas are encouraged and developed (Hirschheim and Klein, 1994).

If freedom is defined as "opportunities for choice, this choice assisting the attainment of a desired and beneficial future", then information systems have to be carefully managed to achieve these things.

> For choice and decision to reflect the wishes of a group two conditions are required. The first is "participation". A design group should contain all interested users of the new system or their represent-atives. The second is "effective communication". All potential users must be able to discuss their needs freely and openly, to accept challenge and dissent, and to want to negotiate an acceptable outcome. They must also have the communication skills to speak clearly, unambiguously and with confidence.

In effect we are seeking to achieve fearless and open communication based on an understanding of interpersonal relationships. Here the work of the Tavistock Institute[1] can act as a guide and inspiration.

Both classical and modern ideas fit with the current view that successful soft-ware development requires the creation of shared objectives and agreement on how these objectives can be achieved. This implies that participation, co-opera-tion and effective interaction take place (Bansler and Haun, 1991). Freedom must also be associated with individuals as well as groups so that liberal theory encompasses particular as well as general interests.

Over the years the author has been following the socio-technical philosophy by developing a structured approach to the non-technical aspects of systems design. This is called ETHICS, standing for Effective Technical and Human Implementation of Computer-based Systems. It has had as its aim the easing of the process by which users can become involved in a meaningful way in the design process. ETHICS requires user needs to be clearly identified and users to be given responsibility for the choice of organisational and technical solu-tions, although the latter will be guided by the knowledge of IT professionals. Successful user involvement requires accurate analysis of needs together with democratic communication and debate so that appropriate solutions can be examined and accepted (Mumford, 1995a).

ETHICS incorporates the philosophies of participation, effective communi-cation and socio-technical design. It assists user design groups to create a deci-sion *structure* that incorporates all interested groups affected by the new system; a *process* which enables the design task to be smoothly carried forward from identification of the need for change to the successful operation of the new system, and an *agenda* that allows business efficiency and employee satis-faction objectives to be considered in parallel and given equal weight. This kind of approach is increasingly being accepted as it is recognised that human consequences cannot be left to chance or to ad hoc adjustments after imple-

---

[1] The Tavistock Institute, London, was founded in 1947 as an independent not-for-profit organis-ation which seeks to combine research in the social sciences with professional practice.

mentation. The analysis and specification of the social system, the design of jobs and of the organisational unit as a whole, have now become as important as the specification of the technical system.

ETHICS provides a learning experience for users and systems analysts, particularly those who are members of the design group. They acquire both diagnostic skills and design skills. They also learn about the various technical options that are available to meet their needs and help solve their problems. The principal objective of a socio-technical approach is to make work more satisfying for the individual and group doing it, while at the same time enabling them to contribute to a high level of technical efficiency. To achieve this, its adherents have developed a number of work design principles. These include the following:

- *Task integration* – the work system, comprising a number of logically integrated tasks or unit operations, becomes the basic design unit; not the single tasks or operations which form it.
- *Team work* – the work group becomes the primary social unit, not the individual job holder.
- *Self-management* – internal regulation of the system is by the work group itself.
- *Multi-skilling* – because the work group is the primary social unit, the jobs of individuals can be multi-skilled.
- *Choice and decision making* – greater emphasis is placed on the discretionary as opposed to the prescribed part of the work roles.
- *Control* – people are treated as complimentary to machines, not as extensions of, or subservient to, machines.
- *Work interest* – work organisation aims to increase not decrease work variety (Emery, 1995).

ETHICS tries to give users design competence through participation and open communication in which all views have validity. Through their informed choice of solution they are in a position to enhance their quality of working life and secure freedom from work that is unpleasant and frustrating.

3.5 Participation and Freedom

The author's experience is that participation does assist freedom. It enables information to be shared, discussion to take place and choices to be made. Those involved also seem to find it an enjoyable and satisfying experience. The reasons for this approval are related to the social consequences of participation.

For example, highly effective groups, with members which communicate well with each other have the following characteristics:

- They are attractive for their members.
- They hold common values and are motivated to abide by these.
- They have a supportive atmosphere.
- Each member is motivated to communicate fully, freely and frankly.
- Each member is anxious to receive communications from others.
- There is a strong motivation to influence and be influenced by others.
- There is strong motivation to use the communication process to assist the goals of the group.

Successful groups also have a good emotional life. Members encourage, praise, harmonise, observe, gatekeep, record and maintain positive attitudes to each other.

The groups associated with user-led socio-technical systems design assume considerable responsibility. This may extend from design and implementation to using the system, monitoring its effectiveness and planning its future development. These groups require time to consider what they are doing. Good analysis and creativity needs opportunity for reflection, thinking through options, and feeling out what is possible politically and organisationally (Morgan, 1986). Freedom for a group as opposed to an individual also requires an agreement on values and a willingness to negotiate, even compromise, to secure a mutually desirable end.

All the evidence suggests that participation has a positive effect on organisations as well as individuals. It is a necessary condition for effective communication and consultation and this is required at all levels in the organisation when major change is being introduced. Nevertheless it can sometimes produce negative attitudes in technical and managerial groups. These may interpret requests for participation as an unwillingness to accept the proposed technical processes. Specialists and managers see this as being so advantageous that further discussion is superfluous. These groups may also see too much participation as having a paralysing effect. It will stop things happening or it will impede efficiency. Yet participation, discussion and effective communication are usually an intrinsic part of the viability of major change. The success of new technology depends on the co-ordinated, disciplined action of various sub-groups including R&D teams, designers, accountants, project managers etc. (Wynne, 1991).

The design world appears to be more sheltered than the real world. In the design world introducing innovation and managing change is often seen as simpler than it really is. Because technical commitments are made at an early stage, participation can be seen as implying resistance, yet participation is usually a facilitator rather than an obstruction. Today, people want open communication and information. They want the opportunity to discuss and criticise with ideas being judged according to their quality and validity. This need to think, talk and evaluate can conflict with the technologists' desire to get innovation in quickly.

3.6 Freedom, Participation and the Future

There seems to be good evidence that participation does increase freedom of choice when new systems are being designed. There is also evidence that people like participation. They like the sense of being in control, of learning and of interacting successfully and positively with other members of a group. But communication is not just a question of words. We interpret what people say and make our response as a result of their facial expressions, the voice intonations they use and their physical movements (Caroll, 1974).

Personality and charisma are also important and these are most effectively communicated through face-to-face convesation and meetings (Zuboff, 1988).

At present, it is those facilitators, project managers and systems developers who support and lead design groups who have the responsibility for helping the group members to achieve these things. In pursuing mutual understanding they elicit, through interaction, a shared understanding of the obstacles to good communication. Progress comes from improved face-to-face contact and conversation and from the learning process that takes place in a social situation. All of these contribute to an 'ideal communication' situation which assists an agreement on systems objectives and on the manner of design and implementation. In this way we achieve better, more acceptable and more liberating systems (Hirschheim and Klein, 1994).

An interesting question is: what happens as technology moves on and the face-to-face group is increasingly replaced by the remote group in which each individual is at a different location and conversation is through electronic messaging systems? Can a socio-technical approach still be used? Can participation, communication, choice and freedom continue to evolve as electronic interaction increasingly becomes the norm?

Many writers believe this is possible. An article in the *Sloan Management Review* maintains that new applications to support team work and participation will evolve. It speaks approvingly of how electronic mail, bulletin boards, and conferencing systems already provide a basic infrastructure for communication and collaborative working (Benjamin and Blunt, 1992). It is also suggested that the anonymity of electronic messaging can improve the quality of participation. This will be less influenced by power relations than it is in the face-to-face context and this can reduce the obstacles to free and unrestrained inquiry. Others maintain that we are moving towards a network nation in which vast amounts of information and socio-emotional communications will be exchanged with colleagues, friends and strangers who live in distant places and whom we rarely meet (Poster, 1990).

Other writers see problems ahead. They point put that computer conversations bear little relationship to face-to-face conversations. At present, although this may not last long, they are written, not spoken. They extend the writing domain to cover areas of communication that until now were restricted to face-to-face interaction, mail and telephone. This is a major change. The communicators now become sexless and faceless, their personalities are diminished to what they write and they have no hierarchical positions. In other words they are not "real" people. There is also the possibility of "silent rejection". Today, those who use electronic mail are frequently anxious that their messages will elicit no response and many individuals are casual about replying to electronic messages even though they would not react the same way to verbal messages.

Technology has always offered a promise of Utopia and a threat of disaster, for example, John Bunyan's *Promised Land* and his *Slough of Despond*. What actually happens depends on our values, priorities and needs as well as who is taking the decisions. Tomorrow's information systems can improve our work, our social interaction and our personal and group freedom, providing we make informed and socially responsible choices.

Social responsibility requires a knowledge of what people want and regard as improvement. This, in turn, requires mutual understanding and shared meanings and these are achieved through good communication in which all can take part. Lastly, progress requires a common set of values, norms and beliefs in which freedom to choose and freedom from unwanted constraints and hardships are priorities to be striven for.

We can contribute to this by striving to increase participation and effective communication in systems design so that users can choose and create the work and social situations that they like and value. If we do this we shall have taken a major step on the road to freedom and towards the socio-technical goals of freedom, choice, compassion and learning (Poster, 1990).

Chapter **4**

Searching for New Grounds in STS: Beyond Open Systems Thinking

Frans M. van Eijnatten and E.C. Lieke Hoogerwerf

4.1 Introduction

Since its conception in Britain in the fifties, the sociotechnical systems (STS) paradigm has travelled the globe. A number of local STS varieties were produced in Europe, North America and Australia. Changing the division of labour within firms to achieve a participative democracy is the main focus of all STS variants (Eijnatten, 1993). Open systems thinking (OST) provided the systemic basis for a whole family of sociotechnical application strategies. Although existing STS models are still being improved by practitioners using past experience, their reflections normally do not take OST into account. In this chapter we suggest – by addressing anomalies at both the theoretical and practical levels – that the next iteration of the STS paradigm should go beyond OST.

We take the Dutch STS approach of integral organisational renewal of the firm (IOR) as an example, which illustrates our search for new grounds. To begin, we summarise some major characteristics of IOR's design model that was developed in The Netherlands, using action research from the seventies and eighties. Next, we present a concise synopsis of IOR practice in Dutch industry. Although IOR applications have resulted in significant changes in the structure of many companies, the pace of transformation of organisational behaviour was much slower and took more energy than was originally expected by both managers and change agents. We continue by exploring some desirable futures for IOR. More specifically, we outline two theoretical models that might be helpful in this respect. The first candidate is called chaordic systems thinking (CST). In essence this is a new lens – a way of seeing reality – that might be a successful competitor of OST as the systemic basis for IOR. The second prospect is the so-called learning network theory (LNT), which focuses on the interaction of individual learning and organisational change.

We conclude that both CST and LNT reveal new opportunities for IOR, supplying sociotechnical change agents with a richer and more dynamic way of thinking, and offering new ways to solve the problem of the slow organisational behaviour transformation process.

4.2 Dutch Integral Organisational Renewal

IOR is a cybernetic, open systems approach that provides a sociotechnical basis for the design of business processes, organisational structures, and human work. IOR aims to create a "balanced production function":

> *"Not only a competitive product, but also a non-polluting product. Not only healthy and safe work, but also inspiring work with reduced risks for stress and alienation and more opportunities for developing one's own resources. Not only a structure ensuring optimal control of the current process, but also a structure that fosters innovation by learning. Not only optimal QWL, but also optimal product quality. Not only profitability in the short run, but also employment in the future." (Sitter, 1993)*

Although modern enterprises should be adaptive systems, able to generate added value for both internal and external stakeholders, most firms find it difficult to answer a multitude of functional requirements in a balanced way.

In the IOR model, the *architecture* of the actual division of labour is taken as a central point of departure. In order to transform this architecture, a normative design theory, called "modern sociotechnical theory" is being used. To avoid the pitfalls of an expert-driven approach, IOR embraces a participative re-design strategy, called "self-design by knowledge transfer". Also, IOR contains a rich set of analysis and re-design tools, originating from both the industrial engineering discipline and the organisation and team development disciplines.

The result of a typical IOR implementation process is a flat, team-based organisation, composed of self-managed product creation and production teams, decentralised self-governed multi-functional staff teams and a business-unit executives team (see Fig. 4.1). This picture only represents the structural characteristics of the division of labour. A typical IOR process would include information about continuous mutual adjustments within and between teams, all being involved in routine and non-routine problem-solving activities

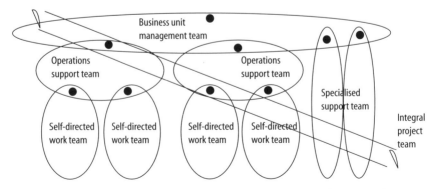

Figure 4.1 Results of a Typical IOR Implementation Process (Amelsvoort, 1992).

related to the co-ordination of primary operations as well as the organisational design, competence development, and overall governance of the firm.

4.2.1 IOR's Design Theory as a Grounded Theory

IOR's normative design theory can be regarded as a grounded theory (Sitter et al, 1997): "i.e., a theory using abstract concepts to describe and analyse a series of general phenomena, but based on practical experiences". The primary design object is the organisational architecture, more specifically the pattern of division of labour, that is, the very structure of a production system (Sitter, 1993). IOR's design theory explains how specific architectures of structure determine the opportunities for coordination, adaptation and innovation, and specifies how alternative architectures change such opportunities and which direction they take. IOR's design theory prescribes that the division of labour should be kept minimal: no complex organisations with simple, highly fragmented jobs, but simple organisations with complex, holistic jobs. Similar lines of thought are found in STS variants that favour "redundancy of functions" instead of "redundancy of parts". The latter represents a maximum division of labour into functional specialised organisational parts (Emery and Emery, 1995). In IOR's design theory, a labour process is defined as a selective interaction process (Luhmann, 1984) controlled and performed by organisation members. *Control* is defined as goal-related selection of actions with respect to system relations (what will be done, by whom, when and where), *performance* is defined as realising actions. Both control and performance should be integrated in each individual job.

IOR's design theory is aimed at creating an organisational architecture conducive to "variety balance" both at the level of the individual workplace and at the levels of teams, business units, and the firm as a whole. This can be accomplished through the design of both the performance structure and the control structure. Such designs offer organisation members ample opportunities to vary their actions according to the demands with which they are confronted in their work. This is called "controllability". Controllability can be characterised as adaptability. This "model of balance" is in fact another application of Ashby's law within the Modern STS paradigm.

IOR's design theory specifies the following major design rules: (1) re-design the performance structure top-down, from macro to micro (parallelisation and segmentation of order flows); (2) re-design the control structure by a bottom-up allocation of control cycles (local, interlocal, global); (3) re-design the performance structure aspect system first, and then proceed with the design of the control structure; and (4) the re-design of the performance structure precedes the re-design of process technology (Sitter, 1997).

One of the central concepts in IOR's design theory is "control capacity". Control capacity is a function of a labour process. It is by no means a nominal attribute of a labour task. Control capacity is not the power to control human actions, but what options there are for the control of the labour process to increase the probability that desired outputs will be delivered. The quality of work is defined as the relative amount of control capacity built into each task. By increasing the relative amount of control capacity into each task, IOR's design theory simultaneously aims at purposeful "mobilisation" of human resources and improvement of the quality of the organisation as a whole. See next section for a further explanation of the theoretical position.

4.2.2 IOR's Design Theory as Contrasted with Other Approaches

In IOR's normative design theory human needs and values are not seen as constants, but rather as process-based variables (Luhmann, 1984). Therefore, the content theories of motivation (Herzberg, 1968) are rejected as valid explanations for emerging organisational behavior. As a consequence, the criterion for good quality of work is control capacity, not individual satisfaction with the job. The art of giving meaning is seen as a prime objective of working life, and is only feasible in interactive contexts. Interactive systems produce meaning by selecting relations and by doing so, they create structure (Herzberg, 1968; Einjatten, 1993).

IOR's design theory rejects the conventional definition of a sociotechnical system as consisting of both social and technical systems, viewed as sub-systems. IOR's design theory uses the so-called performance structure and control structure as basic aspect systems, instead. As a consequence, the classical sociotechnical construct of "joint optimisation" has become obsolete in IOR, and is replaced by the construct of integral systems design (Einjatten, 1993).

The heuristic for integral systems design offered by IOR's design theory demonstrates affinity with the viable systems model, presented by Beer (Espejo and Harnden, 1987). Starting from Ashby's law of requisite variety, both address the allocation of complexity, which is the need for control, towards (abstract) capacities. The central design issue is to determine which capacities should be present in sub-systems. The viable systems model proposes designing recursive structures in which distinct types of capacities are integrated into every sub-system. In a similar way, IOR's design theory advocates the integration of different types of performance capacities (operative, preparative, supportive) as well as different types of control capacities (strategic, tactical and operational) into every organisational unit. Figure 4.1 serves as a model of the recursive structure that may be designed.

4.2.3 Self-Design by Knowledge Transfer

Applications of IOR's design theory in practice converged into a so-called "theory of practice". This is a modelled repertoire of application strategies that builds on successful interventions. Typically, a theory of practice is a set of principles, constructs, methods, action models, and evaluative data, developed both on the content and process levels (Zee, 1995). Over a period of 25 years, the IOR theory of practice was gradually shaped in a number of projects by several stakeholders: consultants, practitioners, action researchers and academics.

Basically, the IOR approach advocates an application strategy that is called "self-design by knowledge transfer". This strategy invites organisation members both to learn to understand and to apply the IOR's design principles for re-designing their own organisation in a participative way. Several coherent pro-grammes for the arrangement of both types of activities have been designed. The earlier models are considered to be participative variants of top-down change strategies, while more recent variants strongly emphasise bottom-up processes (Amelsvoort, 1996). In all models, design activities are supported by substantial IOR-oriented training courses of executives and staff people at top and middle management levels. During the implementation phase intensive training programs for workers and work teams also take place (Amelsvoort and Scholtes, 1993). Knowledge transfer is mainly done by discussing elements from IOR, during both training and design group meetings as well. More recently, more activating training modes have been introduced, to uncover experiential learning and to enable bottom-up re-design processes (Amelsvoort, 1996; Hoogerwerf, 1998). Here are six examples:

- redesign simulation games for all organisational members;
- search conferences;
- design conferences;
- large-scale work team conferences (simultaneous workshops with all work teams, facilitated by specially trained internal staff);
- problem-oriented learning groups at top and middle management levels; and
- individual coaching of employees facing role transitions.

Although discussions are minimised at this stage, self-disciplined thinking which is consistent with IOR's design theory is highly encouraged and system-atically checked.

4.3 IOR Evaluated

IOR evaluation studies focus mostly on structural design and more specifically on the work team level: what is changed in the work system and what are the effects on performance? The target perform-ance improvements clearly have been realised, like indicators such as costs, quality of product, delivery reliability and absenteism illustrate (Amelsvoort and Scholtes, 1993). Structure characteristics indeed have changed in accord-ance with sociotechnical design priciples. These results indicate that self-design by knowledge

> Concepts and heuristics offered by IOP's design theory prove to be a useful frame of reference for engaging in joint creation activ-ities concerning the architecture of work systems, involving most relevant stakeholders.

transfer is effective in realising fundamental changes in organisational structures and performance improvement (Hoogerwerf, 1998; Haak, 1994). However,
a recent evaluation of some IOR cases indicates that individual and collective
learning processes do not keep pace with the actual structural changes
(Hoogerwerf, 1998). Managers as well as workers and specialists need precious
time to relate their actual theories-in-use to the new frame of reference that they
enthusiastically embrace. Ambivalent attitudes towards issues of development
of their theories-in-use indicate that organisation members get caught between
two worlds in IOR: the world they already know from past experience, and the
one they just learned to imagine as a desirable future.

4.4 Desirable Futures for Integral Organisational Renewal

We conclude that in IOR practices the challenge is to deepen further the
process of learning. Moreover, we suggest linking it up with the process of creating, in which structural re-design and implementation are produced. As
Dutch practice has shown, abstractions offered by IOR's design theory are
quite helpful in creating new organisational structures. For that purpose, self-
design by knowledge transfer proved to be a most effective strategy. But IOR's
design theory is not very efficient in enabling individual processes of learning,
that is, in stimulating organisational members to adapt their mental models or
theories-in-use. Although the use of dialogue methods in IOR change projects
improved that condition a bit, we have the impression that the problem should
be tackled at a more fundamental level. In order to further improve IOR, we
think systematic attention should be paid to new lenses that enable sustainable
change, and to new models of learning that incite the development and use of
action theories by all stakeholders in an organisational renewal process. Two
promising candidates for those purposes are chaordic systems thinking and
learning network theory.

4.4.1 Chaordic Systems Thinking

Chaordic Systems Thinking (CST) is "a lens, a way of thinking, and
subsequently an approach to designing a complex organisational system that
recognises the enterprise not as a fixed structure, but as 'flow'; a dynamical
process passing from one attractor basin to the next in an incessant journey
toward the 'edge' of chaos" (Einjatten and Fitzgerald, 1998).

Since the legendary coal mine studies carried out by the Tavistock Institute in
the 1950s, OST has been quite successful in the theoretical foundation of STS.

Up until now, all sociotechnical varieties have had solid roots in this system of thought. For OST, systems seek Equilibrium, and can reach the same final steady state regardless of their initial conditions or the paths they take. With the emergence of CST as a new root metaphor, the once dominant OST lens seems to have been pushed closer to the end of its life cycle, due to a number of anomalies (Fitzgerald, 1997).

Maintaining a steady equilibrium state, as OST proclaims, is no longer desirable. On the contrary, systems that thrive in the flux of far-from-equilibrium conditions, at the very "edge" of chaos, seem to be more sustainable (Stacey, 1996). Also, the above-mentioned principle of equifinality is contradicted by the sensitive dependency on initial conditions (the "butterfly effect"), which illustrates how a meticulous change in the system's initial conditions can have dramatic effects on the outcome (Lorenz, 1963).

CST is a lens that can be used to describe and analyse complex, nonlinear, dynamic systems. In such situations patterns of behaviour may be difficult to recognise and almost impossible to predict, but they are there, and can be repeated, though slightly differently every time. CST distinguishes between multiple equilibria or attractor states (equilibrium, near-to-equilibrium, far-from-equilibrium, fatal chaos), and therefore, might be more efficient in describing the complex, dynamic, nonlinear behaviour of organisations. Moreover, chaordic systems have five distinctive properties (Fitzgerald, 1996):

1. *consciousness*: mind, not matter is the ground state;

2. *connectivity*: nothing can exist independently of the whole;

3. *indeterminacy*: any link between cause and effect is obscured;

4. *dissipation*: falling apart and then back together again in a novel new form; and

5. *emergence*: creating new order out of chaos.

In general, Dutch IOR can benefit from CST by giving up any form of dualistic thinking: CST abandons "either…or" in favour of "both…and" solutions (i.e., both order and chaos, both design and development, both part and whole, both form and wave, both analysis and synthesis, both matter and mind). In particular, IOR could profit from CST in the following ways (Einjatten and Fitzgerald, 1998, pp. 7–10):

- *Broadening its focus.* Facilitating "learning from within" by means of extensive dialogue and creative thinking, on top of mere "surface learning," to meet the CST characteristic of consciousness. The value added to traditional IOR is the system's interiority, the collective development of the "organisational mind", a vision that is continuously created and shared by all. Storytelling and narratives can be used as a means of transferring learning to others. The inclusion of so-called "soft" issues is mandatory here.

- *Expanding its scope.* Concepts such as individuals, groups and teams should be re-defined into "holons", to be in line with the CST principle of connectivity. Holons are entities that are both wholes and parts of a greater whole at the same time (Koestler, 1967). This minor difference has a major theoretical implication for IOR: it is not either…or, but both…and. Holons are both autonomous and dependent structures at the same time. Therefore, it is plausible that even in organisations that thrive in far-from-equilibrium conditions, individuals, groups or teams, will produce emergent new order out of chaos at each level of the organisation, provided that they are functioning as holons. This ability is called "holonic capacity": "Holonic Capacity is the potential intrinsic in a chaordic system for self-transcendence. One can see how the structure of the Chaordic Enterprise continues to evolve towards a vibrant team-based network in which the locus of control is internalised, not the responsibility of management" (Fitzgerald and Einjatten, 1998, p. 267).

- *Further loosening any attempts to control.* IOR already avoids the detailed mapping of "interference" in the local environment for the benefit of some future governance. IOR change agents have to fully accept the fundamental unknowability and unpredictability of future occurrences, to be in concordance with the CST characteristic of indeterminacy. Instead, one should try to grasp patterns and probabilities in the midst of complexity. Hannon and Atherton (1997a) call this process "orienteering": "The successful orienteer needs no directional signs pointing in a specific direction or to a clear end-point" (p. 2). Therefore, IOR should fight any managerial desire that is aimed at controlling the process in case the system moves beyond its steady state. Managers should stimulate change, not focus on control (Fitzgerald and Einjatten, 1998).

- *Creating a culture that anticipates change.* Re-directing the basic organisational renewal strategy from "reacting" – or active adaptation – to changes in the environment, to "initiating" or deliberately changing the system long before it is time, to fit the CST characteristic of dissipation. Crossan, Lane, White and Klus (1996) have called this the "improvising organisation", an art learned through continuous practice. It is the strive for self-renewal – breaking up the status quo – that is key. According to Markides (1998, p. 38) successful innovators are "not afraid to destabilise a smooth-running machine and to do so periodically but continuously". IOR could gain a lot by combining both structure and culture creation in its design approach.

- *Tapping the system's holonic capacity.* The organisation should trust increasingly on the self-organising, self-referential, self-replication and self-transcendental capabilities of its individual holons as they climb the holarchy (hierarchy of consciousness), as to equal the characteristic of emergence. IOR should incorporate the theme of "bifurcation discretion" in its design theory: i.e. both the goal and the discretion for individual holons to transcend to higher levels of complexity, whenever necessary (Fitzgerald and Einjatten, 1998).

More than any other lens CST stresses that time is irreversible. Therefore, the history of the holon's patterns of behaviour becomes an important factor in IOR's analysis. Periods of relative stability are alternated with episodes of relative instability.

4.4.2 Learning Network Theory

In IOR, as in other STS variants around the world, the creation of labour systems is the main focus. Learning is seen as a highly valuable human capacity, an essential resource that enables the system as a whole to be adaptive and sustainable. Work structures should offer sufficient opportunities for learning.

In the so-called "learning network theory", which was designed by Van der Krogt (1995), a double focus is presented, in which a learning system is supposed to exist next to and partly coincide with the labour system. Through the learning system, organisation members continuously develop action theories, and use their simultaneously developing skills to perform better in the labour system. Both systems are seen as networks, built by individuals or collectives. LNT offers a framework showing how organisation members (workers, managers and specialists) and external actors (consultants, trainers, unions and vocational institutions) – guided by their respective action theories and applying all kinds of strategies – organise their labour network and simultaneously organise their learning network.

On the basis of existing management models, LNT distinguishes between four main directions for organising:

1. *vertical*, based on hierarchical coordination;
2. *horizontal*, based on coordination through mutual adjustment within collectives;
3. *external*, based on coordination through professional or vocational institutions;
4. *liberal*, based on coordination through negotiation between individual actors.

As liberal organising is just the opposite of both vertical, horizontal as well as external organising, these four directions compose a three-dimensional space (liberal/vertical, liberal/horizontal, and liberal/external). This cataloguing space allows us to relate labour system models – like bureaucracy, adhocracy and the sociotechnical model – to learning system models – like models that propose formal training arrangements, self-managed individual learning or work-related learning projects (Poell and van der Krogt, 1997).

LNT demonstrates the multidimensional framework not only to be helpful in understanding how actors organise their respective labour and learning networks, but also how they may change them, trying to solve perceived, assumed or expected misfits between required and available qualifications. LNT provides insight into the construction of respective labour and learning networks as both a design activity and a change process at the same time.

In general, LNT can support Dutch IOR practices by directly addressing issues of learning using a pluriform change strategy: Learning is perceived as a serious and complex object of change. IOR may benefit from LNT in the following ways (Hoogerwerf, 1998):

1. *Multi-focused change process*

- Collaborative work system re-design and implementation certainly offer ample opportunities for learning. The act of learning is in the hands of learners, it is the result of what they intuitively decide to do with learning potentials that exist at their workplaces.

- Also, learners are not solely dependent on work as a source of learning: their learning network also includes other social contexts.

- Trying to establish a sociotechnical labour-network architecture without taking into account concurrent changes in the learning network, will cause serious qualification problems, which organisation members find hard to solve (Hoogerwerf, 1998).

- Self-design by knowledge transfer is effective – especially when supported by dialogue methods – but only when issues of individual qualifications are explicitly dealt with.

- In addition, organisation members should be stimulated to self-organise their learning network.

- Frequently, management-imposed work system designs do not meet the criterion of humanity, as individual differences in interests, aspirations and learning abilities are only partly taken into account.

- For that reason, initial estimations of learning effects in a change project should be rather conservative.

- In order to significantly improve personal learning in IOR practices, the learning network should be changed at the same time as the labour network in a similar, fundamental way. Therefore, LNT should be integrated into IOR's design theory.

2. *Action theory perspective*

- LNT adds an intentional perspective to IOR, which brings action theories and strategies of individual organisation members into a clearer focus.

- In LNT-inspired IOR, management and workers are not only seen as behaving functionally in a work system; their intentions and preferences are also viewed as important triggers for organisational behaviour.

- This action theory perspective opens the way to the unexpected, the existence of parallel universes, and "escaping the swamp by pulling on your own wig" (Watzlawick, 1989).

3. *Emergent properties of learning*

- In original IOR, learning is instrumental to the process of structural re-design and implementation: the IOR process is managed by trying to control what organisation members learn.

- The LNT perspective shows the limitations of this approach, and emphasises the emergent properties of learning.

- By stimulating multiple modes of learning, it is expected that organisation members will be more likely to start orienteering activities and initiate improvisation.

- The results of that process can make a big difference with respect to both the internalisation of renewal concepts and pace or amount of change as well.

4.5 Conclusions

1. Before trying to revive the STS approach, it is recommended that its foundational paradigm, open systems thinking, should be replaced by chaordic systems thinking. CST introduces time as a basic dimension and distinguishes between multiple holon states and consecutive levels of complexity.

2. IOR could evolve into a more integral approach to design by engaging in both structure and culture creation as well. This will enable the organisation to collectively develop the "organisational mind", a vision that is continuously created by dialogue and is shared by all. The inclusion of the interior of the system allows us to consider both the emotional and spiritual dimensions of work.

3. The learning network theory provides insight into the construction of respective labour and learning networks as both a design activity and a change process at the same time. LNT should be integrated with CST-informed IOR, so that learning issues can become part of the unfolding "organisational mind".

The sociotechnical systems paradigm definitely is at a crossroads at the end of the century. After almost 50 years of diversification and regional developments, it is time for a big change. Certainly, it is not recommended to try to unify the different local sociotechnical theories of content, as they developed in the course of time. Thus far, these variations have proved to serve the different world contexts fairly well. Rather we advocate a qualitative leap from one foundational paradigm to another: OST to CST. In the case of IOR, we argued that CST and LNT may improve the efficacy of the approach by an order of magnitude, to guarantee its fitness for use in the world of work in the twenty-first century.

Chapter 5

Sociotechnical Perspectives on Emergence Phenomena

Angela Lin and Tony Cornford

5.1 Introduction

The sociotechnical approach, as applied in the field of information systems, has been based on the assumption that more effective and successful systems can be designed if human and social considerations are taken into account. The contribution of sociotechnical theory has informed and extended the design process to include a consideration of individual and group interests, as well as providing a means for their expression as new work systems are developed. However, many contemporary information systems, and the information technologies that they embody, are not exclusively based on an isolated process of design.

It is now common place to speak of information systems, and their associated work practices, evolving through time so that they end up doing things that their designers did not – could not – anticipate. This sense of systems altering their character through use is what we refer to here as phenomena of emergence.

The aim of this chapter is to consider the relevance and utility of sociotechnical approaches from an "emergence phenomena" perspective, with reference to the idea that the design of a system is an ongoing process rather than a distinct prior activity. This perspective places a particular emphasis on the life of a system in use as well as recognising that the character and form of an information system (in technical and social senses, and in the combined emergent sense) continually changes through a complex interplay of multiple elements. In this new context we present a critique of the traditional sociotechnical practice of matching social and technical analyses in design. We then go on to suggest how the principles of sociotechnical design might be reinterpreted to accommodate emergence phenomena. Illustrations are drawn from two case studies in the CSCW literature.

5.2 Sociotechnical Ideas and Principles

In her book, *Systems Design: Ethical Tools for Ethical Change*, Mumford (1996) traces the emergence of the sociotechnical tradition. Starting with pioneering work at the Tavistock Institute in London, she outlines the successes and failures of the early Tavistock ideas as they evolved in various industrial and managerial settings around the world from the late 1940s onwards. Her account describes how sociotechnical concepts related to different periods and how they can influence the macro environment of national industrial relations. In particular she identifies key sociotechnical design ideas such as:

- incorporation of *ethical* choices and principles that affect social outcomes;
- commitment to *participation* in developing work structures;
- focus on *design* to accommodate new technologies; and
- the *autonomous workgroup* as a self-organising entity which is able to take responsibility for its own design activities.

Cherns (1976) expresses the underlying assumptions of sociotechnical design as nine key principles. His formulation is also influenced by the notion of a participative process which has the potential for both exploiting the knowledge of people within a design activity, and delivering improved and flexible work practices for organisations. As he expresses it, the goal of sociotechnical design is "a system capable of self-modification, of adapting to change, and of making the most of the creative capacities of the individual".

These nine principles are described briefly in Table 5.1. We feel that they fall essentially into three categories. In the first category are principles that express ideas about the nature of the design task. In this category we see *compatibility*, *minimal critical specification*, and *incompletion*. The second category expresses some aspects of the ethical and ideological assumptions of sociotechnical ideas in terms of design goals. In this category we would see the principles of *multi-function*, *information flow* and *design and human values*. The third category, including the *sociotechnical criterion*, *boundary location* and *support congru-*

Table 5.1. Principles of sociotechnical design – adapted from Cherns (1976)

Principle of:	
Compatibility	The process of design must be compatible with its objectives.
Minimal critical specification	No more detail in design than is needed, but design must express the essential requirements.
Sociotechnical criterion	Control is local and awarded to the immediate work team – the aim is to make supervision minimal.
Multi-function	Individuals and groups need a range of tasks to provide satisfying jobs and for redundancy and flexibility.
Boundary location	Boundaries are political – boundaries are to be managed.
Information flow	Eschew information intermediaries – information should flow initially to the prime user or group.
Support congruence	Systems should be established within a framework of social support for desired behaviour.
Design and human values	Emphasis in design is placed on quality of working life.
Incompletion	Design is iterative and continuous.

ence principles address issues of how well-formed sociotechnical systems fit within organisations and work practices.

Sociotechnical themes have been used widely in information systems development (Mumford, 1996). From the early 1970s through to the 1990s, the information systems field has generally accepted the idea that involvement of "users" within a formal design activity is a central and critical factor in achieving success (Land and Hirschheim, 1983). More recently these ideas have found a new impetus in the Scandinavian tradition of participative design (PD) (Kensing and Munk-Madsen, 1993). In terms of Friedman and Cornford's (1989) historical account of systems development approaches, this corresponds with the era of the "user relations constraint", reflecting "changing shades of problems resonating in the literature and a changing mix of managerial strategies" (p. 59).

5.3 Sociotechnical Reflections

In reviewing sociotechnical ideas we should recognise that technical and social aspects are both valid and appropriate instruments that developers work through and influence. There are various possible interpretations of this. One account might say that technology is a "given", and that systems developers (including future participants in a system) are encouraged to focus on finding ways to "fit" people to strong, even dominant, technological structures. This seemed the case in the original Long Wall studies (Mumford, 1996). If design is pursued in terms of "fit", the choices seem to be around what degree of freedom is available to achieve this fit, and what social and organisational characteristics are seen as most pertinent. As Friedman and Cornford (1989, p. 196) express it, "[Sociotechnical design] is based on the idea that there is considerable freedom of choice in organisational design because technical factors do not *completely* determine social factors" (our emphasis).

> Going a step further, we could say that not only are people fitted to strong technological structures, but that organisations themselves are formed and shaped around dominant technologies.

In the sociotechnical tradition this is not a narrow form of technological determinism, but a sense that the values and ambitions of the sociotechnical approach require a more comprehensive design approach than just that of the job, the task or even the workgroup. In this way, the sociotechnical approach seeks to differentiate itself from the broader, more palliative, tradition of the Human Relations School. Even so, such positions still have some element of Taylorism within them, if only in the emphasis on a rational analysis of work and work structures; the assumption of a predictive and perfective capability as new sociotechnical systems are conceived and evaluated. The particular emphasis that sociotechnical design has placed on measures of job satisfaction suggests echoes of a metricated scientific management, though this might be a response to the need for organisational credibility as much as being a central part of the sociotechnical approach.

There is another possible position to explore, one in which technologies are becoming more amenable to shaping through design. Throughout the last 30 years, information and communications technology (ICT) has been changing rapidly. The development of minicomputers in the early 1970s, of distributed architectures in the same decade, of query languages and 4GL, of microcomputers and networks, all potentially allowed the developer of a new system some new freedom to recast technological manifestations within reformed working practices. For example, the centralisation of power strongly implied in mainframe and batch processing systems is less apparent in a world of networks and distributed systems. Today's technologies are more "plastic", malleable and indeterminate, and can empower all who take the role of systems developer. There are choices open to the systems developer that technology might be used to support. We should recognise that while such decisions may be initially supported by the technologies as an aspect of design, they may be later reversed or subverted when a system is put to use.

The wider question is whether system developers have used their power to recast and reshape technological manifestations to meet social requirements. The answer would have to be "No": "shaping technology" to (new) reformed working practices has been a minor theme. This has perhaps been most recently highlighted in the "softer" end of the business process reengineering movement, where talk of technology as an "enabler of change" is commonplace – even if the motivations for change are essentially serving managerial agendas, not sociotechnical ideas (Avgerou, Cornford and Poulymenakou, 1995).

5.4 Design and "Matching"

We have shown that sociotechnical ideas came to be associated with a distinct discipline of design in the field of information systems. Using this design approach, a proposal for change can marry the needs (or rights) of interested parties with the desire for efficiency and effectiveness. In this respect Mumford's ETHICS methodology has been particularly influential. Her approach to design activity is characterised by twin streams; one focusing on human objectives and social alternatives, the other on efficiency objectives and technical alternatives (Mumford, 1996; Mumford and Weir, 1979). A key design step is matching the elements of these two streams as *sociotechnical alternatives*, and selecting the "best" option. This notion of matching is based on a sociotechnical model where the realities of organisational and working life are sought in the interactions between social and technical factors. Much of the sociotechnical literature uses the term "optimisation" – an implied predictive and perfective. Other development approaches, such as Avison and Wood-Harper's (1990) *Multiview* build on this theme. The separation and "matching" of social and technical aspects in this way is seen to be a worthwhile endeavour.

Using the contemporary language of information systems development we can describe the above as a mixture of analysis and design, with some substantial emphasis on analysis. But the self-declared primacy of a design agenda (a social design agenda) within the sociotechnical tradition must be acknowledged. Sociotechnical ideas aim to be different, more effective and more ethically based – they claim to offer particular visions and characteristics for new working practices based around participation. Expressed practically as "how it will or could be done", sociotechnical approaches seek benefits that would accrue to the individual, the team and the organisation through participation. However, if systems analysis is divorced from systems design (the *what* from the *how*), and given a primary position, then the potential for effective participation is diminished. Furthermore, if design is undertaken by technical and managerial specialists, then no amount of participative analysis will serve.

> Within the sociotechnical tradition, therefore, *design* is central

5.5 Design and Emergence

The discussion above has highlighted an emphasis on design within the sociotechnical tradition, and assessed the balance of the social and the technical that are drawn into this design activity. However, this approach is associated with the traditional lifecycle model of information systems development, based on:

- analysis of a problem domain;
- design of a "solving" system;
- implementation and use of a "solving" system.

The sequence is: analysis, design, use. Such a sequence of systems development was almost universal in the 1970s and 1980s when information systems tended to be built in-house on the basis of bespoke specifications. However, such a systems development model needs to be reconsidered today. General purpose applications are now readily available in the market, and many organisations choose to buy and configure off-the-shelf packages rather than building systems themselves.

In the second part of this chapter we examine a different and contrasting model, where information systems are developed through:

- the use of information technologies;
- reflection on and refinement of use;
- reflection on the significance of use.

> This sequence is: use, design, analysis

These two perspectives may not be totally incompatible. For example, Ciborra (1996) states that "groupware presents itself as a technology that tends to drift when put to use. By drifting I mean a slight or significant shift of the roles and function in concrete situations of usage, that the technology is called to play, compared to the planned pre-defined and assigned objectives and require-ments" (p. 8). In the same volume Orkikowski (1996) states it rather more strongly, speaking of changes that were "opportunistic and emerged from the ongoing practices [of the users]" (p. 24). Of course, this is not to deny any design in conventional terms, but it does suggest that things continue to change, in significant ways, after systems start to be used.

From this point we could develop the argument in two ways. We might wish to consider what the nature of conventional design (pre-use design) becomes if it is strongly informed by a concept of "drifting" or emergent change – how might a sociotechnical design approach, in its conventional sense, support or reflect a stronger sociotechnical flexibility in the system in use? Some authors, such as Fitzgerald have approached this as an issue of a system's essentially technical flexibility, but such work is largely based on a conventional model of analysis as being a process of predicting required change, rather than one of supporting emergent change (Fitzgerald, 1990).

On the other hand we might observe that systems are rarely sociotechnical during their inception and construction, that we fool ourselves if we try to think that they are. Even if we consider all the principles of sociotechnical approaches during the stage of the initial analysis and design of systems, the gap between "should" and "does" remains as wide as ever. Contemporary information technologies, in contrast to the coal-cutting machines of the Long Wall method, are sufficiently flexible to be shaped in use, rather than in a separate phase of design, however enlightened. If this is so, the key insights of the sociotechnical approach may be better focused on the question of how systems mature, emerge, or mould themselves in use; that is, a sociotech-nical perspective on in-use design and one which addresses phenomena of emergence.

5.6 Emergence in Organisations

Here we offer two examples of information systems exhibiting emergence phe-nomena and various degrees of in-use design.

Orkikowski (1996) describes a software company that installs a groupware application (Lotus Notes) to support Customer Service staffs. Tracing the system over a period of time, she documents a sequence of changes, adapta-tions and organisational consequences that the system seems to manifest. For example, new ways of knowledge sharing, new norms of reciprocal help-giving over the network, and new intermediary roles emerged over time. Orkikowski provides some classification of such emergence phenomena. Thus she speaks of anticipated, opportunistic and emergent change, and relates these to aspects of the new system:

"These changes had not all been anticipated or planned by the department in question, rather some had emerged as the department evolved in its understanding and experience not only of the technology, but of how the technology could be utilised to modify and improve the department's work structures, processes and policies" (p. 53).

It is interesting that the result of this emergent change (up to the point where the study stopped), produced a work process that was described as effective, appreciated within the work group, but also increasingly control-oriented in a Foucaultian sense. Orkikowski suggests that an obvious technological dependence developed as this successful system was established in use, and notes a "psychological dependency" on knowledge contained within the technology, particularly amongst those who had never experienced the work before the new system was installed.

Bowers (1995) provides a contrasting study in the sense that the system in question was largely rejected, and those working with it found ways to isolate themselves from it. The study was carried out in a Central Government Office where a CSCW Network was installed with the aim of improving document productivity. The CSCW Network allowed not just the documents to be available on-line to be shared by others as they were developed, but also allowed the documents to be visible, inspectable and manageable. These functions gave senior managers the opportunity to pursue their aim to become a "quality organisation" by allowing them to trace the history of the documents (e.g. who does what part) to support quality reviewing and inspection.

Employees, however, were not willing to put their contributions on-line if their preliminary draft would be inspectable by both the branch head and line managers. To these employees the CSCW Network was understood as a means for managers to carry out surveillance rather than a means to help them to increase their productivity. As a result some members decided to make their work "invisible" to their managers. In this case, the staff chose to use the old working methods, and to "work around" the system.

"...by having a 'peek in' at the status of work, Jon could ensure that work was being done according to approved 'quality methods' and was on schedule and so forth" (p. 199).

These two cases suggest that systems in-use are manifestations of emergent change, of worked out human interests, and of creative and collective responses to work and technology. They both offer illustrations of emergence phenomena. The first example places emergence in an improvement of work structuring and knowledge utilisation, with a strong emphasis on new actions and interactions: "contextualised innovations in practice". In the second example, emergence can be seen in the response to a challenge to established working practices, as people discover ways of working around a new system.

Generalising, we offer a typology of emergence in terms of three inter-related processes: learning, structuring and responding. Learning reflects the experience that people gain as they start to work within a new system, and in particular what they learn about the technologies, their constraints and potentials, and how they relate this new knowledge to their work situation. Structuring expresses the achievement of new and different organisational forms, work roles and control mechanisms based on experience within a new system, and implies some degree of considered managerial response as events unfold. Responding reflects the more direct reaction of people to what they are being asked to do and how they relate new circumstances to their ideas of the old. We suggest that these three processes need to be understood as emergent, in-use design activities with social and technological dimensions.

5.7 Sociotechnical Principles and "In-use" Design

This final section briefly considers Cherns's nine principles in relation to emergence phenomena as a system is shaped, formed and designed in-use. Certain of the principles are as broadly applicable to design activity taking place after a system starts to be used as they would be to more traditional pre-use design. The principle of *compatibility* ("a participative social system cannot be created by fiat"), and the principle of *incompletion* ("at the end we are back at the beginning") seem, in general, unproblematic. The principle of *incompletion* is perhaps more challenging in that we recognise emergent change as being a form of design, rather than decay, entropy or departure from an "optimal" match achieved earlier.

Other principles are more problematic when interpreted against a background of emergence phenomena. For example, the *multi-function* principle implies that elements within a system need to have multiple capabilities. The idea of in-use design is challenged if information systems are differentiated and refined, and emergent change introduces unintentional fixity, specificity and inflexibility. Similarly, the principle of *design and human values* suggests that quality of working life is a key objective of organisational design. Bowers' study shows that this was not so, as people defended their private work space and work pace in a direct challenge to new working practices.

Within a process of emergence it seems there is no guarantee that the principle of *design and human values* will be sustained though perhaps the principle of *support congruence* might elicit the social support required. Each of the cases above offer some insight into these terms. In Orkikowski's study, support systems at first challenged the new information system, but were in time won over; in Bowers' study the support systems clashed with the new structures and developed their own parallel interpretation of it.

The principle of *information flow* suggests that information should be first provided where it will be acted upon. In traditional sociotechnical theory this need for information is related to the concept of a variance – an unanticipated event that is better managed locally. Sociotechnical design seeks to identify and isolate variances through appropriate information, but it is variances that drive the adaptation of a system and provoke emergence. From an emergence perspective variances are perhaps to be welcomed rather than controlled.

This brings us to the *sociotechnical criterion*, which suggests that control must be local and supported in the team, with the goal of minimal supervision. When discussing the *multi-function* principle, there is no guarantee that in-use design will be sustained, and it may well be subverted unless there is strong *support congruence*. Similarly issues arise when considering the principle of *boundary location*, which suggests that "the more the control of activities becomes the responsibility of members, the more the role of the supervisor is concentrated on the boundary". This can be seen in Orkikowski's case study, in which the teams of support personnel developed a valuable informational resource, and the managers then focused on managing and sustaining this resource across the wider company.

Finally, and most problematical, we come to the principle of *minimal critical specification*, concerned with the designer's balance between minimal expression of three key aspects of a system, described by Cherns as: *what* is to be done, *how* it is to be done, and *who* is to do it. (In a network-centric world perhaps we should add the idea of *where* too.) Emergence phenomena can certainly challenge any and all of these key aspects of a system in-use, and challenge them repeatedly, but the real issue is in the very existence of a specification in any conventional sense. As stated earlier, if systems are developed according to the revised sequence then surely specifications are redundant, or at best achieved through in-use design?

5.8 Summary and Conclusions

This chapter is concerned with recognising and understanding a process of in-use design, the design activity undertaken on the basis of the use of a system, and considering what the sociotechnical approach might offer to it. Sociotechnical approaches to information systems development were introduced to assist lifecycle-based projects in the 1970s and 1980s. The environment of information systems development has changed substantially, as have the processes by which they are shaped and formed. Increasingly packages and other infrastructure technologies (e.g., networks, groupware) are used, rather than approaches based on building systems from unique specifications. This trend challenges the utility of conventional sociotechnical approaches within a development model based on the traditional lifecycle sequence of system development: analysis, design, use.

Here we have suggested a reinterpretation of sociotechnical ideas within a new model of development: use, design, analysis. Rather than focus on pre-use design as the locus for working out the social and technological dimensions of new systems using the concept of "matching", we have argued for a shift of focus to in-use design and indicated the contribution that sociotechnical principles might make. Such a shift is challenging. Much of the conventional use of sociotechnical ideas within information systems development has been driven by an amelioration of the consequences of technical factors. However, contemporary technologies are "plastic" and malleable, and they can support multiple possibilities for their use through configuration/reconfiguration. The implications of sociotechnical ideas need to be reconsidered against the emergent, in-use interactions of technical and social factors.

Chapter **6**

From Socio-Technical to Critical Complementarist: A New Direction for Information Systems Development

Steve Clarke and Brian Lehaney

6.1 Introduction

"There is, at present, no single theory around which system thinkers of the hard and soft schools might reasonably unite. Viewpoints and methods they invoke tend, even today, to be either hard or soft" (Hitchens and Shrivenham, 1991).

Early information systems development (ISD) was firmly rooted in the functionalist traditions of the natural sciences. This history has given rise to a problem-solving, reductionist focus which is still in evidence today, but which in the 1980s and 1990s has been challenged by alternative soft approaches. These soft methods treat information systems as human activity systems, and concentrate on interpretation of the problem situation from the viewpoint of those involved in and affected by the system.

The socio-technical school seeks to resolve this problem by developing approaches which address both social (human-centred) and technical issues within a single intervention. Traced from its roots in the Emery–Trist paradigm, this offers a number of possible development routes, one of which, critical theory, has been largely neglected in information systems development.

This chapter looks at the development of this thinking, and argues for a future direction within which both hard and soft schools may contribute: arguably the goal of socio-technical thinking. The proposition posed is that a higher level, complementarist view should now supplant the current arguments; a view in which all methodologies may be employed where they can make a legitimate contribution. From this research a framework is suggested within which this can be achieved.

Throughout this chapter, reference is made to systems, information systems and computer information systems. The term "system" within this context is used to describe all activities which fall within the boundary of a given investigation. The information system is the part of the overall system of concern that deals with storing and manipulating information, whether or not this is based on technology. The computer system is the technology which may be used to enable the information system.

6.2 Information Systems Development: The Functionalist View

Pick up any standard text on ISD and certain factors consistently appear.

> Lyytinen and Hirschheim (1987) make a compelling case for the argument that few information systems can be considered a success.

1. A strong adherence to pragmatism, with little or no explicit recognition of underlying theory.
2. ISD is generally treated as a technical, problem solving domain.

The lack of theory and strong adherence to methodology leads to the development of information systems being perceived as a problem to be solved. The methodology is seen as the series of steps by which the solution can be reached, and techniques are developed as the means of achieving those steps. The result is that ISD texts almost universally recommend the use of project management techniques in order to build an information system.

This adherence to pragmatic problem solving leads to tensions when the information system or systems to be developed require significant user input. Just as most information systems development texts stress the project management, methodological, pragmatic approach to ISD, so they also emphasise the need for discovering the requirements of users, basing this view on the observation that information systems frequently fail to meet user needs. Most commonly, the incorporation of user requirements into ISD is achieved by including a user analysis stage within the existing problem solving approach (Wetherbe and Vitalari, 1994). Advice on how to undertake this user analysis is often addressed only weakly, reinforcing the functionalist, problem-means-solution view of information systems development: goal oriented, and with little explicit theoretical underpinning to the points made.

The reason for claiming success is, they argue, largely based on an erroneous classification of how such success should be measured, which usually focuses on the extent to which the completed information system meets the requirement specification laid out in advance. The main measures are negative ones, principally the so-called correspondence failure, whereby objectives are set, and failure is defined in terms of these objectives failing to be met. Lyytinen and Hirschheim (1987) promote the notion of expectation failure, or the failure of the information system to meet the expectations of the key stakeholder groups, as conveying a more pluralistically informed view, and adding weight to the critique of the functionalist position.

If functionalist approaches cannot adequately address the problems of development for information systems, what alternatives are available for this purpose?

6.3 Information Systems Development: The Interpretivist View

The interpretivist, or human-centred approach to ISD, has focused on the use of so-called soft, interpretivist methods. Soft systems methodology (SSM) (Checkland, 1981) for example, incorporates human factors into the development process by taking a more holistic, systemic view:

> "Focusing on one aspect or even several aspects of a situation is unsystemic, and at best systematic. The systematic nature of IT clashes with the systemic nature of IS...coping with this tension between systematic and systemic natures is a challenge which has to be taken up by the IS profession" (Angell, 1990, pp. 168–74).

Stowell and West (1991) take a similar position, differentiating the idea of information system from that of computer system, two terms which from their perspective are too often viewed as synonymous. The information system is seen as a more systemic whole in which the computer system may play a part. Stowell and West promote the client led design (CLD) methodology, arguing that since the information system results from social interaction, participants in that interaction ought to be central to information systems analysis and design. Information systems development therefore needs to be *driven* by interpretivism, and not, at the technical development stage, "engulfed by functionalism". Consequently Stowell and West are critical of methods whereby soft, interpretative approaches such as SSM are used to front-end a technological development, arguing that once the soft analysis is passed to the technical specialists the benefits of that soft analysis are largely lost.

These, and other contributors to the soft school, effectively indicate a need to combine hard (technical) and soft (social) aspects within a single intervention, and this is the thrust of the socio-technical approach, which is discussed briefly in the following section.

6.4 The Socio-Technical Approach

Many would trace socio-technical thinking from the work of Emery and Trist, itself located within the field of human relations, and beginning with the now seminal longwall mining study (Trist and Bamford, 1951).

Socio-technical thinking has been applied widely to ISD, an early example being the ETHICS methodology (Effective Technical and Human Implementation of Computer-based Systems). ETHICS (Mumford, 1985a) was developed in the 1970s to combine organisational, administrative and quality-of-working-life factors, and is an explicitly socio-technical methodology.

Multiview (Avison and Wood-Harper, 1991) similarly enables the combination of social and technical issues, and is based on the assertion that at any stage of information systems development the approach is contingent on the circumstances met at that stage. It differs from traditional "systems development life cycle" (SDLC) based methodologies in that it is not seen as step-by-step problem solving, but as an iterative process in which different approaches may be used at different times. Multiview accepts the view that no one methodology can be seen to work in all cases, and explicitly recognises the need for participation.

Participation is one of the key issues in socio-technical studies, where recent work has suggested that, whilst crucial to ISD, participation is often pursued in ignorance of political conflict (Bjerkness and Bratteteig, 1995). So we have identified two key developmental areas for socio-technical analysis: participation and methodological mixing. These issues lie at the heart of critical theory, and it is therefore from this grounding that further development is sought, based initially on Jackson and Keys (1984) "system of systems methodologies" (SOSM) (see Fig. 6.1).

The Jackson and Keys framework seeks to classify organisational problem contexts along two dimensions: the complexity of the system of concern (simple or complex); and the degree of agreement among participants (unitary, pluralist or coercive). Whether a system of concern is seen to be simple or complex is determined by two factors: the number of sub-systems and interactions; and the amount of human activity (increased human activity

	Unitary	Pluralist	Coercive
Simple			
Complex			

Figure 6.1 The system of systems methodologies.

means more complexity). The degree of agreement is unitary if all participants agree; pluralist if there are multiple viewpoints but there is seen to be a possibility of reaching agreement (for example, through debate); and coercive if power structures are preventing effective participation and therefore blocking agreement.

The relevance to the socio-technical domain can be seen by addressing the unitary and pluralistic contexts. Where there is agreement (unitary), there is little requirement for debate, and problems become design-focused or technical. Where the situation is pluralistic, the initial focus has to be on debate, and hence is located in the social arena.

This gives rise to the argument that information systems development perceived from a socio-technical perspective offers a limited view, particularly when faced with coercive problem contexts. Recent thinking (Clarke, 1997) has sought to develop ISD beyond this debate by pursuing the complementarist strand in management science. The following section points to an alternative conception of ISD.

6.5 Information Systems Development: The Complementarist View

The proposition put forward here is that the development of information systems can no longer be perceived as purely social or technical. There is a need to move beyond this perception, and look at the issues involved in attempting to combine both hard and soft methods in a single intervention: the objective that lies at the heart of the socio-technical approaches. Within this section, the current status is first developed through a critique of hard and soft thinking.

6.5.1 Hard and Soft Thinking: A Critique

We begin this critique with Jackson's analysis of Checkland's views on hard systems thinking, categorising them as being: "Guided by functionalist assumptions. The world is seen as made up of systems which can be studied 'objectively' and which have clearly identifiable purposes." These functionalist roots of hard systems thinking severely limit its domain of applicability, but equally soft systems thinking suffers from its own limitations:

"The recommendations of soft systems thinking remain 'regulative' because no attempt is made to ensure that the conditions for 'genuine' debate are provided. The kind of open participative debate which is essential for the success of the soft systems approach, and is the only justification for the results obtained, is impossible to obtain in problem situations in which there is conflict bertween interest groups, each of which is able to mobilise differential power resources" (Jackson, 1990, pp. 657–68).

It may therefore be concluded that, not only might a view of only the functionalist elements of a problem situation prove inadequate, but adherence to any single methodology or paradigm cannot meet all the needs of a given problem context. An approach is therefore needed which can combine methodologies from different paradigms in a wider systems context, and the way forward has been sought from a critical or complementarist position. An early recognition of the theoretical validity of a critical approach to information systems development was by Hirschheim and Klein (1989), who saw neither the functionalist nor the interpretivist approach as adequate. Hirschheim and Klein viewed functionalism as the "orthodox approach to systems development", and characterised it as means and ends dominated but with little discussion about the ends, since these are taken as given: "there is one reality that is measurable and essentially the same for everyone ... the role of the developer is to design information systems that model this reality." The ends can seldom be assumed to be agreed, and in modelling reality the question of whose reality becomes paramount. Whilst interpretivism offers an alternative to functionalism, in so far as it does not accept there to be an objective reality but only socially constructed reality, its relativist stance makes it "... *completely uncritical* of the potential dysfunctional side effects of using particular tools and techniques for information systems development" (Hirschheim and Klein, 1989, pp. 263–280). Different information systems development outcomes are simply viewed as the result of different socially constructed realities. Through critical social theory there is the possibility of moving to a critically reflective, radical position. This critical social stream has been taken up by critical thinkers in the domain of management science, under the banner of critical systems thinking, and it is from here that a way forward for ISD is to be found.

6.5.2 Critical Systems Thinking

Critical systems thinking (CST), it is argued, accepts the contribution of both hard and soft approaches, but exposes both as special cases with limited domains of application and, through critique, enhances awareness of the circumstances in which such approaches can be properly employed.

CST draws its theoretical support from the theories of Habermas, and in particular Habermas's "Theory of Knowledge Constitutive Interests" (KCI), in which it is argued that all human endeavour is undertaken in satisfaction of three cognitive or "knowledge constitutive" interests: technical (prediction and control), practical (human communicative interaction) and emancipatory (social relations of power and domination). The value of CST in information systems interventions can be demonstrated through the Burrell and Morgan grid (1979, p. 22). Burrell and Morgan's work, together with contributions from Oliga (1991), may be interpreted as shown in Figure 6.2.

This position explicitly draws on critique and complementarism. Critique in this sense "[consists of] examining and re-examining taken-for-granted assumptions, together with the conditions which gave rise to them" (Midgley,

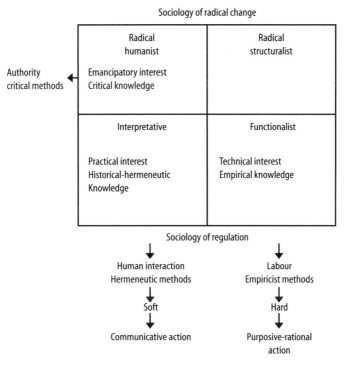

Sociology of radical change

Figure 6.2 The social validity of hard, soft and critical approaches.

1995a, pp. 61–71). This Kantian notion of critique enables participants in an IS intervention to look beyond the boundaries traditionally set, and challenge the development process from a position of practical rather than instrumental reason: that is to say, it is *dependent on* a dialectic or debating process. This position is developed by Oliga (Fig. 6.2). Beginning from Burrell and Morgan's (1979) classification of social theories, it could be argued that most ISD work is at worst located in the functionalist paradigm and at best in the interpretative. A functionalist approach to ISD, following Oliga's reasoning, casts the intervention in satisfaction of humankind's technical interest, applying hard methods in an instrumental manner. An interpretative approach sees humankind pursuing the practical interest; using soft methods to support communicative action. Fundamentally, in theoretical terms, the functionalist is seeking an *answer* (or the "truth" or "facts"), whilst the interpretivist is aiming to surface the many different *viewpoints* and, ultimately, attempting to reconcile them.

The difficulty with this is that, in terms of social theory, both approaches are firmly set as *regulative*, or unable to affect the status quo. The solution, for critical theorists, is seen to lie in a move to the radical humanist paradigm, where the aim is to challenge existing power structures, most often through emancipatory action.

Complementarism rests on the encouragement of diversity and the concept that methodologies can do no more than "legitimately contribute in areas of specific context" (Flood, 1990, p. 28). In other words, the interventionist should not be looking for the "right" hard or soft methodology, but should be using methodologies or even parts of methodologies together in a single intervention according to the nature of the problem context. However, this is more than a simple "pick and mix" problem. In ISD, our experience of working with computer systems developers and systems participants confirms communication to be blocked by each group becoming locked in its own paradigm: the complementarist aim is therefore to address this by taking a "multi-paradigmatic" approach, where action is undertaken in satisfaction of the basic cognitive ("knowledge constitutive") interests.

The objective of human emancipation, from an organisational standpoint, is to enable the achievement of human potentiality, which, it is argued, is enhanced where information systems are implemented in a way that promotes human well-being. The work particularly of Klein & Hirschheim 1993 and Lyytinen & Hirschheim 1987 gives further support to this view.

6.5.3 A Critical Framework for Computer-based Information Systems Development

The work of Jackson and Keys (1984) (Fig. 6.1) proved to be a major turning point in the development of a critical framework which is true to the commitments of critical systems thinking. By looking at the range of problem contexts and at the systems methodologies available for addressing these contexts, Jackson and Keys provided a unified approach which draws on the strengths of the relevant methodologies, rather than debating which method is best, and argued for a reconciliation focusing on which method to use in which context, controlled by a "system of systems methodologies". The key developments from this initial work (Midgley, 1995a) are:

- total systems intervention (TSI) combined with SOSM;
- TSI reconstituted;
- the creative design of methods; and
- critical appreciation.

In developing a framework for information systems development (ISD), TSI in its various forms currently emerges as the most promising basis, offering as it does a solid framework of inquiry, design and critique which most comprehensively actions the commitments of critical systems thinking. In the following section, TSI is discussed as a basis for a 'critical complementarist' interventionist framework for ISD.

6.5.4 Total Systems Intervention

The application of TSI to information systems development works in the following way (Fig. 6.3):

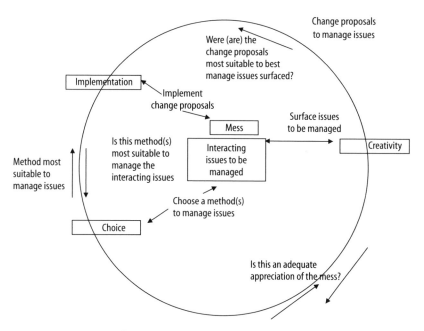

Figure 6.3 The Process of TSI (Flood, 1995).

1. In the clockwise mode, TSI addresses the problem situation by means of creativity, choice and implementation. Creativity uses creative thinking techniques (e.g. brainstorming, lateral thinking, metaphor) to surface the issues to be managed; choice determines the selection of method(s) to manage those issues; implementation implements the change proposals using the chosen methods.

2. In the anti-clockwise mode, TSI supports critical reflection at each phase: does choice express an adequate appreciation of the problem situation?; is implementation using the methods most suitable to manage the issues surfaced?; if we think creatively about the change proposals are they the most suitable to manage the issues surfaced?

So, for example, faced with the "problem" of installing a communication network, it is not uncommon to see the "solution" in terms of a technical specification of computers and network hardware and software.

TSI sees it rather differently:

1. The issues to be managed might surface, through a brainstorming or lateral thinking exercise, as a need to support decision making throughout the organisation by improved information handling.

2. The method chosen initially to "manage" the process might be a combination of (say) interactive planning with a software development method. Further critical analysis might surface the rich pictures of soft systems methodology as an addition to the approach.

3. Implementation of these methods changes (and hopefully improves) the original "mess", at which point the process continues, probably with further creative analysis.

The value of TSI lies in its ability to allow the complementary use of methodologies in a single intervention, and its critical reflection, which is explicitly lacking in the predominant hard and soft methodologies. Where an intervention is complex, and is likely to require multiple methodologies, TSI further offers a framework for choice, into which may be inserted any methods relevant to the intervention in question. This is presented (Table 6.1) together with an assessment of how a selection of methodologies may address the technical (designing), practical (debating), or emancipatory (disemprisoning) issues encountered within a given problem context. The framework of designing, debating and disemprisoning promoted by Flood corresponds to other classifications used in this chapter, listed for completeness in Table 6.2.

Table 6.1. Methodological choice matrix (Flood, 1995)

	Designing		Debating			Disemprisoning
Methodology	SDLC	VSD	SAST	IP	SSM	CSH
Common Principles	Communication Control Efficiency Effectiveness Emphasis on location and elimination of error		Participation Learning Understanding			Identify whose interests are served Link org. power structures to biases in society Identify how biases are mobilised in the org. Identify experts and their position in the power structure
Distinguishing Principles	Design Control Structure Prime	Process Control Environmental Analysis Organisation Prime	Attenuating Adversarial Debate	Diversifying Consensual Debate		Identify source of: motivation control expertise legitimisation

Key:
SDLC   Systems Development Life Cycle
VSD   Viable Systems Diagnosis
SAST   Strategic Assumption Surfacing and Testing
IP   Interactive Planning
SSM   Soft Systems Methodology
CSH   Critical Systems Heuristics

Table 6.2. Different representations of the socio-technical debate

Author / School	Categories ...		
Flood	Designing	Debating	Disemprisoning
'Hard / Soft	Hard	Soft	Critical
Burrell and Morgan	Functionalist	Interpretivist	Radical Humanist
Habermas	Technical	Practical	Emancipatory
Socio-Technical	Technical	Social	Coercive
Jackson	Unitary	Pluralist	Coercive

This framework may be used to help with choice of any methodologies; for a range of methodologies available and further developments in the process of assessment and choice, where a number of methodologies addressing hard, soft and critical issues, and a framework for facilitating choice between them, is presented (Clarke, Lehaney and Martin, 1998).

The application of TSI to information systems development has been undertaken in major interventions within the health service and higher education (Clarke, 1997, Lehaney and Clarke, 1997). The outcome of these interventions supports TSI as a "critical complementarist" framework for ISD, but also poses questions which are currently the subject of further research effort.

To use TSI requires a grasp of an approach which operates in three modes and three phases, is recursive and iterative, and is a far from simple undertaking. Since such an approach is unlike the methods used by most interventionists in the information systems domain, the learning process is made even more difficult. Added to this, human-centred intervention techniques, which are implicitly dependent on theory and practice from the field of action research, must be mastered. All of this represents a significant barrier to the use of these methods in the operational and strategic development of information systems, and the likelihood is that for the foreseeable future most interventionists will continue to use, at best, single methodologies and, at worst, the pragmatic techniques with which they have become familiar.

6.6 Lessons Learned and Signposts for the Future

1. Information systems have been characterised as functionalist (technical) or interpretivist (social): this characterisation is cast as an impoverished and partial view.
2. Advances made from the functionalist / interpretivist to the socio-technical position have been outlined.
3. Socio-technical developments have been classified as unitary/pluralist on the SOSM.
4. The perceived problems of socio-technical approaches have been outlined as an inadequate enabling of participation, particularly in coercive environments, and weak support for multi-methodological intervention.

5. Signposts point to a "critical complementarist" approach, framed within the radical humanist paradigm, underpinned by critical social theory, and aimed at emancipatory practice.

6. A discussion has been put forward of the theoretical grounding of the critical approach in critical systems thinking and the critical social theory of Habermas.

7. The use of total systems intervention, as an application of critical theory within the domain of information systems, has been described and critiqued.

8. A way forward has been suggested, highlighting problems and further developments necessary to the approach.

9. The perceived benefits of enhanced "complementarist" mixing of methodologies and improvements to participation in coercive contexts have been outlined.

Chapter **7**

Socio-Technical Systems: Technique or Philosophy?

David Sutton

7.1 Introduction

In this chapter I suggest that the term "socio-technical systems" (STS) has been presented as either a method addressing a four-faceted view of enterprises, or as a set of principles originating from a desire to counteract the excesses of Tayloristic management. Problems arise when either position is adopted without regard to the other. I propose a third position on the nature of STS practice which underlies the first two positions. This third type of STS is based upon the total dependence of enterprises upon human interaction. I argue that this third type of STS explains how the four facets of enterprises interact, and why participative approaches underpin STS practice.

Practical studies suggest that enterprises are composed of, or are intersections of, different types of entity or concern (Trist and Bamforth, 1951; Emery and Trist, 1961): the stereotypical "Leavitt diamond" is perhaps the best known (Leavitt, 1958). It has also been suggested that STS principles have emerged as a response to the excesses of the mechanistic/scientific view of management labelled as Taylorism (Emery and Trist, 1961; Gill, 1991). STS design has a considerable following and some impressive achievements in producing high quality work systems (Perry, 1984; Hanna, 1988; Mumford and Macdonald, 1989; Mumford, 1993). However, there still seems to be a need to make the link between STS principles and STS practice more widely accessible.

During my 20 years as an independent consultant, I have studied and employed STS philosophy, principles and practice, and should like to offer some suggestions on the clarification and unification of these distinctions.

Like STS, the problem-solving approach known as "soft systems methodology" (SSM) was developed as a response to the deficiencies in the "RAND" approach to "systems analysis" (Checkland, 1981). The "RAND" approach was seen as a mechanistic approach well suited to analysing complex engineering projects but inappropriate for handling problems in complex social systems. But although intended as a flexible, facilitative approach to assist groups of stakeholders, a review of SSM found that it was being used by some in a very rigid and prescriptive manner. This identified "Type I" and "Type II" uses of SSM (Checkland and Scholes, 1990).

It seems that there is a parallel situation with STS, and this chapter considers the value of making an analogous distinction in the case of STS. Let us first consider some of the typical forms in which STS is discussed.

7.2 Forms of STS

STS can be introduced in a number of guises. Some exponents present STS primarily as a technique with quite rigidly defined features that differentiate "true" STS from imitations. I will call this position "Type I STS". Other sources make reference to STS principles, implying that it is philosophy rather than the detailed practice that characterises an STS approach. I will call this position "Type II STS".

7.2.1 Type I STS

The practical recognition of STS is that all work situations, whether factory or office, large or small, have characteristics that are governed by more than the primary activity of the organisation. Perhaps the best-known expression of this was provided by Leavitt in his "diamond" model depicting the four interdependent factors he considered to exist in socio-technical systems, as shown in Figure 7.1.

The diagram in Figure 7.1 shows that any organisation both shapes, and is shaped by, these prime components, and their interactions. Enid Mumford (1983a) has emphasised the necessity of appreciating the dynamic nature of these practical issues, thus:

- changes in *technology* will alter the nature of the *tasks* and vice versa,
- changes in the *tasks* to be done will affect the *people* and vice versa,
- changes in *organisation* will influence the *people* and vice versa.

But although Figure 7.1 seems to indicate that such practical considerations follow naturally, not all the features of STS come from this framework. For example, some of the important aspects of the socio-technical movement are stated to be:

Figure 7.1 Key domains of a socio-technical system (Leavitt, 1958).

- the shift in emphasis from the analysis of solely techno-economic factors in conventional systems design to the consideration of behavioural factors too;
- the understanding that behavioural factors tend to dominate the other factors in achieving the desired performance from a system;
- that peoples" values are accepted as an important driver, and that these include not only those who sponsor and design the system but those who will perform within the system;
- analytical tools, developed within the movement, which help to define the social ends that systems also have to meet (Holti and Sutton, 1992).

Whilst behavioural factors seem to refer clearly enough to the content or implications of Figure 7.1, the others do not. These other aspects of STS emerge from an inherent value position that was clearly articulated from different origins.

7.2.2 Type II STS

Turning to the philosophical nature of STS, the following principles were originally stated by the late Albert Cherns in a 1976 article in Human Relations as a guide to designing technology and organisational systems in general:

1. **The principle of compatibility**
   If the objective of design is to create a group structure where staff share problem solving and decision taking, then the design process must also involve shared problem solving and decision making.

2. **The principle of minimum critical specification**
   Staff should be given the freedom to decide how they work. Jobs should not be too tightly structured although essential tasks need to be identified.

3. **The principle of solving problems where they arise**
   Groups should take responsibility for identifying and correcting any problems that arise in and from their work. This should not be done by other groups

4. **The multi-skill principle**
   Individual staff members should be assisted to acquire a number of different skills and to participate in complex tasks that require a variety of skills for their completion.

5. **The principle of boundary management**
   The boundaries between the work of one group and the work of other groups should be clearly defined. However, boundaries should be carefully managed to fit the logic of the processes and to ensure that there is good co-operation and co-ordination between the groups.

6. The principle of information flow
Information systems should be designed so that information goes first to the group that will use or has produced it, before it may be accessed by other levels.

7. The principle of support congruence
Systems of social support should reinforce required behaviour (e.g. group work should have an element of group payment).

8. The principle of design and human values
The objective of organisational design should be to provide a high quality of working life for all participants in the work situation.

9. The principle of incompletion
This acknowledges that design, for organisations operating in the real world, is an iterative and continuous process.

The issue is how to reconcile the two presentations of STS when they seem to operate in different ways and have no necessary connection between them.

7.2.3 Linking the Two Categories of STS Features

One important link is that both positions recognise the limitations and undesirable effects of adopting a purely mechanistic view of an enterprise. Both presentations of STS reject the validity of Taylorism, one by challenging the facts (i.e., organisations equate to machines), the other by challenging the principles (i.e., quality is defined purely in techno-economic terms).

Type I STS emerged from practical studies in the field and relates to a model of the key features of an enterprise. By working from "what's the essential nature of an enterprise?" we might say that Type I STS challenges the presumption that organisational processes are executed entirely by unconscious cogs. Here, Taylorism is challenged on scientifically logical grounds by disputing the ontological assumptions implicit in viewing an enterprise as a machine.

On the other hand, the Type II STS seems to imply a set of operating principles or even human values about how one "ought" to behave in the creation and management of enterprises. Type II STS argues that measurement of value should not exclude human or subjective factors. In this mode, Taylorism is challenged on value grounds by disputing the assumptions that total production "per operating unit" is the prime objective to be pursued.

Thus STS takes positions upon the two core matters:

- what people think organisations are,
- how people think they should behave in organisations.

The first of these is an ontological position, the second addresses values or ethics. It is my view that the essence of STS lies in embracing *both* facets of STS in practice, and that failure to do so creates many problems. To see why we need to pay attention to both facets, and what happens when we don't, we need to consider how values and ontology link together in a unifying framework.

7.2.4 Unifying Framework

In practice, what we think is important, and why, and what we therefore consider we should do, are all linked together. In other words, all values, ontology, epistemology, methodology, methods and tools are linked into a hierarchy of enterprise issues of different logical type and scope. The definitions I use here are as follows:

Ontology	concerning the essential nature of whatever we are considering. Basically, "what is it?" with regard to any feature of our "domain in focus".
Epistemology	concerning the nature of the knowledge that may be gained and discussed about features of our domain in focus. In essence "what may we know about it?"
Methodology	covering not only actions to gain knowledge of entities but also the nature of the thinking about and interventions in the domain that are possible (conceivable) given the ontology and the epistemology. Basically "how do we interact with it?"
Methods	concerning specific techniques for achieving the above mentioned "interactions".
Tools	concerning specific artifacts that are designed to support specific methods.
Values	affecting all of the above, they concern the core criteria to which we refer whenever we make choices – what shall I consider important?, worth looking at?, worth finding out?, worth striving for? etc.

The interrelationships between these levels of focus is a dynamic one, as shown in Figure 7.2.

Using this unifying framework, Type I STS starts with an assertion that in enterprises there are sets of issues and elements that relate primarily to people, organisation, task or technology. Thus Type I STS takes an assertive position at the ontological level.

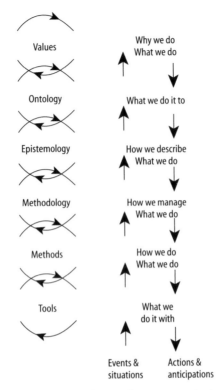

Figure 7.2 Logically distinct types of issue relevant to organisational interventions.

Other than suggesting that there should be two "streams of analysis", the technical and the social, Type I STS has no strong position on what might be the nature of the critical entities in each of the categories of task, technology, people and organisation. It seems that choice of what is significant at this level will be a matter of local context or "fit". It is therefore non-committal at the epistemological level.

At the methodological level, however, it strongly asserts that the design methodology should incorporate "participation". Type I STS is therefore quite positive at the methodological level.

Typically, the elaboration of STS practice then moves directly to specific questions that determine technical and job satisfaction needs (Mumford, 1993; Mumford, 1983a). This alternation across logical levels between being normative or neutral is seen as an alternative between assertive and non-committal, or it may be simply positive or negative. Judgements about what should be treated as important and relevant (epistemology) and what methods are appropriate to use, arise not from the ontology of STS but from the values, that is, the Type II STS presentation.

It is possible to follow the implications of the value position of Type II STS and see that it is positive with regard to values (e.g. the principles of

STS), epistemology (e.g. the job satisfaction analysis) and methods (e.g. formal STS methods such as ETHICS). On the other hand, Type II STS authorities are less definite on matters of ontology, methodological frameworks or tools.

Thus it is argued here that a full STS approach must specifically acknowledge and explicitly consider the implications of both ontological (Type I) and value (Type II) positions. What happens when only Type I or Type II is adopted is the theme of the next section.

7.2.5 Hazards of Fragmentation

Some suggest that the US view of STS is rigidly prescriptive on how an intervention is managed and activities carried out. Such a requirement to automatically implement a detailed procedure may be seen as allowing the ontological (Type I) view of STS to predominate. This position might also contravene the original motivation for both forms of STS, namely to counteract the excesses of the mechanistic, Tayloristic approach to management. Another example of Type I is the introduction of organisational change claiming to be based upon STS without the advance participation and acceptance of those affected (Mumford and Sutton, 1991).

Others suggest that the "European" approach to STS is more pragmatic. However, over-emphasis on the principles of STS without regard to the realities on the ground can produce equally undesirable results.

An example of pursuing values without regard to organisational reality can be found in the attitudes of some to the "multi-skilling" principle of STS. The early days of STS were devoted to work situations that predominantly featured process operatives of relatively low skill: the multi-skilling principle may simply be a feature appropriate only to those types of situation. There are now many professional and scientific areas where expertise can only be acquired through long-term practice and is a key source of status and job satisfaction. I have encountered many situations where the notion of multi-skilling was introduced into such environments with disastrous results.

Principles cannot be applied dogmatically; regard must be paid to the ontological realities. To see the truth of this, ask yourself just how a Professor of Organisational Design would feel on being told that henceforth she and her colleagues in Marketing, Finance, Computing and Creativity will be required to cover for each other, "Oh, and you will each need to provide a brief manual on all your routines so that anyone else can easily pick up your tasks where you left off, and hand them over to anyone else".

This discussion is seeking to suggest a third way of using STS models and principles: to help people understand, respect and negotiate each other's positions and agendas, rather than to provide a direct input to plans for action. This third type of STS may be termed "appreciative": it is employed to enrich the reflections of groups and individuals about the nature of the situations in which they find themselves.

7.2.6 Type III STS

In this "appreciative" mode, STS models and principles are introduced only to help people raise, discuss and resolve issues. Used in this way, the original "Leavitt diamond" in Figure 7.1 can be used as a starting point for broad discussions. These discussions then elaborate multiple issues whilst keeping in mind their relationships.

In my early use of Type III STS, a frequent criticism was that people were insufficiently emphasised. Organisations consist of *people*, and indeed could not exist without them. *People* do the *tasks*, and *people* use the *technology*. It is through people that all the interactions are actualised and all the organisational activities conducted. To better support this message, it was necessary to remodel Figure 7.1 so that people are central in its configuration (Sutton and Sutton, 1990). This "person centred" depiction is shown in Figure 7.3.

Using an STS model like this allows us to understand why it is not possible to take a strong position at the epistemological level. Each of the four facets represents a different focus upon what constitutes an enterprise. Each viewpoint or focus recognises different important aspects of an enterprise and is unable to comprehend other viewpoints. This helps us remember that we always need to consider these four very different perspectives, without insisting that any enterprise is a simple combination of these viewpoints.

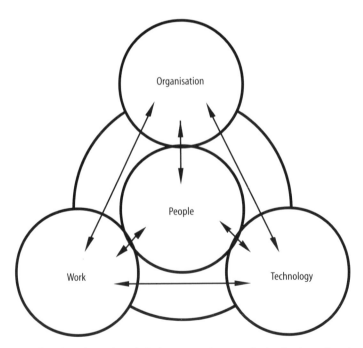

Figure 7.3 Key domains of a socio-technical system redrawn to depict the dynamic nature of the interactions (Sutton and Sutton, 1990).

There is a parallel to this in physics. Light may be discussed and experimented with quite successfully as if it were a solid particle. Equally light may be discussed and manipulated as if it were an immaterial wave. Thus, light is neither a wave nor a particle, it is something "meta" to both of these concepts, but which we are able to appreciate using the two, quite incompatible, metaphors.

The importance of this STS model with respect to enterprises is that it reveals at least four significant viewpoints that need to be considered when discussing what should be looked at, measured, taken account of, and so on (i.e. when adopting an epistemological stance). These viewpoints will be "incompatible" in that they are likely to use different languages, and use different methods and tools. But all these viewpoints can be accommodated through the conversations and interactions of people involved in a real situation.

This may be seen to be the practical justification for the methodological emphasis upon "participation" in STS. Only if all stakeholders are in constant dialogue can all the strands of analysis and intervention proceed to achieve mutual recognition and dynamic accommodation.

7.3 Type III STS in Use

When this model was used to clarify situations, we were often drawn into elaborating the content of the individual viewpoints or components. A recurring theme began to emerge. All enterprises have a purpose or mission. They interact with an environment which in turn influences what the enterprise does. In addition, all enterprises have their own infrastructure and culture which governs the way things are done within it.

So our STS model can be extended to include a breakdown of the interrelated factors operating within the "organisation" component. However, it is people who agree and define the enterprise's "Mission". It is people who recognise and interpret the "Context" and people who design and implement the "Infrastructure". Therefore, principal sub-components of the organisational forces are represented in Figure 7.4 with, again, "People" at the centre.

This representation depicts two "people cycles" and they allude to two different groups and two different perspectives. At the broadest level of focus, the "people" represented by the large circle in the centre of the model refers to the organisation-wide people and people issues. At the second level of focus, the "people" depicted at the centre of the organisation component, refers to the people and issues concerned with the stewardship of the organisational factors. For example, they might be those at board level, followed, at deeper levels of recursion, by departmental directors or, indeed, any people focusing upon management aspects at whatever level. The general form of the more developed model is represented in Figure 7.5. A fuller description of this elaboration of the person-centred STS model is given in Sutton and Sutton (1990).

This recursive socio-technical model is not intended to be a portrayal of the fine structure of enterprises in any real sense; rather it is employed in a variety of ways to assist reflection and communication amongst participants in

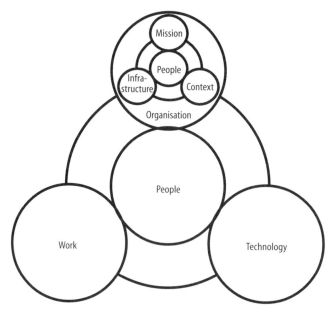

Figure 7.4 Organisation component of a socio-technical system.

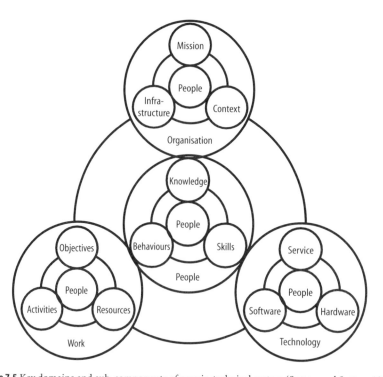

Figure 7.5 Key domains and sub-components of a socio-technical system (Sutton and Sutton, 1990).

problematic situations. The extent to which you sub-divide any cycle into sub-cycles will depend on your reason for doing the exercise. Analysis of your organisation, department, role or whatever, in any cycle of concern, can be a valuable aid in resolving many managerial/operational issues and problems. For example, mapping your own work domain as a sub-cycle of the department and/or organisation as a whole could provide the necessary structure to help you clarify your position and whether that is where you want to be. It can also help you to highlight resource deficiencies, human or material, and to pinpoint missing links in communication or co-ordination.

A final feature to be emphasised is the centrality of people and inter-personal communication as a critical element in the effective functioning of any enterprise. It is precisely through the joint preparation of the basic model, and the consequent planning, discussions, actions and sharing of experiences that the required constructive interaction between the four STS "forces" is achieved.

7.4 Summary

The main point of this chapter is to suggest that the term STS is a combination of technique, philosophy *and* interpretive device. The implications I have been seeking to highlight are:

- The application of STS principles must take account of local realities. The use of formalised STS "methods" must remain in touch and harmonise with the principles.
- The unifying framework and the recursive model can help to clarify and relate the different elements of STS to the local concerns and context of all participants in a systems development exercise.
- STS has three strands: one working "top-down" from principles, one working "bottom-up" from the realities of situations, and one working "inside-out" to achieve the dynamic accommodation between all the relevant aspects which constitutes the "fit" required. At every level, account must be taken of the constraints and opportunities afforded by all three modes of STS use.
- STS can be more than a technique; it can also be a framework to assist the appreciation of complex situations, and the management of interventions that employ a variety of methods to effect co-ordinated change in several of the STS domains.
- The only way that "fit" can be achieved in enterprises is through the mutual accommodation of the four interdependent components. This accommodation can only be reached through constant dialogue amongst all stakeholders, i.e. "participation".

Chapter **8**

Sociotechnical Design and Economic Objectives

Richard T. Grenci

8.1 Introduction

Joint optimisation is one of the defining principles in sociotechnical systems (STS) design; it directs organisational change based on the trade-offs between technical, social and economic objectives. In essence, STS design seeks to achieve certain economic gains by balancing (or jointly optimising) social and technical change. Most business managers would relate economic gains with higher-level measures such as profitability or return on investment. Yet, STS practices tend to disregard profitability by focusing on operational outcomes or behavioural objectives. Consider the recent redesign of the services provided by the Oregon Department of Motor Vehicles; the massive effort failed because the new systems and processes were designed to benefit the users, not the customers (Hayes, 1997).

> In other words, an STS intervention is often targetted at increased process efficiency; but increased efficiency might not translate into economic gains for the firm.

Not only that, depending upon the organisational and environmental context, a traditional approach to joint optimisation can turn out to be less than operationally efficient.

Ensuring efficient STS design requires joint optimisation to be extended beyond the idea of balance or trade-off. In essence, joint optimisation should be associated with the concepts of interdependent features and increased benefits. For example, given the relationship between team-based structures and team-based incentives, there is an increased benefit to employing both features.

By thinking in terms of increased benefits, it becomes evident that there is an advantage to interrelated changes as opposed to isolated change, particularly when costs are considered. This broader view of joint optimisation has interesting implications for organisational design decisions. In particular, it implies that an STS intervention should not focus on preferred (ideal) practices; rather, it should consider the entire organisational configuration as a comprehensive set of interrelated factors. This is consistent with a study of more than 100 change efforts that concluded that the breadth and the depth of the change are critical to achieving long-term, bottom-line gains (Hall, Rosenthal and Wade, 1993).

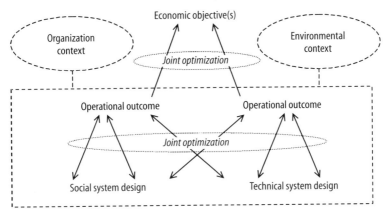

Figure 8.1 STS design and economic objectives.

The relationships between organisational factors may be the key to a successful STS intervention; and despite the emphasis on a balance between the social and technical systems of an organisation, relationships within each system are also relevant to achieving success. However, interrelationships at higher levels in the organisation must be considered. In fact, given a more direct impact on economic performance, the higher-level interdependencies are perhaps of greater consequence than the lower-level design interdependencies. Taking a multilevel perspective will allow design practices to be targeted at both operational and strategic objectives relative to an underlying goal of economic gain. At the same time, contextual conditions and realised outcomes will shape the direction of sociotechnical change (see Fig. 8.1). Ultimately, STS tenets such as joint optimisation can be framed within (and shown to be compatible with) the economic objectives of a firm.

8.2 Sociotechnical Perspectives

With origins in human relations (Perrow, 1983), sociotechnical systems design primarily focuses on the social systems of an organisation. In particular, STS interventions often favour certain practices such as creating autonomous work groups and developing technical skills (Pasmore, Francis, Haldeman and Shani, 1982; Beekun, 1989). Despite this focus, joint optimisation prescribes a balance between the social and technical systems of an organisation. It even allows for equifinal solutions by accepting that different technological alternatives could be employed for a given social structure (Herbst, 1974). However, the scope of past STS interventions has been "restrictively narrow" (Pava, 1986). In that respect, a closer look at STS interventions reveals that:

- only a small percentage of STS designs have tended to utilise a change in technology;

- of the features generally included in STS designs, technological change has been related to the least success in terms of productivity; and

- the greatest increases in productivity have been associated with more comprehensive STS efforts that employed a large number of changes. (Pasmore et al., 1982; Beekun, 1989).

This last point regarding comprehensive change can be emphasised by the tremendous success achieved at the Saturn Corporation.

8.2.1 Comprehensive Change

Comprehensive organisational change was at the forefront of General Motors' (GM) vision of their new Saturn subsidiary. In 1984, a group of people at GM went in search of a better way to build a better car. Seven years later, the first Saturn model rolled off the line; and it took only three more years for the subsidiary to turn a profit. Many would say that the groundwork and inspiration for the new organisation was laid in part by STS theory; others have prefaced that sentiment (Bohl, 1997).

> "Indeed, the early 1980's were a time for learning. Philosophical changes were in the wind, originating from the somewhat obscure concepts of 'socio-technical design'…"

Far from being obscure, the solid theoretical basis of STS design is (and has been) a key factor in directing social and technical change. Regardless of the underlying viewpoint, it is evident that STS principles were at the root of Saturn's success.

To begin with, the design and staffing of the Saturn Corporation followed the STS principle of involving the employees in all decision making. Employee participation was enhanced by an underlying commitment to build the company from the ground up. The combination of these factors served to solidify employee dedication as well as their sense of ownership of the success of the corporation. Perhaps more importantly, starting with a clean slate enabled a break from the mostly adversarial employee-management environment of the automobile industry. In fact, by physically removing the entire operation to a remote location, the environmental context was altered such that a new and cooperative culture was possible.

Starting with a clean slate also enabled the organisational structure (particularly the social aspects) to be designed truly as a comprehensive set of interrelated factors. Thus, instead of just offering lifetime employment, GM did so in conjunction with incentive-based pay. Instead of just creating autonomous work teams, GM did so in conjunction with consensus decision-making and team-based rewards. Instead of just broadening the scope of employee responsibility, GM did so in conjunction with an extensive and ongoing training program that covered practically all aspects of the business. More detailed descriptions of this "grand experiment" (Bohl, 1997; Solomon, 1991; Geber,

Table 8.1. Saturn's comprehensive design

Employee participation in organisational design
- onducted extensive fact-finding
- developed mission and goals
- agreed on start-up decisions
- determined plant location
- hired personnel

Union/management partnership
- shared decision making
- advisors and counsellors
- no privileged parking
- casual dress for all
- no private dining

Self-managed production teams
- self-directed budgeting and scheduling
- consensus decision making
- rotation of duties
- self-monitoring
- elected leader

Extensive and ongoing training
- technical, business, and personal
- internally developed
- scheduled by team
- tied to incentives
- cross-training

Incentive-based pay
- productivity-based incentives
- quality-based incentives
- 20% of salary at risk
- no hourly wages
- no time clocks

Lifetime employment

1992) make for a rich example of STS principles in action (a summary of which is provided in Table 8.1). Essentially, GM recreated the success of the Japanese auto industry, not with a piecemeal adoption of specific ideal practices, but with an implementation of a comprehensive set of practices that worked together. If the organisational design had been restricted to a preferred set of ideal features, the result could have been less than optimal.

8.2.2 Interdependencies

A restricted focus may be the reason for the unpredictable and often unproductive outcomes (Bleakley, 1993) that characterise interventions labelled as reengineering or business process redesign (BPR). The BPR prescription primarily emphasises information technology (IT) as the key enabler of process innovation. The attention placed on IT is embedded in an approach that calls for the identification of enablers as a whole. To that end, a sociotechnical view is advocated, and emphasis is given not only to information and its associated technology, but also to organisational and human resource enablers. Yet emphasis is not given to the interactions that exist between the enablers. For instance, the reengineering literature justifies the benefits of team structure by referring to Japanese productivity; likewise, lifetime employment and its beneficial effects in Japan are also discussed (Davenport, 1994a). However, even though each practice on its own can contribute to productivity, their coexistence could increase the overall benefit. There even could be a negative impact to adopting one of the practices in isolation. Nevertheless, the reengineering literature focuses on identifying ideal practices based on past successes rather than on the interdependence of factors.

It is possible, then, that the inconsistent success of reengineering efforts may be due to organisational designs that exploit interdependencies to varying degrees (Barua, Lee and Whinston, 1996). With IT-enabled reengineering, part of this problem may stem from an over-reliance on the benefits of technological change at the expense of social change. Similarly, in STS design, failure to recognise interdependent factors may be exacerbated by a bias towards social aspects such as group autonomy and reward systems. As discussed, even though STS theory subscribes to multiple technological alternatives, STS interventions frequently maintain existing technologies; thus many designs may be limited in the degree to which technical resources can be exploited as a complement to human resources. As a result, the optimisation of process performance can fall short of expectations. In fact, the tendency for STS interventions to optimise process objectives as opposed to economic objectives presents a problem in itself.

8.2.3 Strategic and Economic Objectives

The costs of investing in organisational change will offset, to some extent, the operational and market level benefits of the investment (Barua et al., 1996). Thus, success at the design level will

> Specifically, increased productivity does not always translate into optimal value; that is, an investment in technical and social change can be operationally optimal but economically inefficient.

not necessarily translate into economic success. Ultimately, decreased operating costs and increased revenues (due to strategic benefits) collectively must outweigh the capital costs of new technology or new social structures (see Fig. 8.2).

Consider the following example (Milgrom and Roberts, 1990). A decrease in the cost of computer-aided design (CAD) and computer-aided manufacturing (CAM) can lead to the adoption of both of these technologies, each resulting in its own operational and strategic benefits. But as CAD makes it less costly to employ a broader product line, and CAM makes it less costly to switch between products, there is an interrelationship that makes it profitable to adopt both technologies. More importantly, it may be unprofitable (in terms of bottom-line impact) to adopt a CAD system without adopting a CAM system. In essence, the economic success of technological or social change is determined ultimately not only by operational efficiencies, but also by the interrelation-

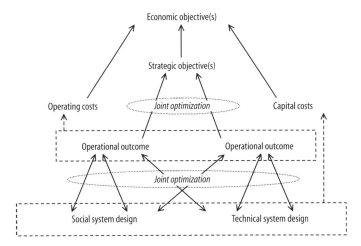

Figure 8.2 STS costs and benefits.

ships and the strategic benefits stemming from the change. This point is emphasised by Greyhound Lines' failure with the implementation of a computerised reservation system.

As the only national bus line in the United States, Greyhound Lines Incorporated gambled on a complex computerised reservation system (CRS) to pull the company out of bankruptcy. Even though the CRS required experienced operators with 40 hours of training, Greyhound maintained policies that fostered turnover so as to hold down wages. As the vice president for customer satisfaction recalled, management reasoned that "if people stayed around too long, they would get too sour and cynical" (Tomsho, 1994). This disregard of the social aspects of work, exacerbated by an unstable system, led to immediate operational problems. Not only did the time to issue a bus ticket initially double, but sales fell 12 per cent upon roll-out (Tomsho, 1994). Greyhound acted quickly to harness the new system; ultimately, customers could be efficiently scheduled for long-distance service throughout the United States. However, the increased efficiency in long-distance ticketing did not create a strategic benefit given the type of service being offered. To be more specific, a long-distance bus trip is an undesirable product given the time and cost associated with it, particularly when compared to low-fare airlines. Thus, the sole focus on operational objectives as opposed to strategic interrelationships resulted in economic inefficiency and poor financial performance.

8.3 Design Implications

With respect to interrelated organisational factors, a multilevel and comprehensive perspective offers interesting implications for STS design. These implications, as described in the preceding pages, provide for the following additional observations.

8.3.1 Bottom-Up and Top-Down

Since the context of every STS application is different, each intervention requires the revelation of a comprehensive set of relevant design features, task characteristics, and organisational and environmental factors. Ultimately, the goal is to evaluate the interrelationships between all of the factors in order to increase process performance. However, process efficiency must be considered with respect to higher-level strategic and economic objectives. Therefore, the evaluation of design alternatives should be embedded in a combined bottom-up and top-down approach with a continual focus on the higher-level objectives of the firm. For example, in the case of the Saturn Corporation, GM had a higher-level objective of utilising customer satisfaction to drive demand. More specifically, the primary goal was to compete head-to-head with Japanese imports both in quality and price. So GM linked employee incentives not only to productivity but also to quality measures. In addition, the extensive employee-training program enabled a focus on market-level factors and helped to place priority on the customer. Thus, GM selected, customised and combined numerous practices based upon a larger goal.

8.3.2 Costs versus Benefits

In general, the underlying goal is not to optimise (in isolation) social behaviour or operational efficiency. This is made explicit when costs are brought into the equation. For example, the maximisation of productivity without regard to cost may result in an overall negative effect on the bottom line of a firm. Therefore, the entire STS design should be evaluated in terms of costs versus benefits, particularly since equifinal solutions may exist. Although costs and savings generally are readily quantifiable, strategic benefits may be elusive. Nevertheless, these benefits should be estimated. This is exactly how retailer JC Penney Company handles every major internal request for new information technology (LaPlante, 1994). In addition to quantifying expected costs and savings so as to forecast a "traditional" return on investment, JC Penney business units must describe expected non-quantifiable benefits such as improvements to customer service or competitive position. This allows for a more complete bottom-line analysis of proposals for IT investment.

8.3.3 IT and Services

The role of information technology presents an interesting twist to STS principles. Much of the discussion concerning organisational change tends to conceptualise technology in terms of processes that "transform objects into other objects" (Barry, 1989). In that sense, IT and services have received less attention in comparison to manufacturing systems. On similar lines, sociotechnical applications and theories have been centred primarily on production systems where technology tends to be transactional in nature. Thus, commonly employed interventionist techniques may not be applicable to the "types of nonlinear work systems that develop with integrated information technology" (Pava, 1986). For instance, one common STS practice has been to target the operations of specific organisational functions. However, evaluating IT-enabled work systems will require a refocusing to cross-functional and business-unit processes. Given the current technological and organisational trends, designing for cross-fun ctional and IT-intensive processes is an important factor in STS interventions.

8.3.4 Case in Point

Consider mortgage loan processing as a cross-functional and IT-intensive activity. Most major US banks utilise loan originators/officers, processors, underwriters and closers. In general, the originator sells the loan, the processor collects and verifies information, the underwriter approves the loan, and the closer prepares the documents. These employees frequently are located in different areas of the bank, and sometimes are dispersed geographically. Efforts at STS intervention can include changes aimed at reporting structures (e.g., creating teams), compensation programmes (e.g., incentive pay for all members as opposed to just the originator), scope of employee responsibility (e.g., cross-training to efficiently handle customer contact), and information technology (e.g., system generated notifications of task completion). Ultimately, given a cross-functional, interdependent, information-intensive, customer-oriented service, STS intervention will be quite different when compared to a manufacturing environment (see Table 8.2).

For example, changes to reporting structures need to take into account that service providers frequently rely upon job roles with multiple duties and responsibility centres (e.g., the bank branch manager who doubles as a loan officer). Likewise, changes to incentive systems need to take into account that services frequently are structured such that the "sales representative" (e.g., a loan originator) is also part of the service-providing team. In addition, STS intervention should consider that the nature of many services often requires immediate customer response. This has implications for the scope of responsibility as well as for the availability of personal customer assistance.

> Personal contact also is important to the building of a team culture.

However, geographic dispersion is not conducive to face-to-face meetings; this has implications for both

Table 8.2. STS considerations for cross-functional and IT-intensive work

Multiple responsibilities

Integrated sales and service

Geographic dispersion

Exposure to customer

organisational and technological structures. In particular, information technology could play a significant role with the ability to provide videoconferencing as well as other enhanced communications.

A large regional US bank considered these factors during a recent redesign of the social and technical systems surrounding the bank's mortgage loan processing activities. Initially, the goals of the bank were centred on improving productivity and processing time. However, it was soon realised that the ultimate objective was to increase profitability, not just operational efficiency. Thus, the goals became concerned with strategic positioning as well as process improvements. At a strategic level, improved response time needed to be accompanied by improved selling effectiveness as well as improved loan decision making. This realisation shifted the organisational design from one that relied on technology to one that included social change. Ultimately, at the social and technical systems level, a comprehensive design was positioned within higher-level strategic and economic goals.

The social redesign was anchored on the roles and expertise of the loan officers and processors. The bank had been operating with officers who functioned as originators as well as the sole points of contact for the borrowers. Processors reported directly to the officers. The redesigned structure created a pseudo-team environment in which the officers and processors were placed into an interdependent relationship. The responsibilities of the officers were focused on origination (i.e., selling), which was enhanced by sales commission incentives. The processors were centrally located (under the supervision of an operations manager) and were teamed with the officers. In addition to collecting and verifying information, the processors became the post-origination points of contact for the borrowers. Not only did this allow the officers to be dedicated to selling, but it also allowed the processors to realise that the borrower (not the officer) was the true customer. In addition, the processors received sales and productivity incentives, though to a lesser extent as compared to the officers. Overall, this team structure created a constructive environment that served to maximise both employee and customer satisfaction.

Technological changes were implemented not only as an enabler of the social design, but also as an enabler of the higher-level strategic goals. Perhaps most importantly, the centralisation of the loan processors required a supporting information network that could tightly link together the processors and officers. This network was the basis for a workflow system that automated the exchange of documents within computer-generated reminders and triggers. In addition, the focus on selling required the use of mobile computing as well as an expert system for greater efficiency and objectivity in loan decision making. In turn, the mobility of the loan officer required an interactive mortgage loan analyser system that would enable customers at a branch to apply for loans in the absence of an officer. The system included a videoconference link to the centrally located loan processors so as to allow customers to consult with a loan expert. It is important to remember that the latter of these technologies were not crucial to lower-level process or social improvements; but they were crucial to the larger strategic and economic framework.

8.4 Lessons for the Future

Although just recently implemented, the social and technical changes described in the preceding paragraphs have been quite successful. The social structures helped to create a highly motivating and productive environment, and the information technologies created operational efficiencies and strategic advantages. So, not only have productivity and response time improved, but mortgage loan revenues have also increased. In addition, the return on the technology investment includes an increase in other revenues due to the cross-selling of banking products. Of particular significance with respect to sociotechnical objectives, the loan officers and processors have become highly motivated by a strategic perspective that includes a sense of employee ownership of specific customer markets. In essence, a strategic perspective served not only to increase profitability, but also to place the employees into a higher-level cause. The implications for employee satisfaction are considerable.

A strategic perspective also serves to enhance the STS practice of employee participation in the organisational design process. Such participation is perhaps the key to the success of the Saturn Corporation. By emphasising customer satisfaction and a responsibility to company-wide competitiveness, Saturn employees removed themselves from a stifling focus on production quotas and cost reductions. Instead, productivity was placed within a more meaningful higher-level objective, thus allowing strategic direction and economic momentum to motivate the employees. In addition, Saturn's comprehensive approach allowed for the STS design to go beyond the restrictive (and often sub-optimal) notion of trade-offs. Instead, the interrelationships between social and technical factors were fully exploited.

The success of Saturn can be contrasted to the failure of Greyhound Lines. Not only did Greyhound management exclude the employees from the decision-making process, they also failed to recognise and exploit social and technical interrelationships at the operational level. At the same time, Greyhound's strategic objectives were detached from organisational and environmental realities. Ultimately, Greyhound ignored the comprehensive picture and relied upon information technology alone to advance their objectives. The result was disastrous to employees as well as the company.

Over the past several decades, sociotechnical systems principles have provided a basis for successful organisational change. The Saturn Corporation is just one example of the magnitude of success that can be achieved by a comprehensive STS design. On the other hand, Greyhound Lines offers an example of the failures that can result by disregarding interrelationships and strategic factors. Many other interventions offer additional perspectives for organisational change. Collectively, the successes and failures of STS interventions provide a basis for justifying a comprehensive, multilevel view of interrelated design factors.

In summary, any organisational design should consider the following perspectives:

- joint optimisation is more about interrelationships than it is about trade-offs;
- STS success is due to comprehensive change, not just preferred practices;
- process performance should be placed within a strategic perspective;
- an increase in benefits is just as important as a decrease in costs.

In addition, it is important to remember that STS design is not limited to the manufacturing sector and production equipment; and it should not be targeted solely at specific functional areas. It is just as much relevant to the service sector, information technology, and cross-functional processes. In fact, advancing STS design beyond its boundaries will help to ensure the relevance of STS principles as we move into the twenty-first century.

Chapter **9**

The Role of Socio-Technical Thinking in the Information Systems Curriculum in UK Universities

Brian Hopkins

9.1 Introduction

This chapter considers the continuing tension within the UK university curriculum in the Information Systems (IS) field between concepts which are grounded in, or have an affinity with, the socio-technical systems (S-T) approach on the one hand, and those which are a legacy of the more instrumental, engineering tradition. In this chapter a distinction is drawn between computer science (which has as its primary focus the knowledge and understanding of the principles and theory underpinning our application of computers) and information systems (in which our major concern lies in the efficient, effective and successful introduction of systems which deliver information to our clients in an appropriate and timely manner).

The essence of the message is that, although we may argue cogently for the validity and pragmatic relevance in IS development of the S-T tradition, the reality in our university departments and courses is that there are powerful, entrenched countervailing views.

This chapter traces the author's experiences since entering the higher education (HE) sector after fifteen years as a practitioner in the IS field. The chapter opens with a description of the environment (cultural, intellectual and technical) in which IS were developed, implemented and managed in the UK in the 1960s and the early 1970s. Reflective lessons are drawn and the hypothesis is posited that in the HE sector we are in many ways the inheritors of attitudes and worldviews which can be traced to that period (and, indeed, to philosophical positions dating from the Enlightenment).

The second section in the chapter focuses on the author's early experiences and impressions of the teaching of IS in our HE institutions. It continues with a description, both reflective and analytical, of his transformative journey from the initial pragmatic, positivist position (which assumed certainty regarding the goals of the process and the content of the courses) adopted on his entry to teaching, through a series of challenges to the present stance of confidence in the relevance and importance of S-T principles in the effective development and implementation of IS. This stance is, however, tinged with diffidence regarding our preparedness, as an academic and practitioner community, to acknowledge the centrality of those S-T principles to our processes.

> Repeated attempts – many successful by their own lights – to improve the products of our development efforts by the use of more sophisticated tools and techniques frustratingly often leaves that client perception unaltered.

Underpinning and reinforcing this transformation has been a persistent and growing apprehension that, in spite of the most radical technical developments in IS, we still find ourselves, at the end of the twentieth century, with a largely dissatisfied clientele (Kavanagh, 1998).

The chapter concludes on a more hopeful and optimistic note (from the point of view of the prospects of an S-T revival) by briefly evaluating the potential for winning "hearts and minds" to a more human-centred approach to the development of IS contained in the burgeoning multimedia (MM) discipline. With its interwoven links with IS it represents a force for change in our teaching philosophy and practice; a force which, interestingly, emanates from the student body rather than (as in traditional IS departments) from the academic staff.

9.2 The Early Years

The period of rapid, enthusiastic, but largely uncontrolled, development in IS occurred in the 1960s when the major focus of our efforts in the IS community was on transferring to computer-based systems those operating and administrative procedures within organisations which could be described as fundamental to the day-to-day health of the organisation, primarily in terms of cash-flow. These systems were characterised by a definite (and definable) set of goals, a well-understood set of rules governing the procedures and experienced administrators who ensured that these vital clerical systems operated effectively.

It is important to capture (or recall) the spirit of the times and to delve more deeply into the attitudes and mindsets of all parties to that mushrooming development. On the one hand, we, the burgeoning IS practitioner community, were partly thrust into and partly assumed the roles of "experts". Indeed, in the spirit of "the kingdom of the blind", we deserved the title, but in another way we found ourselves cast in the role not merely of technical expert but also, due to some strange metamorphosis, as a group who were eminently knowledgeable about information systems in the fullest and widest sense. The outcome of this process was that the staff who had previously been (quite properly) seen as having experience and expertise in that particular adminstrative area were gradually demoted – often metaphorically but occasionally literally – in favour of the new generation of IS practitioners.

This transformation was to lead to a wide range of very significant results as far as the S-T project was concerned. An analysis of the reasons for, and causes of, these developments makes fascinating reading. The philosophical background which informed (and continues to influence) both the user community and the IS practitioners was one which was firmly rooted in the ideas of the Enlightenment. Manifestations of this thinking appeared in the brash confidence with which we proceeded into socio-organisational areas in which we had little or no experience or knowledge, believing that so long as we perfected the technical solutions to the users' "problems" then that was sure to lead to satisfactory outcomes. When this did not materialise then we assumed that the fault lay with the users and their inability to define their requirements accurately, plus their ignorance of the technicalities of computing.

In other words, we were locked into the cosy and arrogant belief that, within organisations, we could reduce complex, interlocking problem situations to ones which could be rendered simple through the reductionist approaches used with such success by scientists and engineers for several generations. We were encouraged in this self-deception by a largely compliant set of users at all levels in organisations who suspended scepticism and joined the rush to elevate the IS practitioners to some kind of guru status. The result of this process was a reinforcement of the already existing cultural norm regarding problem-solving in organisations, namely, the rationalist approach in which a logical, sequential, deductive procedure was deemed to have a high likelihood of success.

> After all, people were often considered to be a major element of the problem

It is now clear how deeply-entrenched such worldviews were in those early days (and indeed, why such a worldview had gained precedence generally throughout Western societies). It is also clear that in the IS field at that time, given the cultural climate described above, the incorporation of S-T thinking and practice would often have appeared to be an alien intrusion. Much IS development was predicated on the perception that human input to the systems should be minimised if the system were to stand a chance of being successful.

So were built the foundations to which many of the attitudes that informed later IS development thinking could be traced. This period coincides neatly with the duration of the author's experience as a practitioner and many of the observations are the result of a process of reflection and critique which has been undergone since his move into academia. It is an important characteristic of the pervasive nature of the then current culture within IS that it was not until several years later, after much soul-searching, extensive reading, continuous (often heated) debate and recurring observation of IS which obstinately refused to meet their clients' needs (Duffy, 1993; Page, Williams and Boyd, 1993) that an awareness grew of the possibility (eventually, necessity) and potential of a more human-centred approach to the use of IS in organisational problem-solving.

9.3 The Process of Reflection

The transformative process referred to above was composed of a combination of internalised reflection on the years of practice, a programme of reading which was both eclectic and focused on IS (but in the case of the latter, opened up new visions of the potential of alternative approaches to the design and development of IS) and above all, an ongoing (and increasingly critical) questioning of the very mainspring of our thinking and practice in the delivery of courses in IS.

The first aspect, internalised reflection, took the form of a debate around the question, initially, of whether or not we could develop a refined form of systems development methodology, which would overcome the multiple problems of project over-runs, inadequate systems specifications and general client dissatisfaction. In other words, the legacy of IS practice was still a predominant and influential feature in my thinking; the quest was for an improved set of techniques **within the existing techno-functionalist framework**.

The other two aspects were probably the more influential and transformative. The reading (over a period of a decade – and still in progress!) was a revelation. To be introduced to authors such as Mumford (1983a, 1983b), Checkland (1981), Checkland and Scholes (1990), Suchman (1987), Hirschheim and Klein (1989), Winograd and Flores (1988), Ehn (1988), plus several other Scandinavian authors and practitioners like Greenbaum and Kyng (1991), Walsham (1993) and more recently Introna (1997), was at the same time both inspiring and depressing; inspiring in the prospect that they held out for an improved approach to IS development; depressing in the observable fact that such ideas were given little credence or weight amongst the IS community at large. One other author whose work was significant in this conversion process was Donald Schon. *The Reflective Practitioner* (1983) spoke eloquently in support of the need for the re-discovery of "artistry" – the encouragement of a humanistic dimension beyond the merely technical (while acknowledging the importance of the latter aspect).

> "From the perspective of Technical Rationality, professional practice is a process of problem *solving*. Problems of choice or decision making are solved through the selection, from available means, of the one best suited to the established ends. But with this emphasis on problem solving we ignore problem *setting*"
> (Schön, 1983; italics in the original).

Although Schon was making a general statement regarding the technical rationalist grounding at the heart of many of the attitudes and techniques across a range of professions, there was a body of evidence to substantiate his claims in respect of the IS profession, in particular its education and training of entrants to the profession (as exemplified in the curricula of our universities and our major professional body in the UK.

From this starting point it was possible to observe the same school of thinking and practice present in a pervasive form within the delivery of our courses and embedded in our pedagogy. So, for example, we could encounter the following learning objectives/outcomes in a module devoted to "Systems Development":

- Review different approaches to systems development.
- Understand the need for engineering principles to be applied to the construction of large software systems.
- Demonstrate an understanding of the skills required to investigate, analyse and design an information system and also some of the techniques used in systems development.
- Account for and illustrate techniques for project control.
- Describe and use in a basic fashion CASE tools for the aid of systems specification and design.

  (Hopkins, 1998)

Here we meet a highly revealing paradox, from the standpoint of the S-T tradition, where the module is ostensibly about the development of IS (presumably within organisations) but it makes no direct reference to the involvement of **people** within that process. Instead the emphasis is on tools, techniques and "engineering principles". This is but one reflection of a range of mechanisms employed within our IS departments and courses – both then and now – to suggest to our students, either consciously or unconsciously, that the design and development of IS in organisations is in essence a technical task, where the efficiency of the system is paramount and the effectiveness and efficacy referred to by Checkland (1981) are either peripheral or simply ignored.

The lived experiences of both practising as an IS professional and teaching the future generations of such practitioners together combined to lead me to a conviction that the marginalisation of socio-technical considerations in both divisions of the IS community was a guarantee of continuing dissatisfaction amongst our clients.

It is instructive to turn to Donald Schon who argued and also posed the question

> Even when practitioners, educators and researchers question the model of technical rationality, they are party to institutions that perpetuate it. (Schon, 1983)

> How comes it that in the second half of the twentieth century we find in our universities, embedded not only in men's minds but in the institutions themselves, a dominant view of professional knowledge as the application of scientific theory and techniques to the instrumental problems of practice? (Schon, 1983)

During the journey of transformation referred to above and in the episodic struggles to win over colleagues to my "discoveries", I regularly and consistently encountered the very obstacles identified and questioned by Schon. It is certain that these obstacles have not been overcome within the IS community, both practitioner and academic. Indeed, it is clear that the worldviews and practices of the latter reinforce the instrumental approaches characteristic of the former, through the provision of a steady supply of "trained" graduates.

9.4 The Continuing Struggle

So, what constitute the mechanisms of influence within our IS courses? What tactics are employed by academics within the IS community to ensure that the *status quo* is not disturbed? Why is it that the IS community resolutely refuses to see the "perfectly obvious fact" that if the people who are inevitably going to be involved in the operation of an IS are not included in the development process leading up to that then the entire project is likely to be jeopardised?

9.4.1 The Mechanisms of Influence

We can trace, within the IS discipline, in our universities a spine of logically and conceptually connected mechanisms which, together, mould our graduates' thinking and practices so that they emerge from the experience ready to perpetuate the traditional, techno-functionalist approaches to IS development which the S-T school has striven to amend.

From their introduction to the university, via the prospectus, the impression is clearly given that this is a discipline which accords priority to the achievement of technical efficiency through adherence to the quality standards associated with engineering. A recent study of UK university prospectuses (Hopkins, 1997) has proved most revealing in this respect. The analytical tool used in the study was discourse analysis (Potter and Wetherell, 1994). The outcomes pointed clearly to the fact that the worldviews of the authors of the IS sections were firmly rooted in that engineering-orientated, scientific tradition.

Two points should be noted here. First, of course, the survey is based on a sample of such documentation and there are certainly some disconfirming instances to be found elsewhere in the project's source documents. Secondly, it is vital to acknowledge that proficiency in tools and techniques in IS is not a skill-set to be derided. In fact the very opposite is true; without such skills in abundance we would (will) never achieve our goal of successfully implemented, generally welcomed IS in our organisations. The core argument which is being advanced is not an anti-techniques stance, rather it is an assertion that **without due consideration and inclusion of people at the heart of IS development then that process is often fatally impoverished and ultimately destined to "fail" in the eyes of its clients.**

However, it is safe to argue that the study revealed evidence to support Schon's critical comments quoted above regarding the instrumental nature of our thinking, outlook and practices concerning the education and training of future professional practitioners in our universities. The clear implication is that, from the very outset, we cultivate an image for ourselves which portrays us to the world as being very much a part of the scientific/engineering tradition, that is, one which certainly has not usually foregrounded (or even accorded equal status and influence) to the socio/organisational aspects of its work.

Therefore, it should come as no surprise to discover that our students not only identify closely with that tradition but that they also expect (and in the current climate, demand) to be taught in a manner consistent with that mind-set. The reality of the delivery of many of our IS university courses is that the primary focus is on instrumental approaches based around tools and techniques. Even in those courses where the human and social aspects are included, the tendency is to treat people as elements in the overall technical system, and thus deserving of similar, mechanistic treatment to their insensate partners.

Further analysis of student handbooks, in-course assignments and examination papers (together with student responses) reveals a consistency of attitudes within both interested parties, the lecturers and the students (Hopkins, 1997). Many of the forms of assessment are of the sort which invite either a unique correct answer or the possibility of one appropriate answer from a strictly limited set of correct answers – an almost foolproof method for inculcating the techno-functionalist paradigm in our students, even if they did not arrive in such a frame of mind.

Finally we have to recognise the influence within our courses of the perceived demands of the future employers of our IS graduates. The nature of employers' requirements as seen by both students and academics is a major influence on our strategic planning in IS, on our course design and on our pedagogy. It is close to heresy to suggest that perhaps we are not so knowledgeable as we pretend regarding the precise nature of the careers pursued by our graduates. However, we proceed on the basis that employers' specified needs are a fixed item, beyond argument. Such an approach has the dubious "merit" of being consistent with, and conforming to, the whole instrumental, goal-driven ethos which pervades our IS departments. Unfortunately, it serves to perpetuate the exclusion or marginalisation of S-T ideas and, more depressingly from the point of view of a philosophical analysis of the broader purposes of higher education, it nullifies any genuine debate about the nature and the aims of the process in which we are involved; the "vocational" argument outbids all others it seems.

9.4.2 Tactics Employed by Academics

Over a period of more than fifteen years the author has persisted in his efforts to achieve at least a meaningful debate regarding the nature and purpose of our undergraduate programmes in IS, in a variety of institutions in a variety of capacities. It is perhaps the most surprising and the most demoralising aspect of these attempts that, in the main, there appears to be little will to engage in such discussions. In the early years the response was almost dismissive; a period when ideas such as those embodied in S-T thinking were regarded by many as intellectually trivial (or naïve) and peripheral to the core knowledge and skill required in an IS graduate. In later years, the emphasis has shifted more towards the "vocational" argument. Throughout, I can recall very few occasions when we truly engaged in an informed and open discussion regarding the merits of the inclusion of S-T ideas and practice **as a cornerstone of the curriculum.**

As with such ideas so with such debates; the best that was achievable seemed to be a token acknowledgement. As a result our IS courses contain an element of S-T thinking but often only as a makeweight or as a concession to fashionable views on the need for "engineering" students to receive a more rounded education with a more humanistic element built into it. In pursuit of these objectives we have designed IS courses which contain modules with appropriate and relevant titles (for example, Methodology in Context, Organisational Processes and Information Systems, Organisation Structure, Social Aspects of Information Systems, Systems and Problem Solving and Users and Systems) but find that these modules are available only as options, or, much more significantly, have not been designed into the thematic mainstream of the course and are thus readily identified by the students as being of secondary importance.

In more recent years one of the repeated claims made by colleagues is that there is only a limited amount of class contact time (and thus of content) available within our courses and therefore we must prioritise the subject matter. In such circumstances the proof emerges both of the resilience of the traditional stances and of the inhibitions surrounding any proper debate on the place of S-T thinking in our curricula. When it is a choice between these ideas and the "core" subjects then the latter are always favoured. This is a perfect demonstration of the automatic assumptions regarding the respective merits and importance of the "technical" modules and the "socio-organisational" modules. It is further confirmation that, when any pressure is exerted, the inclination is to revert to the familiar areas of the discipline. Once again, it is instructive to note that this position is adopted without debate; the moving influence appears to be that, if something must be demoted or removed then those modules associated with S-T ideas are dispensable and are thus the prime candidates.

One other tactic brought into this struggle is the appeal to the requirements of the professional bodies, specifically the British Computer Society (BCS). It is argued that our courses will be more attractive to students and employers if they have been granted BCS accreditation. Analysis of the examination syllabus of the BCS (British Computer Society, 1997) gives a clear indication of the traditional approach to IS which underlies its creators' thinking; analysis of the job advertisements raises doubts about the desirability of such qualifications in the eyes of employers of IS graduates! Nevertheless, the claimed influence of the BCS remains a potent force in the struggle.

These deeply embedded attitudes are not to be airily dismissed in any consideration of a "revival" in S-T ideas and practice. They represent a major obstacle to any advance towards acceptance of those ideas. Their place at the heart of much of the thinking within IS departments ensures the perpetuation of this worldview within the practitioner community.

9.5 Our Refusal to Engage

Of course, the problems outlined above regarding the philosophy and pedagogy underpinning and pervading our university IS courses cannot be seen in isolation. These views are an accurate reflection of a societal perception of desirable approaches to problem-solving. The last two decades have witnessed in the UK an entrenchment of the outlook which argues from a rationalist standpoint – the popularity of "league tables" and other quantitative criteria bears witness to that widespread belief, at least in official circles! Against this background, in the pre-16 education system, in employing organisations and in Government departments, it comes as no surprise to find that our students and our colleagues subscribe to these fundamental ideas.

It can be argued that the perceived unwillingness to debate the place of S-T views in our curricula is a natural and reasonable response to this environmental pressure. This position is tenable only if the outcomes of our IS development efforts are achieving "measurable" improvements amongst our client constituency. All the indicators are that this is not the case. On the contrary, we still seem to be locked into a vicious circle of dissatisfaction. Adoption of S-T thinking and its committed inclusion within our courses offers one way out of this bind. Perhaps the assertions that the present decade is one in which we are more sensitive to the importance of people as agents in a wide variety of organisational and personal situations heralds an opportunity for the advocates of S-T ideas. Perhaps, due to a combination of pragmatism and idealism, the time is ripe for a revival in S-T thinking.

9.6 Lessons Learned

The outcomes of the author's journey, in terms of lessons learned, can be summarised as follows:

1. As a society, we in this country (and probably in the "developed world" as a whole) are culturally wedded to an approach to problem-solving which, having proved its worth in one arena – the physical and natural sciences – has been transplanted, without sufficient thought, into a very different, incommensurate environment – the socio/organisational field.

2. We are unlikely to achieve real improvements in this area until we begin to recognise that it is neither reasonable nor equitable for the IS community (both practitioners and academics) to continue to blame our clients principally for the flaws in their IS; we need to question and reflect upon our own philosophies and practices.

3. The obstacles to change in this paradigm are significant; they are evident in our universities (indeed, in our education systems at large) and, critically, in our organisations, where the over-riding imperative appears to be a combination of a fixation with deadlines and budgets and a (misplaced?) faith in the validity and feasibilty of technically-efficient approaches to the solution of our IS problems.

4. Our clients also cannot escape some share of the responsibility for the unhappy state of affairs; graduates who set out determined to bring S-T ideas into their organisations are often quickly reminded of the pressures and conventions of the "real world".

5. This "real world" of IS comprises a chronicle of unsatisfactory systems (as seen by their clients); a thoroughgoing review of our methods of education, training and practice is long overdue; S-T thinking could and should be a spur to that process within the extended IS community.

9.7 Future Prospects

In spite of the undoubtedly gloomy analysis of the history to date of attempts to introduce S-T ideas as a significant element within IS courses there are signs and indicators which should raise hopes that the desired "revival" may be feasible. One can observe twin transformative themes at work within society at large and within the IS sector of HE in particular.

First, there are pointers in current explorations of attitudes within society and within industry that there is a growing awareness of the importance of human values as almost a tangible asset to be nourished rather than a "human resource" to be exploited. In such an atmosphere it is not surprising that many of the IS community are also beginning to recognise the legitimacy of this stance (*The Times*, Inter//face//, 2/12/1998). It is, of course, only too easy to welcome "false dawns" – the history of the development of IS practice and theory is littered with them – but if we are to assist the progress of acceptance of S-T thinking then we must, of necessity, identify, encourage, consolidate and then propagate these ideas using all possible means and avenues (including, significantly, our IS courses).

The author's experience over the last five years of being involved in the design and delivery of courses in multimedia (MM) has been an enlightening, fruitful and, in terms of a more humanistic view of the IS discipline, genuinely hopeful process. There is a continuing debate about whether MM is about to subsume IS or if the reverse is more likely. In that debate we can detect traces of the tensions referred to earlier when the traditionalists were confronted with S-T thinking. However, this time there are differences which could prove highly influential on the outcome. First, we have a group of students (who will of course be practitioners in a few years' time) many of whom seem to be less imbued with the techno-functionalist paradigms than are their IS peers. They seem to represent a genuine shift in background, thinking and outlook in which there is room for both the traditional IS expectation of technical competence but also an added ingredient, namely, a deeper awareness of the social context in which their "product" exists allied to a readiness to engage with clients in a more open, equal and truly participatory way.

At the same time there is a convergence taking place between the two disciplines – the debate about which becomes dominant is largely academic in the worst sense! – which inevitably means a change in the thinking and practice of IS as taught in our universities. The motor for these changes is the less instrumental, less "expert" driven, more flexible, more people-sensitive and more holistic set of attitudes which many of the students bring to the MM courses.

We encounter a qualitatively different worldview in these cohorts which offers advocates of S-T ideas a springboard for dissemination and application of those ideas; this generation of IS-related students appears to be free of many of the intellectual and emotional constraints which govern their IS counterparts. It should be emphasised that they are not consciously aware of being the vanguard of the "revival". They are instinctively and intuitively pursuing S-T ends and in the process are fomenting radical changes in the approach to course design and delivery in the IS/MM field. The changes are organic and emergent. The seeds for such changes are being scattered; the soil is fertile and the climate is ripe for their ultimate germination and subsequent healthy growth.

Chapter 10

Balancing at the Edge of Chaos in a Sociotechnical World

Kay Fielden

10.1 Introduction

In this chapter the link between educating tertiary technical students to appreciate the importance of valuing people in the workplace as well as technology is explored. Improving the quality of working life with regard to computing goes hand-in-hand with establishing success factors for good information systems (Garson, 1995).

The New Zealand Businesses for Social Responsibility formed in August 1998, promotes the link between financial performance and environmental, social and ethical business practice. Information systems need to be aligned with the strategic direction of an organisation. When students have projects with organisations whose strategic direction incorporates social and ethical business practice then the education provided to these students equips them well to enter a socially responsible business world.

Balancing traditional information systems tertiary education curriculum with creative, intuitive and process-based learning is the challenge we face as tertiary educators in equipping information systems professionals of the twenty-first century with the knowledge, skills and understanding required to manage at the edge of chaos.

> Balancing at the edge of chaos requires stability, flexibility and personal mastery in order to handle the turmoil that occurs in dynamic, ever-changing systems.

Students require the ability to learn how to cope with rapidly out-dated knowledge as well as the ability to manage self-organised systems that change spontaneously to meet an ever-changing sociotechnical environment (Merry, 1995). A core concept of chaos theory is that while there may be a particular stable and predictable pattern of behaviour of the whole system, individual components may exhibit unpredictability. In applying this core concept to periods of chaos in human activity systems, hidden patterns of behaviour of the total system may be uncovered. The move towards self-responsibility inevitably brings with it chaotic situations as outside control is relaxed. This in turn helps to provide better problem solution from a sociotechnical point of view. Strategic information systems in organisations will need to be self-organising in order to align themselves with a dynamic business world.

Educating students to accept this evolutionary nature of information systems design is paramount.

A description of the environment in which learning occurs, is followed by a brief outline of the research methodology adopted. The application of sociotechnical principles to the learning environment is then explored. A link between chaos and control in educating information technology professionals is established. Recommendations for future tertiary education in information systems are contained in the conclusion.

10.2 The Learning Environment

Analysis and design skills acquired in previous information systems papers are put into practice in a project carried out for an outside organisation drawn from the wider business community. Third year Information Systems students at Massey University at Albany spend the whole of the academic year working in small groups (five or six students) to analyse, design and prototype a variety of projects for organisations in Auckland. The experience gained during the project gives students valuable insights into current and future needs of the businesses with which they work. Client organisations find that liaising with student groups is mutually beneficial. "Live" project work also provides the opportunity for students to learn how to cope with problems encountered in groups. Links with businesses that follow social responsibility principles provide not only information technology skills and experience but also exposure to best-practice ethics. Students choose what information systems development methodology is best suited for their particular project. Most groups base their project development on the traditional systems development lifecycle (SDLC). However, in their critical evaluations at the end of the year they acknowledge that while SDLC provides project development guidelines, a mix of methodologies, such as Multiview (Avison and Fitzgerald, 1995), Soft Systems Methodology (Checkland and Scholes, 1990) and ETHICS (Mumford, 1983a), is required at different stages of development. All students stress the importance of sociotechnical principles in their final evaluations. Emery (1995) states that educational systems must be geared to supplying and sustaining a workforce in which information technology is continuously changing the social context of work.

The theory of information systems suggests that a well designed and developed information system will provide a greater level of order and control in handling the information needs of an organisation and thus its productivity (Avison and Fizgerald, 1995). The reality is that even when an information system is well designed and developed this may not happen. The fit between design and development methodology and the organisation, an imbalance between technical and social fit in an organisation or the inability of the design team to communicate with their client, all contribute to greater chaos and less order. Students who learn the importance of finding the right methodology for the client and who value the importance of listening to their user to produce what is required are learning how to balance social and technical fit.

10.3 Research Method

A qualitative, participative research method has been employed over the past ten years to gather information from student evaluations, presentations and discussions as well as researcher observations. Interpretation of results with respect to sociotechnical principles has been refined with each yearly iteration.

10.4 Sociotechnical Principles

> The main design philosophy is that social and technical objectives need to be set evaluated matched and ranked separately in order to define human and computer tasks for the next development phase.

The original objective of sociotechnical systems was to achieve a shift in organisations from a bureaucratic structure to a democratic structure (Emery, 1995). Information Systems development methodologies such as Multiview (Avison and Fitzgerald, 1995) and ETHICS (Mumford, 1983a) outline a sociotechnical approach to information systems analysis and design. The philosophy of these approaches differs from most information systems development methodologies because the philosophy has evolved from organisational behaviour. The development of computer systems is perceived as an organisational issue, which is fundamentally concerned with the process of change.

Avison and Fitzgerald (1995) imply that there are two distinct mindsets – social and technical. This appears to be a simplistic approach. Educating information systems professionals with a holistic approach to sociotechnical

Table 10.1. Principles of sociotechnical compatibility (Cherns, 1987)

Minimal critical specification	Define what and not how Self-managed activities, democratic decisions Self regulation Team members deal with own uncertainties
Boundaries	Minimise inter-group relations
Multifunctionality	Team members capable of diverse range of tasks
Support congruence	Rewards, assessment and training support activities of team
Feedback	Available to person performing the task
Incompletion	Design process ongoing Incompletion result of minimal critical specification
Compatibility	Internal fit between social and technical systems Fit of design process itself
Variance control	Variations from what is planned or expected controlled at point of origin Quality issues local responsibility
Human values	Quality of working life an important consideration for organisation Maximise team and individual autonomy so as to increase commitment and to humanise the workplace

systems achieves a more integrated and balanced approach. A holistic mindset encompassing many points of view – not just two – becomes possible.

10.4.1 Inevitable Change

Part of the learning process in this age of accelerating technology is that change is normal (Bridges, 1991). New and flexible mind-sets are required which accept change as the status quo. Vital skills learned in a "live" project include:

- developing an awareness of personal and interpersonal resistance to change (Boulding 1989);
- learning to assess whether changes are sound;
- appreciating the importance of open, clear and complete communication; and
- feedback on completion of processes to all involved in the change process.

10.4.2 Communication Issues

An invaluable indicator that communication has broken down in a student group project is that inconsistencies appear in system documentation. Even with high-achieving groups, when the quality of the documentation does not match the competency level in the group, this is an indicator that relationships within the group are not smooth.

New technology and new information systems design usually involves revolutionary rather than evolutionary change. Such revolutionary change bears most resistance. Revolutionary change may involve the following:

- Processes out of tune with the competence level within the organisation.
- Processes and technology that do not match the organisational culture.
- Change that does not align itself with the overall strategy of the organisation.
- Change that threatens the diversity of an organisation. This may reduce or lose functions or responsibilities without giving any substitutes. It may also imply a degradation of physical, psychological or social working environment.
- With a down turn in world economies, goals may be formulated with the barest of margins. More than one student group this year knew that their work would not be taken past the prototype developed because the client organisation had been squeezed by the current economic climate.
- Change can also be perceived as a threat to someone's territory. Students working with committees in local government found themselves restricted by what they could achieve because of the perceived threats to committee mandates. Working through the frustration caused has broadened relationship skills for such groups.

Merry (1995) states that the essence of chaos is change. It is stated in chaos theory that when a system is in a chaotic state there is a particular patterned order in the way that it changes as a whole, but the future behaviour of its individual components is totally unpredictable. These uncertain and unpredictable forms of change are in contrast to the regular and predictable ways people expect and believe that most things around them do change. In a complex world, order and chaos are intertwined. Learning to develop an information system for a "live" organisation is a complex activity in which the order of techniques, tools, methodologies and skills learned theoretically are applied to a dynamic, ever-changing organisation in the business world. The orderliness and control of the theoretical world is intertwined with the non-linearity of the "live" project. Politics, personalities, changing business rules and clients unable to espouse tacit knowledge all contribute to a complex and chaotic world that exhibits randomness, uncertainty, unpredictability and irregularity (Merry, 1995). Coping with sudden and unexpected change also provides the opportunity for a project team to self-organise for maximum adaptability.

Students develop their interpersonal skills and a level of tolerance and compassion is exhibited. The ability to cope with multiple realities in complex systems develops. Serious illness, domestic problems and accidents are treated as group issues and solved accordingly. In this way the students learn to value each other as agents of change and technology as the tool. They learn that people are the most important resource in an organisation especially in an Information Technology business world. People's knowledge, intelligence and technical skills are the most valuable resource. The Information Technology industry would not exist without highly trained people. Training students in a multiplicity of personal and relationship, as well as technical, skills means that subjective involvement in technological areas is valued.

> Regarding change as an opportunity to learn is a valuable experience.

10.5 Managing Change at the Edge of Chaos

The edge of chaos is where complex systems are at their most adaptive. This is where there are the widest range of behaviours from which to choose, where there is the highest level of fitness and adaptability, and the richest choice of alternatives. Merry (1995) maintains that complex systems evolve at the edge of chaos. Equipping students with a wide variety of social skills, the ability to think creatively about technology, grounding in generic technical skills and flexible thinking skills equips students well for a working world that increases in complexity all the time. Important skills for managing change at the edge of chaos are:

- learning to value and to recognise the emotional impact of change and the skills with which to handle this both for self and for others;
- being able to recognise whether reaction to change is appropriate; and

- recognising the edge of chaos and becoming familiar with chaotic states.
- welcoming such states as an opportunity to learn;
- differing degrees of participation, depending on appropriateness to organisational culture.

10.6 The Importance of Initial Conditions

Chaos theory suggests that complex systems have a sensitive dependence on initial conditions (Merry, 1995). In educating information systems professionals a trusting, open, co-operative environment is set from the very first meeting of the class. This is an important underpinning for students to learn how to operate in a dynamic world with maximum effectiveness and flexibility. This mix of interpersonal skills and group dynamics provides the balance required to work in teams on a technical project.

10.7 Participation

Hansen and Christensen (1995) distinguish between three levels of participation.

1. Consultative participation leaves main design tasks to Information Technology specialists but tries to ensure that user representatives are consulted;
2. Representative participation involves user representation in design teams; and
3. Consensus participation, where all user staff are involved throughout the design process.

In practice, participation seems to be more fluid and dynamic than just three categories. Over the years in supervising student projects, the range has been from complete hands-off (a client who asked me to "keep the students away – they were too much to handle"), to complete involvement in every stage of the development life cycle. Most commonly there is heavy client involvement in early stages of planning, feasibility and analysis, little interaction during technical design and a little more involvement with prototyping.

The level of participation depends on many factors. These include:

- client level of technical expertise;
- client time available to spend with students;
- client attitude to interacting with students;
- location – some projects are physically distant and while this is not a major problem with electronic communication, there usually seems to be the requirement for a physical meeting; and

- students may have selected their own project through family, community or work in which case they then serve a dual role as client and as consultant.

Managing the participation process is a valuable skill in learning to balance at the edge of chaos. While the supervisor directs the student process, sensitivity to the client needs, values and culture is essential. For instance, in a project completed for the New Zealand Navy, it was essential for the students to observe Defence Force protocol in the dealings with the client. In another project involving local council committees, an understanding of local politics was required.

A movement from the orderly management of change to building changeability in the organisation and the ability to manage conflict as a necessary skill both indicate a shift in direction in both corporate and personal directions in order to balance on the edge of chaos (Fielden, 1995). Students learn to handle such changeability both within the design group and with clients.

> Students develop an awareness of the difference between the long-term implications of imposed solutions and the spontaneous changes of self-organising systems in controlling their own projects.

10.8 Control versus Self-Organising Systems

Semester and academic boundaries for the project paper are set clearly at the start of the course. Project scope is explored with client and supervisor. Students act as consultants to their client in project work and therefore have the power to set the scope to satisfy their clients. A client's business needs may change. As a client's level of understanding about the capability of the information system being developed increases, more requests for the final product are placed. Students also choose which established information systems development methodology to use in managing their project. Most students discover that the standard methodologies work in an "ideal" world and that modifications are required with "real" projects. The author has discovered that a high level of student autonomy is vital in providing the motivation, dedication and quality of work within a limited time frame that is required for the paper. The paradox associated with relaxing controls is that there is less rather than more chaos. Motivation is high because the students own more of the process. The skilled educator evolves from "the person in control of the class" to "the facilitator of self-directed learning". Much of the control for learning has been handed back to students. Feedback from students suggests that the empowerment and trust they experienced enabled them to learn far more than they would have expected.

> For the facilitator of effective learning, it is essential to establish a trusting and supportive environment. Any threat, fear or lack of autonomy is detrimental to effective learning. Frequent supervisor meetings during the year, a flexible attitude to changing requirements and setting deadlines in collaboration with the student class all increase the level of trust in the class.

10.9 Self and Others in Complex Human Activity Systems

Complex systems are characterised by a combination of openness, interactivity and non-linearity. Vulnerability in complex human activity systems is reduced by the ability to transform themselves within a changing environment (Merry, 1995, Piaget, 1952). Developing listening skills is a necessary prerequisite for a deep understanding of self and others in such complex human activity systems. Without being able to listen to others effectively we cannot learn, intellectually at least.

A deeper understanding of human values in relationships happens as knowledge and ideas are shared. As we share ideas within a trusting learning community, the synergy and collaboration means that the pool of knowledge and skills available to all members of the learning community becomes greater. As our ideas coincide or differ from others, so we have the opportunity to reflect on why this might be. When we share our ideas, we participate actively with others in the learning community. As students work in the same group for the whole academic year they develop a deep understanding of their fellow group members working style, thinking patterns and personality.

10.10 Innovation in Education

Prather (1996) establishes nine dimensions for a climate in which innovation may flourish. These fall into three main themes – resources, personal motivation and exploration. Table 10.2 shows these climate dimensions, and the organisational support required in a rational, structural domain as well as the humanistic, holistic support which he suggests is much harder to change.

Table 10.2. Nine dimensions for a climate in which innovation may flourish

Climate dimension	Rational support required	Holistic support required
Resources		
Idea time	Organisation allows time	Processes in place – e.g. brainstorming
Idea support	Is provided to try new ideas	Encouraged and welcomed
Challenge and involvement		Democratic involvement
Personal motivation		
Trust and openness		Lead by example
Playfulness and humour		Expectation set for fun at work
Absence of interpersonal conflict		Honour disagreements Role model dispute resolution
Exploration		
Risk-taking		Legitimise mistakes as lessons
Debates	Time for public debate	Stimulate debate
Freedom		Democratic decision making Personal autonomy

Lean economic times leave little room for reflection and without this the creative and intuitive ideas languish (Prather, 1996). Time is allowed to explore new ideas and to reflect on possible processes and outcomes. Reflection is incorporated as part of the curriculum in peer evaluation at each phase exit and in the final examination. Both the peer evaluation and the examination give students an individual, rather than a group, opportunity to relate issues such as how consistency, quality, project selection, feasibility and management were achieved, how the group functioned and what their individual contribution was. The students are given the opportunity to suggest what might have been done better, in hindsight. Unfortunately, there is little time for such reflection during the academic year.

10.11 Lessons Learned

1. Mistakes made are regarded as opportunities to learn, changing project conditions as a chance to learn to adapt and to self-organise and interpersonal difficulties the opportunity to learn how to resolve conflict.
2. Students learn that project development is not a fixed process, but rather can be a moving target.
3. Most students discover that the standard methodologies work in an "ideal" world and that modifications are required with "real" projects.
4. Interpersonal skills are vital for effective project work.
5. We must learn to value people as agents of change and technology as the tool to accomplish the change.

10.12 Conclusion

Sending Information Technology graduates into the workforce with the right set of technical and social skills is essential. John Ball, CEO of SoftTech NZ says that while the best technical experts are tolerated if they are difficult people, everyone in his organisation must have technical skills. Feeny and Willcocks (1998), on the other hand, suggest that relationship building is among the core IS capabilities. This involves developing users' understanding of Information Technology's potential, helping users and Information Technology specialists work together, and ensuring users' ownership and satisfaction. Having students developing real projects with clients is building this depth and breadth in these core capabilities.

Besides the traditional technical-skills, information-systems professionals of the twenty-first century need to:

1. develop balanced approaches both structurally and creatively to managing change at the edge of chaos;

2. develop an awareness of the difference between the long-term implications of imposed solutions and the spontaneous changes of self-organising systems;

3. be adept in questioning underlying cultural, political and intellectual assumptions;

4. value people as agents of change and technology as the tool;

5. have a deep understanding of self and others in complex human activity systems;

6. value subjective involvement in technological areas;

7. be tolerant, compassionate and at ease with multiple realities in complex systems;

8. understand the learning process as a meta-skill and to develop flexibility in thinking; and

9. allow time to explore new ideas and to reflect on possible processes and outcomes.

This research, which is also supported by Lee, Trauth and Farwell (1995) has shown that students who extend their human potential as they develop as information systems professionals are more likely to cope with accelerating technological change.

Part 3
Re-Design

Chapter 11

Group Dynamics Meet Cognition: Combining Socio-Technical Concepts and Usability Engineering in the Design of Information Systems

Andrew Dillon

11.1 Introduction

Socio-Technical Systems Theory (STST) has been widely mentioned and applied in the domain of information systems implementation (see e.g. Eason, 1988; Mumford, 1983b). In a review of the theories of models that seek to predict user acceptance of new information technology, Dillon and Morris (1996) noted that the term "socio-technical" has become widely applied to a mix of theoretical positions that do not all share the original psychodynamic views of socio-technical thinkers.

> In current usage, STST is interpreted as referring to almost any view of user acceptance or resistance that emphasises the role of the organisational context in shaping technology use, thus blurring the historical distinctions between structuralist, human relations and open systems approaches.

As such, STST stands in contrast to the user or tool-based models that seek to explain user reactions in terms of individual dispositions (e.g., cognitive style or personality) or tool quality (e.g., ease of use).

Currently, broad based socio-technical approaches tend to deal with issues at one level of abstraction (the group, the organization) while usability professionals deal with another (the user, the interface). The result, in my view, is a joint limitation of these perspectives, which if coupled appropriately, could offer richer insights and practices for all systems design and implementation projects. The present chapter extends this by examining the nature of both approaches and the practical means of utilising both appropriately in context.

11.2 Usability Engineering

Current software design practices place great emphasis on interfacing the tool to the intended users. While the origins of this work are classic ergonomic or human factors concerns with control panels, user-centered design methods have evolved over the last two decades to the extent that usability is now seen as a crucial component of the software engineering lifecycle even by mainstream software engineering theorists (Nielsen, 1993).

Usability engineering (UE) is a term that has come to describe a pragmatic approach to interface design which emphasises empirical methods and operational definitions of user requirements for tools. Extending as far as International Standards Organization approved definitions (see e.g., 1S0 9241 part 11) usability is considered a context-dependent agreement of the effectiveness, efficiency and satisfaction with which specific users should be able to perform tasks. Advocates of this approach engage in task analysis, then prototype interface designs and conduct usability tests. On the basis of such tests, the technology is (ideally) redesigned or (occasionally) the operational targets for user performance are revised.

Usability engineering has been an extremely influential approach to technology design. Conferences, academic articles, job advertisements, professional groups etc., all make reference to the approach and one could be forgiven for thinking that the adoption of this operational perspective is the panacea for information technology design. Its philosophy of specify-design-test-redesign etc., is both action oriented and pragmatic. UE espouses empirical data collection from real users as the only yardstick by which success can be measured. As such, this approach has won many adherents in the literature on human-computer interaction (HCI) and an ability to operationalise and test usability is a de facto core competency of any budding interface or interaction design specialist.

11.3 The Impact of Socio-Technical Systems Theory on Information Technology Design

STST shares the UE concern with understanding users and their tasks, but in contrast to UE, STST can appear to outsiders as cumbersome and ill-defined. Rather than specifying empirical methods to be iteratively applied throughout the design process, the socio-technical approach places greater emphasis on the participation of stakeholders, and the evolution of a planned implementation strategy. Derived from STST's focus on the fundamentally unconscious drives of all organizational members, practitioners seek ways of enhancing the users' working lives through technology. Such concerns are not immediately translatable into interface design guidelines or testing methods.

Faced with a group of designers who demand answers to questions, a socio-technical theorists can appear vague or irrelevant. In my experience, advocating anything other than a quick usability test in these circumstances is frequently a recipe for communication breakdown.

"what size would the window be?"

"which icons are most meaningful?"

One should not be too surprised by the apparent negative reaction here. Software design is a costly and ill-structured process and the search for clear answers motivates anyone seeking to design a usable system. More importantly, STST offers no clear advice on interface design. This is hardly damning, STST makes no claims to unique insights on this matter and relegates it to a second-order concern in conceptualising the users' response to technology. However, the danger is of STST seeming irrelevant at worst, or vague at best in the face of increasing expectations of designers for clear answers to such questions from social scientists. And it is not just the expectation of designers – the lack of specific interface design guidance is a frequent criticism made of many social science approaches to technology (Landauer, 1995).

Aside from the practical concerns of addressing software design appropriately, STST needs to address the theoretical slide that reduces the term to a catch-all, a convenient dustbin into which we all throw the soft, social stuff that we know we ought to consider but somehow is not amenable to testing in our prototypes. Yet it is precisely this form of fossilization that STST faces as the empirical methods of usability engineering gain greater foothold, and as all classes of organizational perspective get lumped together. Can STST regain its practical import? I think so but we may need to do socio-technical analysis under a different name!

11.4 Developing Humanly Acceptable Information Systems

All social scientists and HCI professionals engaged in the production and implementation of software know the importance of being involved from the outset. However we continually face the problem of being seen as "testers" or evaluators who of necessity cannot be employed until there is "something" there for us to test, and this "something" must be built first by the "real" designers.

Over the last 20 years there has been a growing movement towards what is known universally as a "user-centred" design process. In this process emphasis is placed on iterative design-test loops and the desire to "know the user". This is contrasted with the more traditional waterfall models of design that used to impose fixed stages and milestones for development that made revisiting earlier decisions costly. The beauty of the user-centred approach from an HCI or STST perspective is the opening it provides to engage in design at the earliest stages, rather than at the end. Some have argued in fact that the movement towards a user-centred approach is a direct result of STST and related movements (Baecker, Grudin, Buxton and Greenberg, 1995). However, powerful as user-centredness might be, it is clear that UE and STST are not equally served by this approach.

The UE community have perhaps more naturally found a niche in this process. Encouraging testing from the outset, the setting of operational criteria for efficiency, effectiveness and satisfaction, the development of prototyping etc., UE makes a case that seems to immediately support the better development of systems: feedback is quickly gained, design alternatives can be empirically selected and long-term targets can be seen to be attainable. This is positive and renders it easier to engage design at the conceptual stage, but is it sufficient? More importantly, should this be the extent of social scientists' involvement in active design? In my experience it is not, and there are two inter-related short-comings with the UE approach which can be at least partly overcome by employing STST. It is worth exploring these in turn to consider the options for STST in HCI. Let us call these the problem of involvement and the problem of measurement.

11.4.1 The Problem of Involvement

To design for usability, one normally runs candidate designs by representative users until the emerging interface can be shown to support agreed upon levels of performance. In a systematic UE approach this generally entails well-controlled usability studies, often in a laboratory environment, with any user errors or problems noted and analysed for their causes and potential implications. Redesign recommendations normally are made by the testers, designs are then tweaked, and testing is performed again until acceptable performance scores are found. Obviously the tests could vary in form (expert, heuristic, user-based etc.) and location (lab or field) depending on the context.

In itself, UE guarantees some measure of data that is directly pertinent to the job in hand. However, underlying this approach is a rather simple idea that user involvement in the design is primarily as a test subject. While mention is made of participation in standard UE texts such as Nielsen's (1993), this is highly simplified and no mention is made of the importance of psychological rather than just physical participation in the process (Hartwick and Barki, 1994). Users in the UE method answer questions, give reactions, highlight problems and are "called-upon" – they are not active generators of designs. Indeed, part of the UE literature calls attention to the problems with asking users for design ideas since they demonstrate seemingly very poor ability to estimate the impact of any design on their own behavior (Bailey, 1995).

Involving users in a process that is costly, politicised and management-driven is always going to have problems. While UE has found a natural niche in the philosophy of user-centred design, it has done so largely through ignoring the messy issues of really centring efforts on users or for users. This is less a criticism of UE which stands as a pragmatic improvement over once-off testing at the end of the development chain but more a recognition of the need to determine just what involvement or true participation in design processes entails.

Similarly, UE places no emphasis on the key socio-technical concepts of designing for human values such as the provision of work that is reasonably demanding, that supports user learning and incorporates an element of decision making (Cherns, 1976). Lack of appropriate task structures leads to alienation in the long term, but most directly it affects the user's perception of control. Such concerns are difficult if not impossible to articulate in UE terms and thus are cast out of the user-centred design paradigm that rests on usability alone. In this way, participation is limited by the very language we use to conceptualise the human response. The very concepts that drive acceptance from an STST perspective are too easily bypassed in an analysis of effectiveness, efficiency and satisfaction of individual users.

11.4.2 The Problem of Measurement

Measures of effectiveness, efficiency and satisfaction certainly have value, but they tell only part of the story. That I can use a system is in many ways of little interest if you want to estimate whether or not I will use the system once it is implemented. Efficiency or satisfaction measures alone are not likely to be powerful enough to determine this.

STST has long emphasised the psycho-dynamic forces shaping our behavior and the search for control and enhancement of one's position are considered natural phenomena of existence. Such forces are far deeper and more difficult to measure than efficiency etc., yet they are ultimately more powerful in determining our behaviour.

> A highly usable system is always likely to be rejected if users perceive it as increasing others' control over their working lives on leading to a de-skilling or reduction in autonomy

UE offers no insight on these issue, which is fine if one understands what usability testing is all about – measuring if people *can* use a tool, not if people *will* use it – but the term usability is now taken synonymously with anything positive about a technology that enhances its attraction to users. Everyone recognises usability as important, every designer is user-centred, but somehow, we end up with systems that people will not use. In short, this is a natural result of relying totally on a set of measures that reflect only part of the complex determination of use.

Other models of user response, such as the Technology Acceptance Model (TAM) (Davis, 1993) raise the value of usefulness or utility of a new tool but even the best evidence for this model suggests it accounts for only half the variance in user acceptance. Innovation diffusion models (Rogers, 1995) posit characteristics of users and tools that influence adoption but the constructs themselves such as "relative advantage" or "observability of outcome" are open to more than one interpretation.

> STS strongly suggests that the frequently unconscious aspects of human motivation are more responsible for user behaviour than objective reports of utility.

Furthermore, neither perspective seeks to go as deeply into the core forces that shape human responses.

STST has an important role to play here in articulating and, ideally, operationalising the variables shaping acceptance at the human level that could be used to extend the UE measures now so dominant.

11.5 Reconciliation?

Obviously, STST does not offer a ready made set of alternative methods of involvement or of measurement. Enhancement or personal control are intuitively appealing as theoretical constructs, and allow for plausible explanations of resistance to new technology, but they are difficult to clearly measure. Compared to counting user errors in a usability test, they are more difficult to operationalise and harder to observe! Furthermore, it would be foolhardy to ignore the power of UE properly applied. What I would advocate is some degree of reconciliation between the two approaches that might allow STST to display its value in a manner that will allow its application through UE-style practice.

The best way to do this, in my view, is to remind ourselves of some of the basic principles of STST and how they are overlooked in current usability-based approaches. Thus, in reminding system designers to re-address these core issues, we might be able to build further on the work accomplished by UE professionals to date in impacting design processes. Specifically, some of the main principles of STST as outlined by Trist (1993) emphasise the work system as the basic design unit and the need for technology to support a work group rather than just a single user/single task. This places STST in sharp relief to UE which advocates the primacy of task level analyses and evaluations. Coupling this with the advocacy of increased variety, multiskilling and group-level regulation of work activities, it is conceivable that we can propose a richer form of analysis and evaluation than a strict usability approach.

This does not mean, as is frequently assumed, that one must be either STST or UE in outlook. A user is both an individual and a group member; cognition is both internal and distributed and we need to break down the limited barriers of analysis level to understand interaction with technology in its true socio-cognitive form. I propose UE as offering a way of grounding some concerns with users in a measurable form, but that effectiveness, efficiency and satisfaction are insufficient to explain and predict user responses fully. STST affords a perspective that emphasises establishing the value of these measures in group-relevant terms so, for example, establishing faster performance on a given task is not seen as the end of the design, but the point at which we can start to establish the implications of this for the group or socio-technical unit.

The reverse also holds. STST can be employed at the very outset to offer insights into the setting of operational criteria for effectiveness, efficiency and satisfaction so that they reflect better the needs of the real work context in which the technology will be employed, for example, satisfaction criteria can be determined for all stakeholders, not just the direct users etc. Not only would this allow us to exploit the gains made by UE, it would serve to orient UE into a truer representation and measurement of the variables STST has long advocated as crucial.

11.6 Lessons for Learning

- Usability is a necessary but insufficient condition of technology acceptance.
- Criteria for effectiveness, efficiency and satisfaction must be derived from the social not the individual context of use.
- User-centred design must engage real users as more than test participants.
- STST must address the operational measurement of control and enhancement factors.

Clearly these lessons are not simple to learn, but they represent a means for socio-technical perspectives to impact design practices in the immediate term.

11.7 Practical Hints and Tips

- Derive participation through clear stakeholder analysis.
- Expose designers to the context of use for the tools they are developing.
- Continually revise criteria for acceptance through user involvement.

Chapter **12**

Enhancing IS Quality through Design-based Documentation Production

David Tuffley

12.1 Introduction

User documentation occupies an ambiguous position in the information systems (IS) development process. While it is usually an indispensable item on the list of project deliverables, it is constantly seen by IS developers as unimportant in relation to the software itself. Due to its relatively low status in the eyes of many developers, it is common for user manual writing to be a post-design activity. Poor quality user manuals are a cause of user dissatisfaction: they are a social element of IS development that suffers in relation to the technical aspects.

In this chapter I argue that if user manuals are produced earlier during IS development, facilitated by a technical writer, then better user requirements information is generated (Fig. 12.1). Not only is more time available to produce a good quality user manual, but also software is more likely to have the sought-after "user-friendly" quality that comes from improved user involvement.

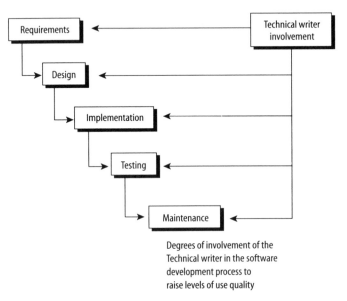

Degrees of involvement of the
Technical writer in the software
development process to
raise levels of use quality

Figure 12.1 Involving the technical writer earlier in the development process.

126

IS quality can be improved by developer/user collaboration, but this seldom happens effectively. The various integrative approaches that encourage this collaboration have achieved success where there is commitment, yet this commitment is not always apparent in IS development. What is therefore needed is an "integrative process" which accommodates the differing cognitive processes of developer and user.

12.2 A Problem Observed

> Poor quality software user manuals, both paper-based and electronic, cause user dissatisfaction.

This problem has become evident to me as a member of IS development teams in both the public and private sectors, in Australia and the United Kingdom, since the mid 1980s.

I draw on my observations of IS development projects as a technical communication consultant over a 12-year period using an interpretivist approach – perceiving the reality of situations via the social constructions of language, consciousness and shared meanings (Burrell and Morgan, 1979).

The scale of projects ranged from small to large, and involved teams of up to 35 (comprising IS developers, user representatives, technical writers and marketing people). My participation in these projects has led to a design-based documentation production method as a way of improving IS quality. Using the technical writer as a facilitator between the user and the developer in the development process is a key feature of this method. The ability of technical writers to understand both the technical and user aspects of an IS development qualifies them for this role.

12.2.1 Shortfalls in User Documentation and User Requirements Specification

Users resort to documentation when they have reached an impasse with the software or want to understand a function, when they have a problem and are looking for the solution. The user perception of the manual is as a problem-solving device, but if the manual then becomes part of the problem instead of the solution, the user is likely to be dissatisfied with it and the IS.

For example, if a user is unable to perform a software function, and resorts to the user manual only to find that it is so poorly written or organised that they are unable to obtain the necessary information, then they are likely to give up in frustration, and are unlikely to resort to the manual again. Although the software may have been produced "correctly" using prescriptive methodologies, resulting in a "high quality" product – software which conforms to its specification and contains few technical defects – something is clearly lacking from the user requirements specification.

A vital contributing factor to poor quality user documentation is therefore inadequate or incomplete requirements elicitation.

The IS developer has not determined the user's complete requirements unless they also know the user's expectations about how they would like the IS to work

12.2.2 Poor Quality Manuals due to Being Written Late

If the user documentation is written during the post-design stage (e.g., implementation), there is too little scope for user-related problems to be resolved, and rarely enough time to produce manuals of a high standard. For example, if a user-related problem arises in the software during the development of a manual, the remedy or lack of it depends on the error observed. If there is a technical error it will probably be corrected. But if it is a matter of making the product more user-friendly, time constraints will normally dictate that this category of problem is not fixed.

Furthermore, if delays have occurred during the production phase, it is even less likely that user-related problems will be addressed. Similarly if the original product delivery date still applies but financial penalties for lateness also apply, then it is less likely that a high quality manual will be produced.

12.2.3 The Link between Poor Manuals and Poor Software

I have observed that there is a link between the problem that made the user refer to the manual, and the quality of the manual itself. If the manual is developed during the post-design stage, it describes functions which already exist. A function that is developed without complete knowledge of the user's needs and expectations is unlikely to be satisfactory.

The manual can therefore be describing a deficient function that probably cannot be changed at this stage of the development process without a compelling reason: complete user satisfaction is rarely seen as a compelling reason.

"It works doesn't it? What are you complaining about?"

"If it's not broken, don't fix it."

The function may make sense to the developer, but the developer's perspective is usually very different from the user's. The developer invariably has a more technical perspective than the user. The developer will therefore tend to make invalid assumptions.

12.2.4 Technical versus Other Perspectives

Difficulties for the user therefore arise when the developer makes invalid assumptions about the user's level of technical understanding. A software function that would make sense to a "technical person", with previous experience of similar functions, may make little or no sense to a person with different expertise. Unless these assumptions are challenged in the design phase, and time allowed to document them properly, the user is likely to encounter problems later.

The problem of user manuals being written in technical language can be solved by recognising the importance of the technical writer in the production process. Unless sufficient resources are allocated to documentation production, user manuals are likely to be written during the post-design phase by a member of the software development team who has a technical rather than user view of the software; or by an administrative support person who may have a user's view of the software, but who nonetheless lacks the skills to produce effective user documentation.

12.2.5 Quality and IS Development

In an attempt to develop a general-purpose quality framework, Garvin synthesised the wide-ranging definitions of product quality, derived from philosophy, economics, marketing and operations management (Garvin, 1984). This synthesis proposes five basic approaches to defining quality: transcendent, product-based, user-based, manufacturing-based and value-based. It was argued that relying on only one approach to define quality could lead to misunderstanding and conflict. For example, a marketing person might define quality in terms of user satisfaction, a production person in terms of the manufacturing process.

IS development faces the challenge of conforming with internationally recognised quality management standards in an increasingly globalised economy (Von Hellens, 1995). IS development services can be readily purchased from international suppliers and a commonly recognised set of IS development standards is necessary to guarantee acceptable levels of quality. The problem for IS developers is how to stay competitive whilst improving the quality of systems through the software development process.

Several prescriptive approaches have been developed, including the ISO 9000 series and the IEEE software engineering standards collection. The aim of these functionalist approaches is to prescribe a comprehensively detailed process which results in quality software. Software quality in this sense can be defined in terms of Garvin's (1984) manufacturing-based definition of quality: "How closely does the software conform to its technical specification; how few defects does it have?"

It is necessary to make a distinction between software quality, which takes a manufacturing-based approach, and the user-based approach to IS Quality. Von Hellens (1997) emphasises the difference between the quality of the software artefact, and IS quality as the use of the artefact in an organisational context.

12.3 IS Quality and Documentation

High user satisfaction is an important contributor to IS quality. If the user-based view of product quality corresponds to IS quality (that the quality of an artefact lies in the eyes of the beholder), then the user-related documentation which supports a system may be assumed to make a significant contribution to IS quality. It has been shown that user documentation makes an important contribution to the success of an IS in the user environment (Torkzadeh and Doll, 1993).

Many organisations have made considerable investments in IS, and the user documentation which supports those systems plays an important role in maintaining user satisfaction. Users need to be able to understand how the system works, and how to use it (Ackoff, 1967). High quality user documentation is important to the user. Yet organisations have, on the whole, failed to provide even adequate, much less high quality, user documentation. In a traditional data processing environment, only about half of the operational applications had good documentation, which in turn led to user dissatisfaction (Torkzadeh and Doll, 1993).

The contribution of user documentation to IS quality is further explored in a survey of Australian technical writers (Fisher, 1998). Here the technical writers' role extends beyond their traditional role of simply writing the user manual to include: acting as a user advocate, writing on-line help and error messages, and helping to design user interfaces. Such activities, with the exception of user advocacy, can still be considered "user documentation" in the sense discussed earlier, since to define the user manual as the only form of user documentation is too narrow a definition.

12.4 Participation and User Satisfaction: The Need for "Integrative Processes"

In an analysis of 151 independent IS development projects in eight different organisations it was found that user participation has a direct relationship with user satisfaction (McKeen, Guimaraes and Wetherbe, 1994). Four factors were examined: task complexity, system complexity, user influence, and user-developer communication, and how these factors affected the relationship between user participation and user satisfaction. In projects where tasks were complex, the relationship between user participation and user satisfaction was significantly stronger than in projects where tasks were less difficult. It was concluded that user influence and user-developer communication were independent predictors of user satisfaction.

This points to the relationship between the level of user involvement during system design, and the level of user satisfaction with the eventual product. The more user involvement, the greater their satisfaction. However there are difficulties in communication between users and IS developers, due to differing cognitive processes. The problem of poor manuals and software leading to low user satisfaction can be seen to be directly related to developers and users not communicating effectively during the requirements elicitation process. A complete set of user requirements is therefore not derived.

Although user participation can lead to enhanced IS Quality, the different outlooks of IS developers and users can cause difficulties. IS developers typically possess certain characteristics which inhibit their working relationship with other members of the organisation (Feeny, Earl and Edwards, 1996). These findings are consistent with earlier research (Edstrom, 1977; Gingras and McLean, 1979; Zmud and Cox, 1979).

> In a survey of IS directors, 46% reported that the culture gap between IS professionals and business counterparts was their most important challenge (Grindley, 1991).

This problem is clearly significant to many IS directors: literature emphasises the need for stakeholders to be involved with each other; to be committed to desired outcomes and collaborative effort. Arising from this need, a range of so-called integrative processes have been proposed (Galbraith, 1977). These processes are meant to bridge the cultural gap and integrate the different cognitive styles of IS developers and users. These integrative processes include the ETHICS model for participative systems development (Mumford, 1983a), Joint Application Development (Raghavan, Zelesnik and Ford, 1994) and the use of particular people as integrators, such as the "hybrid manager" (Earl and Skryme, 1992).

Unfortunately IS developers are reluctant to adopt participative systems development approaches because they are seen as expensive and time-consuming (Feeny, Earl and Edwards, 1996). Such approaches may also pose a challenge to the user's organisational culture, leading to avoidance and subversion of the "integrative process". As participation is crucially important, a process is needed which poses the least perceived threat to the IS developer's established method. Only then is the integrative process likely to win acceptance from both IS developer and user.

12.5 Bridging the Gap

The importance of developing a practical integrative process is highlighted in an analysis of the factors behind the success and failure of IS development projects (Lockett, 1989). Organisational issues were found to be more important than technological issues to the success of a project. One of the major factors identified was a development team which bridged the gap between IS functions and users.

Based on 30 project studies, the most critical area identified is the conversion of business needs into IS requirements. A "project champion" appears to perform this most effectively. In the absence of a champion, the gap is best bridged by either someone moving from the user side to the technical side as a mid-career change, or else by an IS developer with a long working relationship with the users. In simple terms Lockett is referring to someone with the ability to understand both the technical and the general perspectives.

What is therefore needed is a practical way of bringing about a form of collaboration that is acceptable to both developer and user. In theory, the various integrative processes (ETHICS, JAD, Participative Design, etc.) are effective ways of deriving a comprehensive set of user requirements, but in practice they suffer from being seen by developers and users as being costly in terms of time, effort and resources. The problems of poor quality user manuals and incomplete requirements elicitation which lead to reduced IS quality is due to the culture gap which exists between the IS developer and the user.

12.6 A Solution to the Problem

A solution to this problem, and to the related problem of poor quality user manuals is to upgrade the role of the technical writer from being a describer of software artefacts, to the active facilitator of user requirements elicitation as well as the manual writer (Fig. 12.2). The technical writer can encourage participation by reconciling both the technical and general perspectives.

As the technical writer is already a member of the IS development team, it is only necessary for the developer to accept the technical writer's involvement *earlier* in the project than is usual. This acceptance might be facilitated when the technical writer is seen to be co-operatively relieving another member of the project team of the onerous task of "writing down the user requirements".

If the technical writer documents the users' requirements in sufficient detail during the requirements elicitation process they will have produced the first

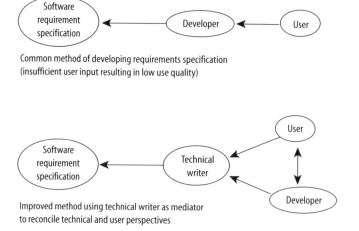

Figure 12.2 Design-phase user manual production as a means to derive improved user requirements information, leading to improved use quality.

draft of the user manual. A user manual produced like this is an effective way to detect user-related problems at a stage when it is still possible to remedy them. The technical writer facilitates participation by engaging the user in an extended session, or series of sessions with the developer. Acting as a "bridge" between the developer and the user, the technical writer can bring about sufficient participation to elicit a complete set of user requirements. In the absence of a facilitator, as Lockett (1989) pointed out, there is a real risk that the differing cognitive processes of developer and user will limit both the time allowed for requirements elicitation and the development of shared vision of the proposed system.

12.7 Summary

This chapter has discussed the relationship between user involvement in the development of user manuals during the design phase, and the users' overall satisfaction. Given an apparent relationship between participation in the design phase and user satisfaction, a practical process that enables the IS developer and the user to collaborate effectively is needed. Such an "integrative process" needs to reconcile the differing cognitive styles of the developer and the user, and avoid the problems that make developers and users disinclined to use integrative processes.

I suggest that the role of technical writer, normally an integral part of the IS development team, be expanded to include requirements elicitation. Technical writers qualify for this role with their ability to interpret technical aspects in terms of the general, and vice versa. In addition to interpreting the different perspectives of each aspect, the technical writer can document the users' requirements in sufficient detail to produce the first draft of the user manual. If this is done early during IS development then the technical writer has more time in which to develop the user manual to a high standard. A user manual thus produced would also be an effective way to detect user-related problems at a stage when it is still possible to remedy such problems.

IS quality would be significantly enhanced by using design-phase user manual production, involving the technical writer as a facilitator of communication between the user and the developer during the requirements elicitation process.

IS quality is likely to be improved because the manuals are not only of a higher standard of usability and usefulness, but also the software is improved because its design is based on the users' real requirements, not just the requirements perceived by the IS developer.

Chapter **13**

Design: A Better Way for Making Systems

John Nicholls

13.1 Introduction

There is no doubt about the stunning success of the computing and networks enterprise, although occasionally a hint of "trouble ahead" catches the public attention. At the time of writing the so-called *Millennium Bug* is making a lot of news. It has that rare quality, a technical problem that everyone can understand, but which has profound consequences, creating fears of a universal disaster. Surely, a little matter like this cannot be so important?

"No-one knows what will happen in the run up to 2000 and beyond. There is no precedent… Most IS systems, and round 5% of embedded systems, process Year 2000 dates in a way that causes a disruptive failure. Many (I believve more than half) of these errrors will not be corrected and, in correcting the others, further errors will be introduced" (Martyn Thomas of Praxis plc).

As the influence of the digital revolution continues to grow and as we, at work and at home, become more and more connected by networks, the need for concern about the social consequences of technical directions in the ITC world will grow. This chapter is a contribution to sociotechnical thinking on the issues that face society. It shows how an established body of thinking, the theory of design, might be adapted to help in dealing with the increasingly complex and seemingly intractable issues that face engineers, policy makers and educators.

13.2 The Technical Basis of Computing

Within a generation, the computing/network industry has been transformed from a minor player of interest mainly to scientists, academics and technicians, to a major force in the industrial and commercial world.

Computing, networks and the emerging digital industries were created as a result of scientific and engineering advances and for the most part remain dominated by technology. You can see this from the shelves of Blackwell's or Foyles, the papers in the BCS *Computer Journal*, articles in the computer tabloids. The technology of computing feeds itself – computers are used to design new computers, software to generate new software, networks to transport designs and programs and enable systems to be developed collaboratively. And so the technical orientation is continuously re-enforced.

In the UK there are perhaps 50,000 people taking part in the development of new computer systems. It is essential that the leaders of these groups, who help to set objectives and establish technical priorities, understand not only the technical implications of their work but also the social, economic, political and legal consequences.

How do developers of computer systems learn their craft? The two main areas of academic research and teaching in computing are *Computer Science* and *Software Engineering*. If we are to understand why some projects fall short in a social, economic or political way, at least some of the reasons may be found by looking at the concepts behind these subjects – both of them are technical subjects and when the chips are down (so to speak), technology prevails.

13.2.1 Computer Science

One of the most telling attacks on the shortcomings of computer science is in the paper by Fred Brooks (1996) who, after a distinguished career as a designer and manager of one of the largest computer projects of his time, became a University Professor.

Brooks would like to be considered a toolsmith – an "honourable trade" – and his case against computing as science can be summarised as follows: (a) it is a self-serving conceit; (b) it confuses the publication of endless varieties of computers, algorithms and languages as being equivalent to the discovery of laws of nature; (c) it leads students of computing to overlook the importance of *users*; (d) that as we honour the more abstract parts of this so-called science we "misdirect young and brilliant minds from a body of challenging and important problems that are our peculiar domain, depriving these problems of the powerful attacks they deserve".

Setting aside the rhetoric (Brooks is an excellent debater) the key point in his attack is his concern that system developers should pay more attention to human aspects of science.

13.2.2 Software Engineering

Software engineering was founded on a more eclectic approach but remains essentially techno-centric. It grew up as a counter to the computer science movement, and was given impetus by the famous NATO Summer School of 1968. This conference was a stage for articulating the growing concerns of industrial computer groups on the practical problems of developing large systems.

In comparison with the approach of computer scientists, software engineers recognised ideas of resource limitations (time, manpower and computers), the economics of development, the dynamics of large development groups and the adaptation of project management ideas to computing.

However, the development of software is not like the old disciplines of engineering, where there is a distinction between the design of objects and their manufacture – in contrast, the manufacture of software is trivial. There has often been an uneasy relationship between software engineering and the traditional schools of engineering.

13.3 The Human Dimension

As we look at the successes and failures of computer systems, we see that many of the failures are due to lack of consideration of the human as part of (and in relationship with) a computer system. Systems developed without thought for their human and social environment can be unpleasant, anti-social and dangerous. The dangers may not come, as the common myth has it, from a crazy computer freak hacking into a military system and taking over the world. They are more likely to come from more mundane sources, as computing and network components become more prevalent but less visible. In many cases, potential dangers are not deliberately covered up, but are simply overlooked by those who give exclusive devotion to technical matters.

Historically, the first and necessary stage was to look at the human individual using a system. What became known as *human factors* and *ergonomics* was based on applied psychology, looking at the parameters that are needed to be understood by every systems designer. For the most part these studies were based on the individual relationship between the individual and the computer system.

> A different approach is needed to deal with groups of people, the place of the individual in society, the impact of ICT on human work. This is provided by the study of *sociotechnology*.

The sociotechnical movement grew up before the computer industry developed, but its theme of paying attention to both technical *and* social aspects in the development of new working systems remains highly relevant to the modern world, and particularly the world of computing and communications. The task of including sociotechnical thinking into computing and network design is not simple. I feel it important to do two things: First, to identify the sociotechnical concepts appropriate to the computing field. Second, to suggest how these concepts can be applied in the development of computing systems.

13.4 The Case for Design

In this chapter I argue that

1. neither computer science nor software engineering is suitable as the primary basis for research and teaching on computing;

2. these subjects should be augmented with an approach based on the concepts of design.

The case for design has been advanced by several writers, including Freeman (1980), Dasgupta (1989) and Denning (1991). In 1989 Terry Winograd wrote:

> "...the current vision of software engineering is too narrow and needs to be expanded into a vision of design. A building is created by a combination of people including both engineers and architects. The architect's skill includes knowledge of materials and building techniques, but has a primary focus on function. The key questions go beyond construction to "What will make the building be appropriate to its uses? What will function as a good design when people move in?" We need to develop effective (and rigorous) training that builds the skills to answer these questions in designing computing systems" (Winograd, 1989, pp. 1412–13).

As we enter the information age, there will be a need for ICT-based systems to serve the entire population, not just the small segment of the population from which current users are drawn (technically aware, affluent and well educated). New systems will have to be developed by those sensitive to their impact on the life and work of a much wider population of users.

The contributions of computer science and software engineering will continue to be vital to the continued development of new technology. It would be foolish to build large, complex, inter-related systems without the technical expertise that can help to ensure their safety and integrity. But we need to move towards a more global view of computing, making use of theories and practices that have been found valuable in developing other "man-made things that change the world" (to adapt a definition of design).

In using the theory of design as a basis for ICT development, we don't just mean making a plan or writing a specification – we mean employing the body of knowledge gained in schools of design since the early part of this century, when the first systematic studies of industrial design were carried out.

13.5 History of Design

An important aspect of design is that its practitioners, even when they are developing new and adventurous ideas, use knowledge gained from past experience. Students of design – whether in architecture, industrial design, fashion or textile design – learn to review and discuss historical styles, to see how one school of design has influenced others, and above all to see what can be learned from successes and failures of the past. One of the things to do in establishing a design basis for computing is therefore to look at the history of design.

I have taken a classic work as the basis for the design history in the past 100 years. The work in question is *Pioneers of Modern Design: From William Morris to Walter Gropius* by Nikolaus Pevsner (1991), a work which has had a considerable influence on design thinking. In the following, the two design masters that Pevsner uses in his book – William Morris and Walter Gropius – are considered, to see how they might affect our thinking on computer design.

13.5.1 William Morris

Writing about the beginning of his period, Pevsner discusses the Arts and Crafts movement in Victorian England. In referring to William Morris's early awakening to the importance of design he writes,

> "we owe it to him (Morris) that an ordinary man's dwelling-house has once more become a worthy object of the architect's thought, and a chair, a wallpaper or a vase a worthy object of the artist's imagination".

A recent view of Morris's life and works is given in the biography by Fiona MacCarthy, *William Morris: A Life for Our Time* (1994). He was a man of outstanding talents, a radical thinker and a political activist. Morris might have been shocked by computers, but would also have been fascinated by them. He liked to learn new skills and crafts, to do things for himself and I suggest he might have emerged as a craftsman-programmer with a profound interest in the quality and potential beauty of the user interface.

His relevance to the sociotechnical movement is that he repeatedly stressed the dignity of work and the qualities of self-expression that he saw being destroyed in Victorian factories and sweat-shops. He was a tireless advocate of *change*, often clashing with the business interests of the time.

"William Morris, a bearded Victorian figure whose talents extended over many fields – artist, book-designer, business-man, craftsman, idealist, novelist, poet, printer, romantic, socialist, weaver – was a man of extraordinary energy. Pevsner (1991) considered Morris one of the founders of the modern design movement, and his influence was acknowledged by that more recognisable figure of modern design, Walter Gropius.

The writings and life of William Morris have inspired many ideas in modern humanist thinking, particularly his ideas about the place of work in peoples' lives. His idealism included the design of work to suit the capacity of the worker, and the emergence of work that

'after a little, people would rather be anxious to seek work than to avoid it, that our working hours would be rather merry parties...than the grumpy weariness it is now.' Not that all work would be pleasure: *'But a man at work, making something which he feels will exist because he is working at it and wills it, is exercising the energies of his mind and soul as well as his body.'"* (from *A Factory as it Might Be,* quoted in Thompson, 1991).

William Morris (1834–96)

13.5.2 Walter Gropius and the Bauhaus

The Bauhaus, founded in Weimar by Walter Gropius, is a more obvious starting point for ideas in modern design and its achievements were recorded in many books and papers.

In 1919 Walter Gropius was appointed to head a new institution, the Bauhaus, in Weimar, the German capital. Germany, crushed in the war and humiliated at Versailles, had a collapsing economy and there were threats of revolution. Against this background Gropius, chairman of the Working Council for Art, worked to bring all of the arts together, within the framework of a great architecture.

Perhaps the Bauhaus' most lasting influence was on applied design. Their view included the idea that it is harder to design a first-rate teapot than to paint a second-rate picture, and their philosophy did much to dignify the work of modern designers. We are now familiar with displays of modern furniture and kitchen pots in museums.

In 1937, as the Nazis rose to power, the stars of the Bauhaus migrated to the United States. Gropius was made head of the school of architecture at Harvard. Moholy-Nagy opened the New Bauhaus, which evolved into the Chicago Institute of Design, and Mies van der Rohe, who had become the head of the Bauhaus in 1930, was installed as dean of architecture at the Armour Institute in Chicago.

Soon, American architects were learning the principles of the new International Style, a name taken from the book, *International Architecture* by Walter Gropius. An American corporation in the late 20th century will most likely be housed in a tall, sleek, glass edifice, deriving essentially from the Bauhaus tradition.

Walter Gropius (1883–1969) and the Bauhaus

The contribution of the Bauhaus is significant for the following reasons:

- It represents a point in time when the modern movement in industrial design can be seen to be emerging.
- The principles of Bauhaus design were explicitly stated – they include:
  simplicity and abstraction;
  respect for the materials of manufacture;
  functionality and avoidance of unnecessary ornamentation.
- The programme of work for the Bauhaus had a prominent place for the education of designers.

Although there is now not much popular enthusiasm for the appearance of many Bauhaus buildings, the influence of their work, particularly in the design of everyday objects, is considerable.

13.6 Systems Development as Design

In addition to a change of name (e.g. from Chief Programmer to Chief Designer), a shift to design as the guiding principle for computer systems development would involve changes to process, organisation, and to the way developers think of their work.

Of course, it is what people *do* that counts, not what they are called, but as the creative professions have known for a long time, it is the vision of those who practise their art that governs what they do.

Here are some of the consequences of a shift to design.

13.6.1 Greater Diversity of Approaches

There is not a single, uniform, universal theory of design that is inherently multi-disciplinary. Designers have welcomed and assimilated contributions by people of all sorts including engineers, mathematicians, economists, applied psychologists, biologists and artists.

> In the Britain of the 1950s there was a great interest in improving the way of "doing things" in the home, in towns and cities, and in the new factories. These ideas were collected to form a *theory of design* – a basis for what the best architects, engineers, industrial designers and others were doing.
>
> The ideas in Christopher Jones's *Design methods: seeds of human futures* (1980) are drawn from many disciplines. One of the delights of this book, my first introduction to writings on design, is the way in which Jones accepts all kinds of ideas and makes the best use of them. He was one of the first academics in the UK to lecture on design to computer professionals and his book deals with computer matters as well as the more usual topics. Christopher Jones was a valued guest lecturer on my courses at the European Systems Research Institute, La Hulpe.
>
> **"Seeds of human futures"**

13.6.2 Models and Mock-ups

In software engineering there is a view that if you get the requirements "right", use these requirements to write a precise specification, and develop the system systematically, you will get a good system.

This is often illustrated by a process diagram of the following kind:

requirements →
  high-level design →
    detailed design →
      final product

This "waterfall" model has been superseded by more modern ideas including the so-called "spiral" model, but the waterfall model underlies a great deal of thinking in software engineering.

The design approach is more experimental and evolutionary, allowing for the fact that the introduction and use of a product changes both the ideas of the users and the environment of the product.

13.6.3 Wicked Problems

An essential part of mathematics, the underlying science of computing, is the establishment of theories which can be *proved*. Once a proof has been obtained, the question is settled and there is no need for further discussion – a "problem" has been solved.

In contrast, a distinguishing feature of design problems is the existence of "ill-structured" (Simon, 1973) or "wicked" (Rittel and Webber, 1973) problems with the following characteristics:

- they have no definitive formulation;
- there is no stopping rule;
- solutions are not true or false, but good or bad;
- every wicked problem is a symptom of another higher level wicked problem;
- no problem, and no solution, has a definitive test;
- each wicked problem is unique.

One of the important things in teaching design is to appreciate that such problems exist, and to show how to tackle them. In my experience this is one of the hardest parts of adjusting from a mathematical to a design approach.

13.6.4 Personal Signature

The emergence of a role of Chief Designer and the encouragement of schools of Computer System Design would allow us to replace the anonymity of current systems with the kind of personal signatures that are so important in industrial design.

Every day, I use a piece of software, a word processor. I do not know who wrote it, nor do I know who is responsible for the operating system on which it works. The vendors of the software do not attribute their designs, though their products are as important and necessary as a table knife. Parts of the sub-package are clumsy, hard to use and contain design faults (i.e. a property that allows or even encourages me to make errors and waste my time). Perhaps they are not particularly proud of their package?

It would be interesting to users (though perhaps not to megalithic computer companies) to know the person responsible for the pieces of software we struggle to use every day.

Some time ago we decided to stop having "best" cutlery in our home but instead to use a single set for everyday use. We bought a set of Alessi knives, forks and spoons called *Nuovo Milano*. The designer of this simple and beautiful cutlery is a famous Italian designer Ettore Sottsass. We know this because Alessi acknowledge and respect their designers.

Not only do we know who designed these knives, we can find out something about what the designer thinks, since he has written about his ideas. He actually mentions what he was trying to achieve with the design of *Nuovo Milano:* simplicity, a sense of tactile feeling, making use of the qualities of the stainless steel. The knife is particularly pleasing, since the handle is hollow and the balance in the hand is just right. The design is successful, sharp and clean and dishwasher-proof, always a pleasure to use.

We know who designed our knives and forks

13.6.5 Evaluation

In early days of programming, there was a lot of emphasis on "bugs" in programs. There was study of the nature of programming errors, meaning programs that did not terminate at all, that ended in a system crash, that gave wrong results. A strange controversy developed, centred on the avoidance of the **go to** statement.

The need for this care is still there, but with a design approach, another and more difficult set of problems becomes prominent. We now need to look at the systems as a whole, consisting of the machine and the human users, working together. With this as the approach, the existence of "bugs" includes:

- over-complexity;
- systems that cannot be understood by their intended users;
- missing or erroneous messages.

> Here is a maxim for users of modern systems: "if you can't use the system that's intended for you, it's not your fault, it's the fault of the system".

This brings a new view of what is a bug, and the need for a new kind of evaluation that will include not just functional, but also aesthetic judgement. Asking questions that extend beyond "is it correct?" or "does it work?", to the more difficult "is it good?". This would lead to the emergence of a school of criticism (different from the Which-report approach now prevalent) and the publication of reviews of software, as we have reviews of books, films, theatre.

In addition designers should get their ideas from artistic sources – from the graphic arts (pictures, icons), poetry (the use of metaphor), music (sound, rhythm), theatre (scenario, dialogue), film (story-boards).

13.6.6 A Sense of History

Designers do not always put the same store by originality as some computer people.

The idea of taking and adapting the best ideas from the past is common in design teaching. It is often the basis of what we mean by style in artistic productions. Perhaps computing is too young to have developed this sense, but there should be greater attempts to develop it.

13.7 Agenda for Research and Action

In this chapter a case has been made for adopting *design* as an underlying framework for ICT development. I believe this approach both embodies and expands the principles of sociotechnical design.

Since there is relatively little tradition of applying design theory to the construction of computer systems, a number of ideas need to be developed in order to take this approach a stage further:

13.7.1 Reviews

Compared with other creative activities which use words, pictures, scenarios and living-spaces, the makers of software come off too lightly. Books, TV and buildings are reviewed by critics who have established criteria by which these are judged. Such reviews are not just concerned with functions and features, but with judgements relative to other activities in the field, with the satisfaction felt by the user, with the social worth of the book, play or building.

I suggest it is time for those who design computer systems to regard themselves in the same light as authors, playwrights, film directors and architects, and to expect the same kind of criticism (and recognition) as in these other fields.

We should set up evaluation exercises to carry out detailed, objective reviews of selected ICT systems. Not just to look at their "features" but at such things as ease of learning and use, compatibility with existing work practices, how they fit in the social environment of their users, their flexibility and ability to change. Above all, at the satisfaction and pleasure to be gained from their use.

These reviews should be published and disseminated. There should be workshops and debates on reviews of truly critical software. In other words we should treat computer systems as other design artefacts (see Gelertner, 1998).

13.7.2 Independence for Designers

If we are to get to a situation comparable to the best in industrial design and architecture, where key designers, working independently, can set up studios and develop their own style and philosophy of design, there would have to be a change in the way in which computer programs are commissioned, developed and paid for.

Computer programs can be roughly subdivided into packages and bespoke software. The importance of packages is such that they over-ride the importance of bespoke software – many ICT systems are simply assemblies of parts of packages.

The development of packages is mostly in the hands of a diminishing number of large corporations who *sell* (not rent) them for what is, comparable to their cost of development, a very small amount of money. Because of their low selling cost, software developers need to produce new versions in order to generate new revenue. Each new version has to be different, bigger and "better" than the previous version, or customers would not buy them.

This situation leads indirectly to two results:

1. the continued anonymity of software designers – and hence to their lack of accountability and their difficulties in establishing their own philosophy of design;
2. the increasing redundancy of current software packages and the lack of an established aesthetics for software.

It is difficult to see what can be done about this, but here are two ideas.

Design Studios

We should encourage the setting up of design studios for computer systems, particularly software systems, independent of software and hardware manufacturers, to develop transportable systems that would have long life and support. The products of these studios would be offered to manufacturers and other vendors, with their guarantee of distribution.

Economic Changes

I believe some of our current problems arise from the way in which software is paid for. If we could pay for packaged software by use rather than by package, this would affect the economics of software packages. With a suitable pricing structure, it might turn out that good designs would persist longer, without unnecessary changes. There could be adequate recompense for developers without the need for vendors to "version" software so frequently.

13.7.3 Making Use of Past Designs

One of the most obvious differences between computing and modern design is that "creativity" in computing tends to be equated with invention. This is partly related to the pricing structure of computing artefacts and the commodification of software and user interfaces. Added to this, there is no tradition of using tradition in software, as there is in other constructive activities such as architecture and the decorative arts. One of the ways this approach has been applied in architecture is by the use of *patterns* – designs for parts of buildings, towns and other things that affect the lives of humans (Alexander, Ishikawa and Silverstein, 1977).

The idea of design patterns has been adapted to the design of object-oriented software (Gamma, Helm, Johnson and Vlissides, 1995) and computer interface design by the Usability Group at Brighton University and at the Massachussetts Institute of Technology (see Brighton University and MIT web pages). The use of design patterns provides a way of avoiding the excessive search for something "new" that besets much of the computer industry and of addressing one of the key deficiencies of and inhibitors of development in computing, the lack of skilled designers.

13.7.4 A New Approach to Research

The last point to be made involves taking a different approach to the way in which computing research (and teaching, and funding, and description) is carried out.

A distinction is traditionally made between the "hard" and "soft" sciences. As examples, physics and sociology are often seen as being at the extreme ends of a spectrum. The hard sciences are seen as stressing the need for precise, quantitative data and unambiguous decisions, while the soft sciences allow for qualitative methods of evaluation. Design is an activity where the means of evaluation are much more at the qualitative end of the spectrum and ideas of "correctness" are not applicable.

13.8 Summary

To sum up, the improvements in systems that will be necessary as computing enters its mature stage will come from a new vision of what computing is about.

Although computing relies on continued growth and adventurous development of technology, the full potential will come about only when the human environment of computing systems is recognised and acknowledged. For the reasons suggested above, this potential may never be realised within the framework of the current bases of computing, computer science and software engineering, though these remain essential for guiding the technical basis needed for continuing development.

It can be argued that each major technology goes through several stages in its evolution, and full awareness of design values does not come until later stages, when appreciation of the social environment of the technology is apparent and recognised.

Once this is done and the profession recognises the value of a more rounded and balanced view of what is involved in developing systems, it will be possible to evaluate the future of computing in a different way. With the freedom of thinking that this will encourage, the computing profession may be able to take the leaps of imagination that have characterised the best industrial designers and to free the computing world of some of what Norman (1998) has called the "fatal flaws" of the most pervasive technology of our time.

Part 4
Transforming the Long Wall

Chapter **14**

Information Systems Implementation and Organisational Change: A Socio-Technical Systems Approach

Margaret T. O'Hara , C. Bruce Kavan and Richard T. Watson

14.1 Introduction

The typical organisation of the information age faces a complex decision making process related to its information systems. Information systems come in an amazing array of shapes and sizes. During the last thirty years, they have evolved from simple systems that automate tasks to intricate ones that transform organisations (Weil M, 1998).

Simple systems are not extinct; they now co-exist with their more elaborate progeny. Thus, organisations deal with information systems in varying stages of evolution. This complex coexistence of information systems in varying stages demand correspondingly complex organisational responses (Eckhouse, 1999).

Organisations also face rapidly changing environments to which they must respond if they are to remain competitive (Hoffman, 1998). The drive to remain competitive often results in an effort to first enhance, and then update or replace the organisation's information systems. Because the response is rapid, needs analysis and understanding may be incomplete. Risk from implementation failure rises, and the chances of a positive, quality outcome are greatly diminished (Wah, 1998, Remenyi, 1997).

One method of understanding this dual-front complexity is to examine the organisational impact of information systems implementation using the socio-technical system (STS) framework. In the STS view, organisational work systems are composed of two subsystems. Each of the two subsystems has two components: technology and task comprise the technical subsystem while people and structures define the social subsystem. STS organisational design seeks to maximise the successful interaction of these components, thereby optimising the entire work system.

In this chapter, we focus on the changes brought about by information systems. Using illustrative cases, we expand the traditional STS model to include an explicit focus on the changes that result from the implementation of complex information systems. We identify the magnitude of change by its direct impact upon the STS components. Such identification is significant because when change is adequately understood and planned, it is far more likely to be successful.

The expanded STS model defines three orders of change, each linked to a component of the STS model. *First order or alpha level change* involves task accomplishment only, and typically occurs when a task is automated in some fashion. *Second order change* (beta) occurs when the method of task accomplishment changes in such a way that people's organisational roles are affected. *Third order change* (gamma) affects task accomplishment, people's roles, and the organisational structure.

When change is unanticipated and unplanned, many undesirable consequences may result. Many projects have failed because the changes they engendered were poorly handled. Managers and organisational theorists alike have spent considerable time and effort attempting to improve change management. Using an expanded STS model, managers can first identify the level of change that is likely to result from an information system's implementation and then respond with the appropriate resources to ensure success.

First, we briefly present the STS concept, and then we discuss organisational change brought about by technology. Next, some information systems implementation examples are presented, and the STS model is expanded to include the change dimension (alpha, beta and gamma) with each example. The paper concludes with guidelines for project managing based upon each unique category of change. These guidelines provide direction for the project manager, the project team and the organisation itself.

14.2 Organisational Change

The concept of organisational change has intrigued academic researchers for years, and managing organisational change effectively has proved difficult. In this section, the authors will briefly review the key concepts of the socio-technical systems approach to organisational design followed by an examination of the relationship between technology implementations and organisational change utilising the socio-technical systems approach.

14.2.1 The STS Approach to Organisational Design

The interaction between technology and the people in an organisation is complex, and one way of understanding this interaction is to consider the firm as a socio-technical system as depicted in Figure 14.1.

The technical subsystem includes the technology that drives the method of task accomplishment (task). While the same type of technology may be present in multiple organisations, the technical subsystem will likely be different within each firm since it is the result of implementing the technology, and the implementation choices are vast.

People and structure comprise the social subsystem. Attributes of people (attitudes, skills and values), reward systems and authority structures are among the concerns of the social system (Bostrom, 1980). Multiple social

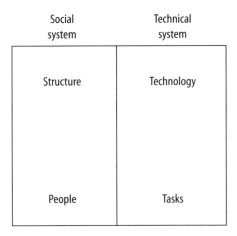

Figure 14.1 The STS model.

subsystems exist within organisations. Each department may form a unique social subsystem, or subsystems may form based on more temporary divisions.

To optimise the performance of the total work system, one must examine all the components of a work system and accommodate their interaction. To focus on only one subsystem or component would, by definition, result in a less than optimal outcome. System developers often inappropriately focus more on the technology and how it will affect task accomplishment without adequate assessment of the interaction of the entire work system.

> "[this] limited focus…leads the systems designer to ignore the fact that these changes cause more changes within other variables in the work system" (Bostrom and Heinen, 1977a, p. 25).

14.2.2 Organisational Change and Information Systems

When change and organisational impact are related to information technology, researchers have acknowledged that different levels of change may result from a single technology intervention (Gash and Orlikowski, 1991; Schein, 1994; and Zuboff, 1988). For example, the first use of a word processing system is typically to perform existing tasks more efficiently. Some workers may be eliminated with improved productivity. After a time, the word processor may be used to add value to or redesign pre-existing work. When this occurs, people are affected because their jobs or roles may be redefined. In some firms, the presence of the word processor sparked interest in other application software and those word processing workstations gradually evolved into highly interconnected office automation systems. Thus, in some cases, the introduction of a simple word processing system initiated a very high level of organisational change.

14.3 Some Illustrative Cases

Data from three information systems projects are presented. In the first case, the new information system was viewed as a way to automate current practices (an alpha level change) and eliminate dependence on a single computer. In the second instance, the new information system reshaped the nature of people's jobs (a beta level change). The third example demonstrates a technology that helped redesign work management and enabled the transformation of the organisation into a new form (a gamma level change). After each case, the traditional STS model is extended to include the level of change.

14.3.1 Case One: Alpha Level Change

In the original information system of this case, stand-alone PCs were used to print customer labels in each manufacturing plant. Because the PCs were not on-line with the main computer system, the information they contained was often outdated. The new information system provided the plants with multiple, networked PCs that were linked to a central data repository. Customer information was updated regularly from the corporate office, and the printed label was far more reliable. The new system did not change the manner in which work was performed (task accomplishment); it simply enhanced the task.

This is change at the simplest level. Easy to plan for and understand, the system was neither disruptive nor a radical departure from the status quo. First order (alpha) change is highlighted in the STS model by an interaction arrow between technology and task (see Fig. 14.2).

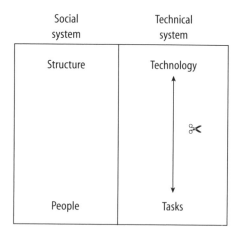

Figure 14.2 First order (alpha) change.

14.3.2 Case Two: Beta Level Change

Prior to implementing a new customer reporting system, sales representatives would either produce a standard report by pressing a single key, or fill out a printed form to request a special report. Their requests then went to the sales manager for approval. Once approved, the request was forwarded to the customer service manager who then sent it to the corporate information systems department. Finally, the programmer would receive the request and create the report. A new information system made the data more readily available to the various locations, and responsibility for report creation moved to the customer service and sales representatives. The reporting process was automated and streamlined, but the representatives roles were also altered. Instead of placing a request and waiting for a report, representatives now needed to understand the report development process and the data structures involved. This level of understanding required significant training for the representatives.

The two interaction arrows: (1) tasks and people, and (2) people and technology in Figure 14.3 represent the second order or beta level change (β) that resulted from the new reporting system. The new technology altered the manner in which reports were processed (task accomplishment). Not only was the method of task accomplishment altered (α), but so were the roles that people assumed in the reporting process. It was not simply one technology substituting for another as in Case One. The arrow between task and people represents the changing roles that resulted from the new system. In addition to new methods of task accomplishment, the manner in which people interacted with the technology was also altered. This is reflected in the arrow between people and technology.

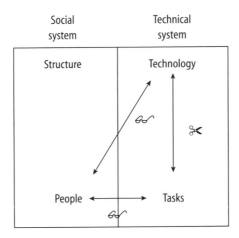

Figure 14.3 Second order (beta) change.

14.3.3 Case Three: Gamma Level Change

The information systems project for this case provided users at a small bank with access to data that previously had been available only in limited format on the mainframe system. Using intelligent workstations, users would download and manipulate the data as necessary. The availability of this information has changed the manner in which many of the bank's employees perform their jobs, and it has re-engineered many work processes.

As more people had broader access to information, the management structure of the bank also changed. Managers became more self-sufficient in that they now generated reports for their own use rather than calling upon analysts to create the reports for them. Information was also more readily available to clerical employees. Thus, the new system distributed information up and down the organisation. Decision making moved down in the organisational structure so that now these clerical employees are given the information and authority to make decisions. There are fewer layers of management for each decision to travel through; thus, the organisational structure has flattened. People, the tasks they perform, and the communications, authority and workflow structures were all affected

This change is highlighted in Figure 14.4 by three interaction arrows: (1) people and structure; (2) structure and task; and (3) structure and technology. In addition to the beta level changes discussed previously, the changes resulting from this system flattened the organisational decision processes (people and structure arrow dynamic). These changes represents gamma order change (γ), the highest order of organisational change that may result from technology implementations. The STS model is now fully developed as a change impact model that reflects the varying levels of change.

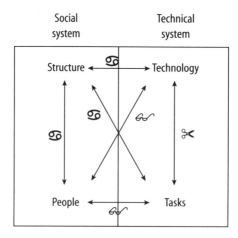

Figure 14.4 Third order (gamma) change.

14.4 Managerial Implications

In order to avoid the undesirable consequences of inadequately planned change, project implementers – acting as change agents – need to be aware of the STS dynamics and the resulting magnitude of intended change. In this manner, these individuals can manage towards the change by adjusting the organisational response to the change based upon its potential magnitude. Ideally, organisations will match available skill sets to projects at the beginning of the project. Each group of stakeholders – management, users and developers – anticipates certain organisational impacts resulting from every new project implementation. Since some of the changes that result may be greater than originally anticipated, resources may be under committed for the project. Conversely, other changes may be less than anticipated, thereby reflecting resource over utilisation (see Table 14.1). Over-commitment often results in waste since projects can expand to reflect resource availability while under committed projects are likely to fail because of inadequate resources.

The first stage of many change models concerns preparing the organisation to change, but many organisations do not undertake implementation planning appropriate to the level of change anticipated. Managing towards the appropriate level of change will permit mangers to match resource allocation to the appropriate level of planned change and orchestrate an appropriate response.

14.4.1 Change Dynamics

The higher the order of change, the greater the implementation complexities. Information systems projects may be divided into three broad categories based upon the expanded STS model. By examining the case database from which the above examples were drawn, the authors have created a set of guidelines related to change management to help managers achieve the desired results. These critical success factors are grouped and discussed along three dimensions: project management, project team and organisation.

Table 14.1. Anticipated versus actual level of change

		Anticipated level of change		
		Alpha	**Beta**	**Gamma**
Actual level of change	**Alpha**	Match	Over-committed	Over-committed
	Beta	Under-committed	Match	Over-committed
	Gamma	Under-committed	Under-committed	Match

14.4.2 Project Management

Just as the complexity of system design increases with the number of other system interfaces, the managerial complexity of an implementation increases based upon the level of interaction within the socio-technical model. This increasing complexity requires that both business acumen and the ratio of business understanding to technical understanding on the part of the manager increase. In alpha level change, the focus is on the task and the technology; thus, a manager needs only limited business understanding along with significant technical knowledge to manage the change. Beta level change requires greater business functional area knowledge, since as people's roles change, their job responsibilities may cross departmental boundaries. With gamma level change, the structures of the organisation change. A manager responsible for such high-level change must not only have true insight into how the business works, but must also be clearly recognised within the organisation as having such insight. In this manner, the manager truly empowers the project team members and users.

Since alpha level change represents the simplest form of change within the socio-technical system, it requires the least amount of business acumen and understanding. Generally, this reflects a participatory management style for the project manager – users participate on the team in the selection and implementation process. When the interaction is between technology, task and people such as beta change, individual roles are altered and a more facilitating management style is required to encourage the people affected by the change to identify role changes, redesign their job descriptions, and bring definition to the new roles. The highest order of complexity occurs with gamma level change. This type of change has the maximum number of interactions (people, task, technology and structure) and thus a more empowering management style is most successful. This management style enables people and teams to redesign both their work roles and the organisational structure, recognising that no single person or group can accomplish this task individually.

14.4.3 Project Team

As projects gain complexity along the alpha to gamma change continuum, the nature of the project team is also critical. For lower order change, the team members are technical specialists who emphasise the technology. As the complexity increases and individuals' roles are altered, team members must be able to deal with greater levels of organisational complexity. Team members need experience to guide and train people in their new roles. When gamma change occurs, the team requires not only technical and training components, but also an organisational design component. The organisational design specialist reviews and develops the structures, reporting relationships, and reward systems that affect the people who perform the work and the roles they assume.

Project success depends upon good communication. As the complexity of a project increases, so does the need for varying types of communications. Lower order change may be handled through simple project status reports accompanied by the current implementation planning guides. When change expands to include role changes (beta change), work flow walk-throughs and redesigned job descriptions are required to help individuals understand the new ways of doing work (i.e., altered roles).

Higher order (gamma) change requires that the organisation prepare in a more formal manner. Change orientation seminars emphasising the problems associated with maintaining the status quo and the opportunities afforded by responding to these problems can be conducted to solicit input as to how the organisation might, should, or could respond. This approach allows the participants to buy into the change process. Additionally, early successes resulting from the change must be highly publicised and rewarded to reinforce the new appropriate behaviours.

14.4.4 Organisational Success Factors

Organisations must also prepare differently for different levels of change. High order change typically requires the entire organisation to be mobilised. In addition to the change preparedness processes illustrated above, organisations can rally around threats such as a major competitor or new regulatory requirements. Such actions lend themselves to contests, testimonials or success stories, all of which provide focal points for strategic planning purposes.

Lower order change may require only motivating people through improved understanding of the rationale for change (alpha) or to generating enthusiasm for the new method of accomplishing work (beta). Training sessions, newsletters, kick-offs, and victory celebrations may all be useful in generating a positive attitude towards change.

Since unanticipated problems often come with every change, the handling of these problems is often as critical to the project success as the handling of the intended change. The higher the order of change, the more deliberate the problem response. Problems associated with alpha change must be handled swiftly by the immediate supervisor. A higher level manager would handle changes affecting the roles of individuals (beta change) after a methodical understanding of the conflicts or problem. Executive level resolution is required to handle gamma level changes, since they may involve organisational competitiveness or other market or competitive positioning. Gamma level problem response may involve significant organisational introspection, and thus may not be immediate.

Training can often minimise problems associated with the change. Alpha level change requires task level training (i.e., how the new technology is to be used). People's roles are changed with beta level change, and therefore training must be extended beyond task level training to work flow training to understand how roles are changed. At the gamma level, considerable care and deliberate planning are needed. When possible, the change should occur in phases to allow the organisation to deal with it in smaller, incremental chunks rather than all at once. In such instances, it is very useful to understand not only the end goal, but also how each phase helps achieve the longer-term outcome.

14.5 Hints and Tips

- All projects are important, but not all projects should be treated in a similar manner.

- Projects associated with gamma level change are difficult to manage:
  the tasks are changed;
  the people are affected; and
  the management structure is transformed.

- To be successful, the project manager must consider *all* the factors mentioned previously; concentrating on only one or two factors may not be enough to produce success. With such projects, the manager must perform a true juggling act, ensuring that all the factors are well managed.

- Most firms have already reaped the benefits of automation in many of their processes. That is, there are fewer alpha level change projects. Additionally, many firms implement multiple information systems projects simultaneously, thus stretching undoubtedly scarce resources. And, this situation will only intensify as the firm's information systems become more complex.

14.6 Conclusion

The concepts of the socio-technical systems model provide a powerful foundation from which to examine the potential magnitude of organisational change associated with information system implementations. The extension of the STS model to consider levels of change suggests that varying dimensions of management style, project team characteristics and organisational preparedness are critical for project success. In this era of mergers and acquisitions, coupled with restructuring and downsizing, reengineering work has become more commonplace. When work systems change, the socio-technical systems model provides tremendous insight into the dynamics among the components of the work system. In considering these dynamics, managers must effect those activities that contribute to project success. Grounding implementation activities in terms of the socio-technical system is not only intuitively appealing but also a logical extension of a well-accepted framework for work system project planning. The model extension will help focus attention on those characteristics critical for project implementation success.

Chapter **15**

Virtual Dynamics and Socio-Technical Systems

Eliat Aram

15.1 Introduction

Networking technologies such as email, the Internet or TeamRoom are at the forefront of developments in information technology. This chapter suggests that they can be seen as a form of virtual semi-autonomous work groups, which can be seen as synonymous with socio-technical systems (Miller, 1999; Trist and Murray, 1993). These recent socio-technical configurations provide an exciting opportunity to explore their impact on organisational life.

Networking technologies can greatly increase and enrich context. The use of virtual space enriches the conversational life of organisations and adds a fresh and exciting flavour to the ordinary, familiar, human interaction. These technologies are influencing our lives by enhancing communication and speeding up the rate of change. They also have more subtle implications for the development of organisations at a deeper level of interaction where the dynamics of anxiety, shame, resistance, envy, authority, power, projective processes, splitting and others, take place in an emergent, sometimes surprisingly escalating manner.

Many of the dynamics that occur in virtual teams are similar to those that have been identified in real life interactions, only faster, less contained and more difficult to work with. This chapter explores the dynamics that arise in using networking technologies in relation to a number of core socio-technical design principles, and supports sense-making using insights from the following theoretical perspectives:

- Complexity with an emphasis on self organising and emergent processes and its implications for control (Gleick, 1987; Kauffman, 1995; Stacey, 1996).
- Psychoanalytic with insights into the unconscious dynamics of groups, and its notion of the primary task, suggesting that virtual teams are characterised by dynamics similar to face-to-face groups, both small and large (Bion, 1961; Main, 1985).
- Gestalt with its holistic approach and its focus on dialogue, both important in exploring the relationship between, and the relatedness of, people using electronic means of communication (Friedman, 1992; Yontef, 1988).

The data for this chapter arises from experience of participating in the virtual (and at the same time very real) life of some groups using different networking technologies. In addition, detail from discussions with people about their experiences are woven into this chapter.

15.2 Networking Technologies and the Individual

The socio-technical principle of system boundaries suggests that "the design process must be careful that boundaries drawn from the system do not interfere with the sharing of knowledge or information which are needed for task accomplishment" (Cherns, 1976; 1987). The fast development of computers, however, suggests a more complex task than simply setting up a "boundary between author and typist" (*ibid.*). Taking this analogy further, when working with networking technologies more than one level of setting up boundaries is possible: one person might be both the author and the typist; a number of authors can work on the same document, therefore, there can be a number of typists; and these can change at any moment of working on a particular task. Moreover, the innovative networking technologies enable more roles than only a typist or an author (a commentator, a supervisor, an observer, etc.). Using networking technologies thus means working with multiple and complex boundaries, and, in fact, it often means working *across* boundaries, including cultural and personal boundaries in all their differing aspects, covering attitudes to work and the use of technology, openness or resistance to change, language differences and the use of humour.

The principle of information flow suggests that "relevant information should go directly to the person" as this "contributes to the control of variance and, thus, to superior performance" (Cherns, 1976; 1987). Many organisations, thus, try to constantly update themselves with the use of technology, absorbing the idea that "fast is good", "the more the better" and that "the world is getting smaller and smaller" so we can all communicate with everyone quickly both nationally and internationally.

Not many, however, stop to think of how potentially risky these assertions are for our sense of self, for our identity, for who we are and what we become when boundaries are so easily crossed and information overwhelms us. Those who try to collaborate and work jointly across such boundaries take the risk of unwelcome and unwilling intrusion that could threaten individual and group senses of self. The fragility of a sense of self (Beaumont, 1993; Mollon, 1994) is heightened when networking technologies come into play. This can be seen in the dynamics of shame and regression and can sometimes take the form of an overt attack or the taking of offence. Moreover, the anxiety that accumulates around this is uncontained and can escalate and burst into the formal, non-virtual, system in unpredictable, potentially destructive, ways, as shown below.

Furthermore, networking technology is, at present, a medium that is very much centred around language. All that is available is the keyboard, the screen, and the person's ability to communicate in a recognisable language, commonly

English. In this sense what the Gestalt perspective (Perls, Hefferline and Goodman, 1972; Polster and Polster, 1973) refers to as the phenomenological *"what is"*, the multi-dimensional and sensual phenomena, to work with, is reduced to that which is communicated on this screen. Much is thus left open for the imagination and fantasy.

Consider the following email exchange (between two people who are working only a few desks away from each other in a large corporation) as an illustration of the impact of fluid system boundaries on the dynamics that occur in what we might call virtual relationships.

- Richard comments on Arthur's tie; Probably a humorous comment.
- Arthur responds pointing to the misspelling of his name; Is that still a humorous response?
- Richard replies by identifying Arthur's national origin; Is this a racist comment?
- Arthur responds with threat, the Blue Form, which is the company's procedure for reporting on racial and unethical behaviour when observed by members of the organisation. Being reported on this from could result in the lossof one's job.

What we see is how the written message can become a sponge for projections because there are no nuances, tone of voice, gestures or facial expressions to accompany the message. Thus, Arthur, reading the word "Pollack" reads it in his context, with his sensitivity to racial comments, leaving out the context of the other. His sense of self is affected and he reacts with an attack. This kind of fragility of self is reinforced by the cultural context of this organisation.

Here we have a large corporation which has implemented, as part of its Codes of Ethics, a procedure (known as the Blue Form) which everybody in the organisation is free to use when they feel unethical behaviour has taken place. On the face of it, the intention behind this policy is good: to have a system where all individuals take part in the monitoring and maintaining of a moral culture in the organisation. In complexity terms it could be seen as an attempt to allow a culture of ethics to emerge out of a self-organising process where each person takes responsibility for his/her actions. While no-one has overall control of the system, controlled behaviour nevertheless emerges (Griffin, 1998; Stacey, 1993).

This Blue Form procedure, therefore, is stepping directly into the space of becoming another one of the many ways that organisations have been using technological developments to increase formal control. By formalising the potentially self-organising shadow process of emergent control in the system, this procedure has become yet another "direct monitoring of an individual's work activities through the immediate, computer-assisted surveillance of what he or she is doing" (Oravec, 1996, p. 69). As the email exchange is potentially "witnessed" by the surveillance it was possible to use it as a threat, as a "method of domination". What could have been an emergent ethical culture out of the ethical behaviour of each member participating in the life of the organisation ended up being a powerful means of control by the formal hierarchy, which in fact is using its members to spy on one another's behaviour.

15.3 Networking Technologies and the Group

The principle of iteration suggests the ongoing monitoring and reviewing of the system to allow continual improvement (Hirschheim, 1985). The principle of minimal critical specification stresses the necessity to identify what is absolutely essential to be accomplished in a task, yet allowing maximum scope for how the task should be undertaken (*ibid.*). Figure 15.1, which addresses these two principles, summarises the progressive stages of technology use by teams until they reach the ability to skilfully use the technology. Using networking technologies, the cohesive work group is inevitably a developmental process. The diagram provides a useful point of reference to monitor at which developmental stage a group is at any moment of using the technology. Initially, the group operates at the bottom left corner, using the networking technology as a point of reference only, and face-to-face meetings are an integral part of the work. The goal is to get to the stage where co-ordinated and collaborative work can be done through the networking technology with very little need for face-to-face meetings.

The group's progression is assumed to depend on two factors: the nature of human interaction (x) and the degree of behavioural change required (y). In socio-technical terms: the minimal critical specification to accomplish the task of achieving real collaboration is that the work needs to be co-ordinated and the feedback in terms of connectivity has to be tuned. Thus, for example, people need to log into the virtual group room and participate in it regularly

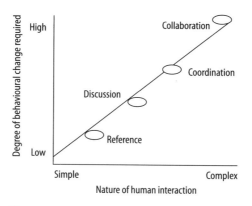

Figure 15.1 Progressive stages of technology use by teams.

(increase in the behavioural change required), so that there is enough rich and synchronised communication among the members (interactions are complex enough).

All these, however, are rooted in linear Newtonian thinking. The figure cannot address the complex meaning that lies within the two dimensions of "degree of behavioural change required" and "complex interactions", and the socio-technical principles do not take into account the increased complexity and unpredictability involved in human interactions. Email facilities, for example, have been made available to enhance working efficiency, as part of the organisation's legitimate system (Stacey, 1993; 1996). Not surprisingly, however, what Stacey calls the shadow system is also expressed in email exchanges.

Stacey's perspective is rooted in research that attempts to understand non-linear dynamics. He suggests that organisations, being complex adaptive systems, operate in a non-linear manner, that is, outcomes cannot be explained only by a cause and effect mechanism. These systems survive when they operate at the edge of chaos, or in bounded instability (Stacey, 1996). Bounded instability is the dynamics of simultaneous order and disorder, predictability and unpredictability (*ibid.*).

Stacey (1996, p. 179) lists five control parameters which determine whether or not a system can operate in bounded instability, which is postulated to be the dynamic required for creative and emergent self organising processes that bring about creative new patterns and change. These five control parameters are: the rate of information flow, the degree of diversity, the richness of connectivity, the level of contained anxiety and the degree of power differentials. When these parameters are at a critical level the dynamics of bounded instability occur, below the system solidifies and above it disintegrates.

The dynamics of the virtual interactions resemble those of **the large group** dynamics (Main, 1985) even when the actual number of people participating is small. These dynamics are particularly likely to occur in organisations, where all members are connected to an internal email system. The dynamics are those in which people have a sense of a loss of individuation, loss of sense of self, by becoming anonymous or by being generalised and labelled into a group without being recognised for their difference. This is accompanied by envy and projective processes (*ibid.*).

These large group dynamics are explored below through examination of two very different groups, designated the "chat group" and the "TeamRoom group".

15.3.1 The Chat Group

This is an informal chat site on the Internet open to anyone interested in joining it. It started off as a political site, that is, an area for people to discuss their political views regarding matters concerning Israel. The target audience is Israelis and Jews living in Israel and abroad. The people in this chat group found their way to this site by word of mouth or by surfing the Internet. People did not know one another before joining the group. The people writing in it now are physically located in different countries, they are from different age groups and have different professional backgrounds. Some of the people who write have introduced themselves and have developed contacts outside the site, over the email and even in person. Others have kept their identity hidden.

Interesting phenomena take place on this site: some people do not use their real names, but invent new identities for themselves and take up various roles ("the provocateur", "the family man", "the wise woman", "the uneducated", and so on); some write under more than one identity. Having begun with one or two people these phenomena have now become part of the culture of this group and other members of the group sometimes know who is writing under what name and sometimes not. In other words, it is practically impossible to know how many people actually participate in this site, how many occasional visitors there are, and who the "real" people are.

This illustration joins the chat site shortly after a period of friction: a few weeks previously the site had split. Some members had left to write in another site, others had stayed, and some (or others?) were writing in both sites, using the names they were known by, or unrecognisable names, or no names at all. This split occurred after arguments and battles between members in the original site became unbearable. However, the battles now continue between the two "war zones" and a regressive dynamic of generalised "good guys/bad guys" is evident.

At the same time that a dysfunctional dynamic of BaF (Basis Assumption Fight-Flight)was taking place, some very creative debates were also going on. The group that had split off spent most of its time complaining and finding excuses for why nothing interesting was going on in their site, blaming the other group and envying their discussions. The group that remained in the original site, however, carried on conversing, only occasionally interrupted by the departed group.

These dynamics are similar to those that have been identified in real life situations: being common in face-to-face interactions in inter-group events. In companies, when competition and conflict is not held or contained, the result is splits and break ups.

Consider another virtual group.

15.3.2 TeamRoom

TeamRoom is a Groupware product of Lotus Notes. Members of the Complexity and Management Centre (CMC) of the University of Hertfordshire have been using this software as an additional means of communication and as a space to store information and share experiences regarding various projects. This use of Groupware is different to the chat group in that all group members know one another well, meet in real life and work together in other places. In this respect it is similar to the peer group.

TeamRoom is operated through a main server and the process by which people interact with the server and with one another is called replication. This is a procedure by which the server updates the person's local TeamRoom copy with the most recent information it holds at the same time as it updates itself with the new information it finds on that person's local copy. Thus, the replication is a two-way feedback procedure. Then, the next person to replicate will receive the new updates. The software stores all the interactions among group members under an indexed list that can be retrieved according to the subject of the interaction, the person who created it or the date it was created.

An example of the use of TeamRoom, is the attempt to develop an MA in Complexity Management in collaboration with a university in Italy and a leading international IT organisation. This was a group of twelve people consisting of three sub groups representing the above three organisations. They had not met before starting to work on the project and worked together for this purpose only. This project did not achieve the desired outcome, but it is interesting to look at the dynamics that took place as the project was heading for its inevitable death.

Cultural differences emerged very quickly. The Italian culture, with its intense daily social interaction, did not seem to lend itself to working in virtual space. Using new technology demands the extension of one's own capability to adapt. The differences in the way

"I think I've got the hang of it now."

"oops, forgot to switch to 'local', this is going to be expensive…":

people respond to the use of new technology came across in the group by voices heard expressing the dis-ease with it. All these were potential obstacles that were probably not addressed. Perhaps there was too much diversity, both cultural and in the capacity to use the technology. Power differences emerged, where CMC members were perceived as holding the theoretical knowledge on behalf of the group, the IT company members were perceived as holding the technological knowledge, leaving Italian colleagues with the perception of being laid back, uninterested and potentially even incompetent .

Using technology played a vital part in the collective memory of this group. The data, impressions and words put on the team space remained there for as long as the space was used and in a way it was as if they were crafted in stone.

"ooooh, it all goes public…"

In addition, there was a perception that computers have a preserving ability. That is, they can capture the meaning of what we write forever because our virtual interactions are being recorded in the mechanical mind of the computer with the possibility of retrieving past discussions.

This perception has implications for the way people participate in the virtual groups. It can threaten the spontaneity of dialoguing: some felt they needed to log in often to keep, others felt they needed to craft very carefully what they were writing and that it could become very time consuming. Others found it easier to write precisely because they did not see the person they were

"I think there is some danger in replicating becoming obsessive"

writing to and thus could be more direct and open. It was interesting to see how the increased frustration arising from the lack of collaboration between the sub-groups on the MA TeamRoom was manifest in the boldness and directness of what people were saying, including the use of calligraphic expressions to replace the vocal and physical ones such as the use of bold letters, three dots, question marks and exclamation marks.

15.3.3 In Summary

The parameters of power and anxiety were enacted differently in the two groups. In the TeamRoom group, power difference emerged in relation to computer literacy and language competence. Anxiety has increased in the TeamRoom group in relation to the need to use the technology and for the Italian group, not having a sense of support around, resulted in the anxiety being uncontained. In the chat group, power and anxiety enacted themselves in a more dynamic way, in the sense that power difference, for example, did not establish itself as a static distinct grouping as in the TeamRoom (e.g., "the Italians" – "the English") but was subtly moving among the various people at any moment of the group's evolution. It seems that in the chat group participants gave themselves fuller permission to engage in the unfolding life of the group, a process which might be more difficult to let happen in a pre-designed group such as the TeamRoom.

15.4 Networking Technologies and the System as a Whole: The Paradox of the Primary Task

Some distinctions need to be made to address the notion of the primary task. First, the perceived primary task, that which involves control and clear goals, stems from the legitimate system and is rooted in linear rational thinking. The use of networking technologies is introduced to the members of the organisation from the legitimate system. On this level, the role of using networking technologies is to increase the communication exchange, keep up with, and be part of, the technological developments in the world. Organisational email assists the work of the formal system, enables cross-cultural work and, in addition, carries an ecological awareness function.

But an informal shadow system is emerging as well and the technological system is developing a dynamic life of its own which is nested within the larger system of the organisation or society and is independent of it at the same time. It is also possible that within the group/s that is/are using networking technologies, further groupings emerge, further conversations take place, smaller and smaller circles are created, to the level of pairs and intimate relationships. There was a level of intimacy created in the various groups by including people's personal reflections, an immediacy created when people respond quickly and by the subtlety of messages which highlighted the uniqueness and individual voices people do have even when writing anonymously.

The virtual primary task is to be able to take part in using networking technologies and to converse. Groups form and develop in a non-linear manner, emerging out of ongoing interactions which no one person or group has control of. They are confirmed and re-confirmed in a feedback process of continuing interactions whose goals are not pre-determined and whose route is not yet known. This process is enabled in the context of networking technologies and, thus, members can fully participate and truly network in the unfolding process of the virtual group's development.

The real primary task is non-linear in its nature and it can only be worked towards in a self-organising, emergent manner. By its nature it involves the emotional dynamics discussed in this paper. The real primary task requires holding together of both the perceived and the virtual primary tasks because the virtual networking system is dependent on conversing for its survival. For a group to be able to work towards the perceived primary task it has to be able to hold the paradox that the real primary task is both a perception and virtual but never tangible. This paradox is a potential source for the increased anxiety and intensity.

With this notion of a primary task in mind it becomes possible to understand how these groups behave. They fluctuate between dysfunctional, destructive dynamics of splitting and basic assumption behaviour, to having some good exchanges of relevant information, be it some free tickets to a concert, report on progress of work or world news and some good conversations about difference, values and others. Whereas the legitimate system tries to suppress the chatty nature of virtual groups, the shadow system undermines the suppression by creating and enabling more and more conversations, emergent of sub groups and pairs, and "hiding" some of the exchanges by sending "private" messages, for example.

Virtual interactions, thus, paradoxically hold very real, very rational as well as very fantastic and irrational dynamics. What emanates is the gap between our perceptions and fantasies regarding computers and what can really happen: we perceive computers as mechanical and logical developments, whereas, I believe, computers should be perceived as providing a vessel for emergent, imaginative and chaotic dynamics, and in that sense a participating agent in a self-organising conversational process. In addition, because of the computer's storage capacity we attribute to it the ability to hold a collective memory for the group and to capture the meaning and knowledge we co-create. We think it can objectively hold knowledge and meaning for us in a safe mechanical brain that we can always look into. We expect computers to help us reduce and manage complexity. Again, we are proved false; we find that computers actually participate in increasing it.

Finally, it is interesting to see how the sense of self and of group identity is maintained when held paradoxically; in the chat group losing the sense of self, who-is-who and how-many-are-one is part of the culture and of the identity of this group. It is a clear example of an identity as an emergent property out of the tension between the shadow and the legitimate; in creating multiple personalities, in acting out different roles and in providing the space for imagination and fantasy to be as wild as they may be, the group has been constantly grappling with issues of identity and task. In the TeamRoom, however, since the group's identity as well as primary task were postulated by the legitimate system and did not emerge out of the conversational life of the group, maintaining and adhering to them have been more of a struggle.

15.5 Conclusion

This chapter has demonstrated the potential impact of networking technologies on the individual sense of self and has addressed the constant demand to re-construct oneself with the ongoing developments of information technologies. I have shown how electronic communication has become an even more intense vehicle for group dynamics than face-to-face groups, albeit similar, including those of large group dynamics, and the tension between maintaining individual identity while being part of a group, or losing one's sense of identity. I have explored the generation of fantasies around computers and have brought forward the paradox of the primary task, including the struggle in maintaining a sense of purpose when the task becomes so multi-layered.

Thus, when participating in and/or facilitating virtual teams one thing that becomes important to remember is that real life interpersonal dynamics emerge virtually as well. In addition, virtual groups are potentially more fragile than real life groups in that they are limited in their dimensions of communication, they are fast and less boundaried and dynamics are thus highly amplified. And, finally, because networking systems are self-organising, participating in them is highly important if one is to make any sense of what is going on.

Chapter **16**

Knowledge Sharing in Virtual Organisations: The Effects of Task, Role, Status and Network Structure

Manju K. Ahuja

16.1 Introduction

Virtual organisations that use email to communicate and co-ordinate their work toward a common goal are becoming pervasive. However, little is known about how these organisations work. For example, in many virtual organisations, much of the knowledge sharing takes place through informal communication (Ahuja and Carley, 1998).

"how does information exchange take place in response to specific knowledge sharing needs in virtual organisations"?

This chapter examines the behaviour of one virtual organisation. The analysis is based on a case study of the communication structure and content of email communication among members of a virtual organisation during a two-month period.

Drucker (1988) has suggested that the new forms of organisation enabled by information technology are most evident in the area of research and development. Therefore, it is appropriate to study in depth one such existing organisation in order to begin to develop an understanding of this new form of organisation (Eisenhardt, 1989), the virtual organisation. This chapter examines data from a field study of a virtual group engaged in research and design of a general-purpose artificial intelligence system – Soar (Ahuja and Carley, 1998).

The Soar group is engaged in the use and development of the Soar architecture. Like many virtual organisations, the Soar group is geographically dispersed and its members share information and co-ordinate tasks by email. Despite being dispersed, the Soar group acts as a cohesive and co-ordinated research group as if all its members were at one location. In addition, distinct roles of student and mentor are played by members thus allowing an examination of information exchange patterns of these roles. Also, distinct occupational roles of user and developer exist. The three main tasks of the Soar group are research and design, group maintenance and resource management, with the group meeting twice a year for workshops where members present their work.

Information exchange through email can take various forms in the Soar group. For example, a member can inform the group through email when he or she finds a bug or discovers new requirements, or members can post a problem on a bulletin board with the expectation of receiving feedback from other members. Someone else who may have encountered this bug or problem may respond with a solution. Practices of making announcements, asking questions and responding to inquiries through which co-ordination takes place are examined. Individuals making announcements can be thought of as sharing knowledge with other group members. Those asking question are clearly seeking knowledge. Members giving responses can be perceived as knowledge providers who are facilitating learning of other members.

The primary goal of this research is to understand the co-ordination processes occurring through information exchange in a virtual organisation. The effects of task, role, status and structure on interaction patterns (who talks to whom) and information exchange (what types of messages, i.e. announcements, questions and responses, are exchanged) are of particular interest.

16.2 Knowledge Sharing in Virtual Groups

A virtual organisation can be defined as a geographically distributed organisation whose members are bound by a long-term common interest or goal, and who communicate and co-ordinate their work through information technology. My focus is on a particular type of virtual organisation, the virtual research organisation, in which members of various corporate and academic research units voluntarily come together to advance a technology on an ongoing basis. These members assume well-defined roles and status relationships within the context of the virtual group that may be independent of their role and status in the organisation employing them (Ahuja and Carley, 1998).

Research on computer-mediated communication suggests that individual characteristics such as role and status are less influential in email communication than in face-to-face communications (Sproull and Kiesler, 1986). However, the information processing needs of individuals varies, based on their role and status in the virtual organisation, resulting in different email communication patterns (networks formed by graphing who talks to whom). Indeed, more recent research has found that these individual characteristics can influence communication patterns (Saunders, Robey and Vaverek, 1994; Cohen and Zhou, 1991; Zack and McKinney, 1995), and therefore may affect communication structure. Task also influences information processing needs and therefore, information exchange. The effects of task, role, status co-ordination needs and structure are considered below.

16.2.1 Task

Studies have shown that task is often a major determinant of organisational performance, indeed, the most effective organisational network by which information is exchanged varies with task (Ahuja and Carley, 1998).

Three types of tasks – group maintenance, resource management and design – represent the central activities of the Soar group. Group maintenance (GM) tasks involve creating and maintaining distribution lists and archives, organising meetings, etc. including personal and social messages,as they are an integral part of group maintenance.

I will be away,

note my new address,

I need a ride to the meeting site,

Included in the resource management (RM) category are allocation and maintenance of hardware, disk space, security, etc.

please clean your disk space

my machine is having a problem

Design tasks involve planning, software features, implementation, debugging, patches, etc.

Within the Soar community, it would be likely that sub-communities emerge based the task being performed. Co-ordination on actions (announcements, requests or questions and responses to questions, requests and ideas) are thus expected to

I need a site licence

there is a bug in the chunker

do you have a patch for this

version 4 is ready

vary by task. For example, individuals involved in GM should interact with each other regarding that aspect of their work and form a "group maintenance information exchange network". Announcements may be a more frequent mode of information exchange than questions and responses in the GM and RM networks because they provide a quick way of relaying the same information to a large number of people. The design group may show frequent usage of questions and answers indicating a greater use of dialogue and discussions, as one would expect in a research activity.

16.2.2 Role

In Soar, individuals sometimes play both the roles of users and developers. It is to be expected that the co-ordination and thus communication needs of users will be different from those of developers. For instance, users are expected to receive information about new versions of the software, and instructions relating to hardware maintenance. They will send in bug reports and inquiries when they run into difficulty using the system. Individuals acting as developers can be expected to play the role of "teachers" and therefore to send to the group information on problems they are working on, code they write, and fixes in response to bug reports. Developers, like users, will receive operating instructions from hardware and group co-ordinators. Developers, in their didactic mode, are also expected to be more involved in workshops where work-in-progress is discussed (GM). Developers may make frequent announcements of new or changed design features as they progress in their work and are thus likely to send more messages than users, exhibiting a higher number of responses than questions with users exhibiting an opposite pattern by asking more questions than answering them.

16.2.3 Status

In Soar, members can have the status of senior researchers and students. The senior research staff within the Soar group include faculty members and full time research staff. As with role, individuals that vary in status should have different co-ordination needs, which in turn should lead to different interaction behaviours. In particular, senior researchers are expected to act as mentors whereas students are expected to be in the mode of acquiring information and performing tasks assigned to them. It is therefore conceivable that senior researchers will make more announcements than students. If, as expected, the flow of knowledge is from senior researchers to students, then students should ask more questions than staff and other faculty. Similarly, senior researchers will respond to more inquiries than students.

16.2.4 Structure

One way of studying information exchange among individuals is by using a social network view of structure (Tichy and Fombrun, 1978; Tushman, 1977; Brass, 1985; Burkhardt and Brass, 1990). This view defines structure "as the enduring characteristics of an organisation reflected by the distribution of units and positions within an organisation and their systematic relationships to each other" (James and Jones, 1976, p. 76).

A variety of measures of group performance based on the distribution of units and positions have been proposed (Ahuja and Carley, 1998). Two measures, which are expected to be important in terms of learning and information exchange, are the degree of centralisation and the degree of hierarchy. The centralisation measure "is an expression of how tightly a graph is organised around its most central point" (Scott, 1991, p. 92) with the degree of hierarchy being based on the prevalence of one-way communication chains (Krackhardt, 1994). These network conceptions of structure are particularly important to examine as informal organisations and , unlike more traditional formal structures, do not conflate status with structure.

It is likely that different task groups in Soar will exhibit different levels of centralisation and different degrees of hierarchy. Group management and RM tasks require someone to be in charge of a task at any given time, which may lead to higher centrality. A design group, on the other hand, will need to engage in discussions and dialogue over design issues, and may be less hierarchical than the other two groups. The members can be expected to discuss abstract issues through questions and answers.

16.3 Data and Method

Data on status and role were collected through interviews and workshop archives. Status was recorded as faculty, paid research staff, or graduate student. For this analysis faculty, paid research staff and corporate researchers are combined into a single status, senior researcher, as they are all typically in an information providing position. Role was recorded as user or developer. Individuals were classified into the roles of users and developers by three core individuals in the Soar group. A secondary measure of topics of workshop presentations was also used. Individuals whose presentations relate to development of the Soar architecture were classified as developers. Those using Soar for different artificial intelligence applications were classified as users. Users are the individuals engaged in research and applications using Soar. Developers are individuals who actually develop and maintain the basic Soar code. There are 41 users and 11 developers.

Data were collected by archiving all email messages sent or received over a two-month period through available distribution lists and archives and pertinent messages among individuals were forwarded to a specified directory. A total of 820 messages were collected during this period. Soar members were notified of the procedure to save messages. Through analysis of these messages, task and interaction pattern data was coded.

16.4 Results

The distribution of members participating in various tasks is shown in Figure 16.1. Fewer individuals participated in the GM and RM activity than in the design activity. Most notably, all developers participated in the design task.

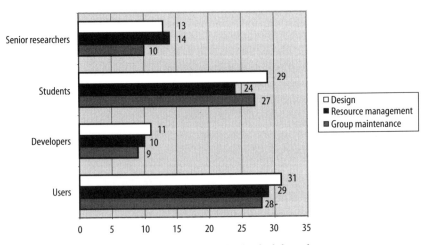

Figure 16.1 Distribution of individuals by task.

Despite the fact that only a few people are the locus for much activity, particularly in the RM and design groups, participation is widespread, with 82%, 84% and 93% of the individuals in the GM, RM and design groups respectively, making announcements, asking questions, and generating responses.

In the virtual group studied, most of the information was exchanged in the form of questions (Figs. 16.2–16.4). This suggests that, in this group, co-ordination is often directed by the individual on an as needed basis. The second most frequent type of message, however, is announcements. This suggests that a great deal of co-ordination is also occurring not just by being told, but by the group being told. This suggests that there should be some uniformity to the knowledge within the group and that the level of socially shared cognitions should be quite high.

Evidence of shared cognition is seen in the frequent use of group-specific slang in these messages.

Further, over half of all information exchanged was associated with the design task (Fig. 16.4), suggesting that most of the knowledge sharing in the Soar group takes place in the area of design. Recognising that the primary reason for the Soar group is research, all related information comes under the design category. That the majority of information exchange is associated with this task suggests that the group is quite actively engaged in research and that the other information exchange and co-ordination is in support of this activity.

In the following section, the effects of task, role, status and structure are discussed.

16.4.1 Task

Out of 820 total messages, the majority (697) had a design content (Fig. 16.4).

GM: As shown in Figure 16.2, 31% of all messages referred to GM activities such as meetings, workshops, publication library, etc. Most of the GM messages were exchanged in the form of questions (35%) and announcements (43%). A relatively small number of responses (22%) were sent to the inquiries made. This may be because the individuals co-ordinating the group activity can answer questions posed by several people through a group announcement. Thus co-ordination occurs both in a bi-directional (through questions and answers) and a unidirectional (through announcements) fashion. This is corroborated by the fact that fewer individuals send responses than send announcements.

RM: Compared to the GM task, many more messages (52%) had RM content (Fig. 16.3). Unlike GM, more questions (157) were asked than announcements (127) made. This may be a result of the academic and research orientation of this group. In this group research involves extensive computational resources and so members tend to be concerned about the resources they need to get their work done (e.g. hardware, disk space, funding etc.). Consequently, members tend to make periodic inquiries about them. Information exchange and hence co-ordination appears to occur in a somewhat more bi-directional

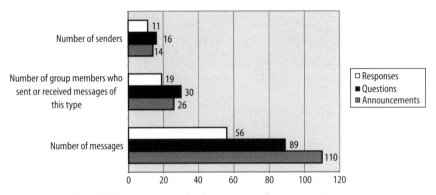

Figure 16.2 A comparison of tasks – messages for group maintenance.

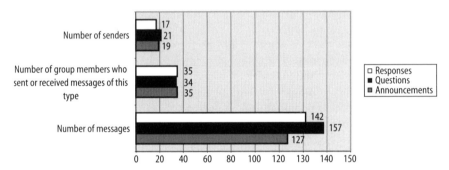

Figure 16.3 A comparison of tasks for resource management.

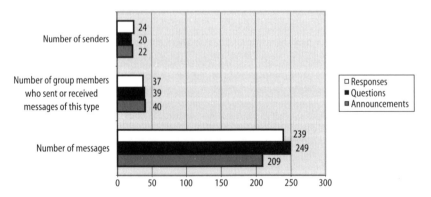

Figure 16.4 A comparison of tasks for design management.

than unidirectional fashion for this task. About half the individuals in the group (45–55%) were involved in the sending of messages regardless of type, with more individuals (both totally and proportionally) sending resource message information than group maintenance information.

Design: Most messages (85%) exchanged by the members of the Soar group during the period examined discussed design issues (Fig. 16.4). This observation also suggests that most co-ordination is focused in the research rather than management area. However, more of this research co-ordination is bi-directional (questions = 249 and responses = 239) rather than unidirectional (announcements = 209). This suggests that there exists an on-going dialogue over design issues as they pertain to the group members' research and also suggests that co-ordination for this task occurs in a bi-directional fashion; that is, they are engaged in "on demand" co-ordination rather than through lectures and other unidirectional modes.

16.4.2 Role

A much larger percentage of the developers (44–90%) than users (12–37%) were involved regardless of task (see Figs. 16.5 and 16.6).

GM: In total the number of developers in this group sending messages was markedly higher (63% on average) than the number of users in this group sending messages (28%) and a higher percentage of the developers, than users, send out announcements. A higher percentage of developers send questions and respond to questions. This was unexpected.

I expected developers to generate more responses (see Figs. 16.5 and 16.6). Users, as expected, asked more questions than they answered. The flow of knowledge was from developers to users, although not by a large margin.

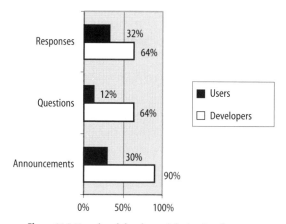

Figure 16.5 Users' and developers' design involvement.

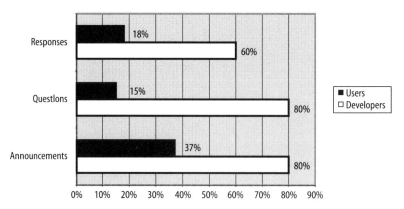

Figure 16.6 Users' and developers' resource management involvement.

RM: As in other task groups, a higher percentage of the developers than users were active in this task group. On average, 73% of the developers in this group sent messages as opposed to 23% of the users in this group. As expected, most developers (8 out of 11) sent out announcements regarding RM (Fig. 16.6). As expected, the flow of knowledge is from developers to users. Developers and users tend to educate others more through announcements than responses. Surprisingly few users ask questions in RM. Interestingly developers ask more questions than they answer. These observations are contrary to the expectations that users will ask questions of developers. As in GM, this may be due to the fact that most of the information exchange needs are being adequately satisfied by announcements making co-ordination unidirectional.

Design: Overall, compared to developers, much fewer users were involved in any information exchange activity in this category. Of those involved, very few users in this group (12%) asked questions (Fig. 16.5). Like other task categories, a high proportion of developers are very actively exchanging information. A high percentage of all developers are engaged in asking and responding to questions. Most developers sent design announcements at one point or another during this period, thus sharing their knowledge with the group.

16.4.3 Status

Figures 16.7–16.9 show information exchange by status. Note that a higher percentage of students than researchers engage in sending messages.

GM: Very few students are involved in the GM activity. However, those involved are very active in co-ordinating group activities through announcements (Fig. 16.7). Interestingly, these active students are more involved in co-ordinating day-to-day activities than researchers. Of all the students, 36% sent GM announcements; whereas 24% of all researchers did the same. Researchers principally asked questions. It is plausible that the researchers have reached a conscious or unconscious decision to let some students perform these GM

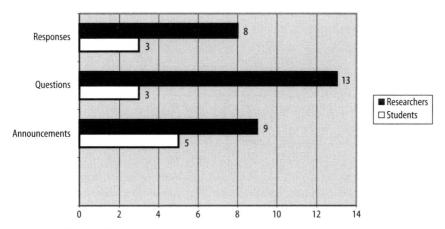

Figure 16.7 Students' and researchers' involvement in group maintenance.

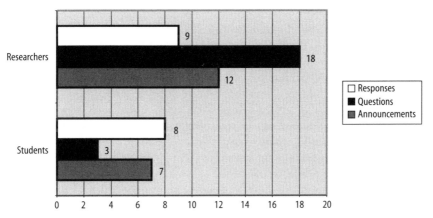

Figure 16.8 Types of messages sent by students and researchers in resource management.

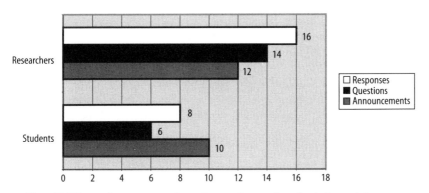

Figure 16.9 Types of messages sent by students and researchers for design maintenance.

activities as a part of their co-ordination process. Co-ordination on the whole takes place in a bi-directional manner.

RM: As shown in Figure 16.8, researchers and students are equally likely to send announcements. However, researchers are much more likely to ask questions (75%) than are students (21%). This suggests that the researchers are controlling the flow and distribution of resources and that there is no co-ordination, except indirectly, by students on how this is done.

Design: Students were very active in information exchange regarding design (Fig. 16.9). A higher percentage of students (77%) than researchers (41%) send announcements. Researchers are more likely to respond in a bi-directional fashion, using responses rather than announcements to transfer knowledge. Both students and researchers are equally likely to ask questions. Co-ordination among researchers and students is largely bi-directional indicating a process of dialogue rather than lecturing.

16.4.4 Structure

In this section, the role of centrality and hierarchy is considered (Figs. 16.10–16.12).

GM: Overall, this task group exhibited a higher degree of hierarchy (on average) than both RM and design. Contrary to the predictions, this group was not as centralised as the design group. One explanation for this may be that the individuals in-charge of group management tasks assigns sub-tasks to other members. For example, the person organising rides to the workshop site may assign various drivers to co-ordinate activities of those who live in their neighbourhood. Centrality scores for questions were particularly high (80%) which may represent such delegation of tasks.

RM: This task group is moderately centralised in general, and highly centralised in terms of questions. One individual is extremely central and appears to single-handedly co-ordinate a great deal of the RM activities. This central individual also asks members to comply with certain procedures (e.g. asking members to clean up their disk space). This may explain the extremely high centrality level in questions (93%).

Design: Contrary to the expectations, this category was highly centralised. This is especially so for announcements. Even though the design group is not very hierarchical, a few individuals make most announcements (89% centrality) and respond to most questions (84% centrality). The data show that while senior researchers have delegated group and RM to students, the major decisions are still made among a few key members and then announced to the group. It also suggests that in this group, social learning and the development of socially shared cognitions should be quite high (everybody is reading the same announcements). This group is also fairly hierarchical in terms of questions. This, coupled with the high centrality in announcements and responses, suggests that while individuals are directed in what they want to learn and only ask "up the hierarchy," answers are given in a socially shared fashion.

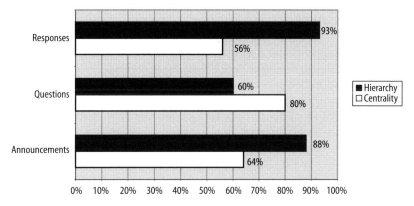

Figure 16.10 Centrality and hierarchy in group maintenance.

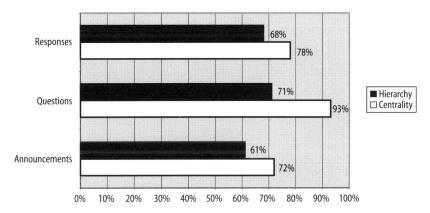

Figure 16.11 Centrality and hierarchy in resource management.

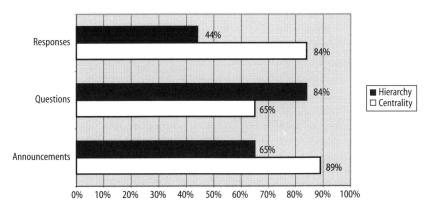

Figure 16.12 Centrality and hierarchy in design.

16.5 Conclusions

This study suggests that task, role, status and structure determine interaction patterns and information exchange activities of an organisation. Table 16.1 summarises the detailed expectations and findings of the study.

It is clear that type of task being performed affects information exchange activities. Tasks like design, which require creativity, tend to be performed through dialogue, and may have a less hierarchical organisation. Surprisingly, in spite of being less hierarchical, these groups exhibited a tendency to be led

Table 16.1. Summary of findings

Expectation	Support	Comments and interpretations
Task : Co-ordination needs will vary by task.		
1. GM will exhibit frequent use of announcements.	Yes	Also exhibits frequent use of questions thus indicating both uni- and bi-directional co-ordination.
2. RM will exhibit frequent use of announcements.	No	RM takes place through inquiries rather than announcements.
3. Design will exhibit frequent use of questions and responses. co-ordination.	Yes	Design is co-ordinated through dialogue indicating bi-directional
Role: Users and developers will exhibit different co-ordination needs.		
1. Developers will send more messages than users.	Yes	Knowledge flows from developers to users.
2. Developers will send more responses than questions.	Mixed	Depending on task, co-ordination needs may be adequately satisfied by announcements (e.g. in RM)
3. Developers will send fewer responses than questions.	Yes	Knowledge flows from developers to users.
Role: Senior researchers and students will exhibit different co-ordination needs.		
1. Senior researchers will send more responses than questions.	No	An opposite pattern was found. See next comment.
2. Students send fewer responses than questions.	No	Senior researchers delegate the co-ordination tasks to students whenever possible through routines.
Structure: The communication structure will vary by task.		
1. GM and RM networks will exhibit higher centralisation levels than Design networks.	No	Design network was highly centralised, indicating a few knowledge centres.
2. GM and RM networks will exhibit higher hierarchy than Design networks.	Yes	GM and RM are co-ordinated through announcements. In Design networks, only a few people make announcements and respond to questions.

by a few key individuals. This may be because a more centralised co-ordination structure is efficient and that over time, groups evolve in such a manner as to take advantage of this efficiency. The GM and RM of tasks seem to warrant more one-sided information exchange indicated by frequent announcements.

Similarly, the roles played by individual members appears to influence their learning (and teaching) activities. Role influences the information requirements which in turn affects how the information is acquired and from whom. Status, too, played a part in determining information exchange patterns. Individuals of higher status tended to delegate routine announcements to others and provide guidance only when asked.

Further, there was an interaction between role, task and status in affecting information exchange patterns of groups. Members in a certain role can behave a certain way in one task group but act differently in another task group. Their information exchange seemed to vary further depending on their status. Interaction and information exchange varied with task and structure.

This study explored the process of co-ordination by examining the information exchange among individuals as it takes place as an integral part of their day-to-day work. The framework for studying information exchange presented here may be valuable in any learning organisation or group. This kind of in-depth analysis in different contexts may reveal effective (and ineffective) co-ordination patterns in virtual organisations. Further, these patterns may be instructive in designing organisational and technological support for virtual organisations.

Chapter **17**

Adaptive Processes for Achieving Socio-Technical Fit in Computer Supported Co-operative Work Groups

Sajda Qureshi and Doug Vogel

17.1 Introduction

This chapter considers some of the social and technical forces affecting computer supported co-operative work groups and suggests how these may be supported in order to achieve the best possible *fit* for the organisation (Trist, Higgin, Murray and Pollock, 1963).

Socio-technical approaches such as Multiview (Avison and Wood-Harper, 1990) among others, described by Avison and Fitzgerald (1988), are seen to be some of the ways in which organisations may adapt their own processes while customising new technologies to their own needs. However, there is a growing recognition that modern organisations need to support formal and informal groups in order to maximise the potential of their information resource. Together, teams and new information technology have the potential to catalyse dramatic improvements in organisations but only when understood and applied consistently with organisational objectives.

> It follows the socio-technical view, that for a system to be effective the technology must fit closely with social and organisational factors.

Communication through the computer network can provide a powerful means of linking a group of widely separated people. In this, the support of remote work can be provided within *virtual structures* through Computer Mediated Communications Systems (CMCS). As defined by Hiltz and Turoff (1992), "these systems use computers and telecommunications networks to store, deliver, regulate and process communication among the group members and between the computer and the group".

Although the most common form of CMCS is electronic mail, other computerised conferencing, bulletin board and shared work software is classified under this heading. A popular term which encompasses both distributed communication systems and face-to-face group support is Computer Supported Co-operative Work (CSCW). Wilson (1991) defines CSCW products as including message systems, computer conferencing systems, procedure processing systems, calendar systems, shared filing systems, co-authoring systems, screen sharing systems, Group Decision Support Systems (GDSS), advanced meeting rooms and finally team development and management tools. The use of computer networks in general, and distributed group support in particular, has opened up a myriad of possibilities to enhance interpersonal communication and co-operation and made possible new forms of work processes and radically transformed organisations. This suggests that when considering the socio-technical alternatives for work groups it is necessary to consider the dynamic nature of the groups and the choice of technologies available and the possibilities offered.

An example of a popular use of CSCW for supporting groups is GDSS used in an advanced meeting room environment for its ability to enhance the meeting environment. Much of the research in GDSS, however, is laboratory based and is largely concerned with the usability of group support and thus pays little attention to the social and inherently political process of influence (McCarthy, 1994). Efforts often concentrate more upon individual differences rather than with understanding how groups and organisations function and evolve (Clegg, Waterson and Carey, 1994). When considering the social and technical considerations relating to computer supported co-operative work support for groups, it is important to note that the implications of face-to-face group support may not be generalisable to distributed group support where there are fewer visual and verbal cues.

The social and organisational context play a major role in the way in which groups use CSCW technologies, but it is difficult to ascertain. The work of Sproull and Keisler (1991) which explores the context of electronic mail, draws attention to context, suggesting that groups learn to adapt to the technology. Studies reported by McCarthy (1994) on real time multimedia conferencing suggest that the technology introduces asymmetries into the interaction between people by affecting social processes. In cases where the technology attempts to replicate the social environment, video images were treated as mere representations of reality making the groups less sensitive to subtle movements. The research evidence suggests that there are a number of organisational factors at work at different points in time, meaning that socio-technical fit at one instance may become a socio-technical *mis-match* at another.

This chapter explores the social and technical considerations that affect the use of computer supported co-operative work groups in context. The following sections explore the implications in the light of three cases and present approaches to enable organisations to manage social and technological considerations when supporting co-operative work groups.

17.2 Organisational Challenges

In their review of electronic communication and changing organisational forms, Fulk and DeSanctis (1995) suggest that new technology brings about changes in relations between organisations and in the organisational form itself. Within the organisational form itself, they describe the formation of leaner forms of organisations associated with the flattening of hierarchies, greater horizontal co-ordination related to electronic workflow, and the rise of virtual organisations. In addition, distributed technologies such as email have been active in facilitating the informal diffusion and dissemination of information throughout organisations which may bring about more egalitarian beliefs and aspirations (Clement, 1994; Schuler, 1994).

In view of these developments, Fulk and DeSanctis (1995) outline four major areas in which the application of new electronic communication technologies in organisations need to be investigated:

1. the study of how organisations emerge, evolve and dissolve over time as being central to organisational form development;
2. situated studies which address the varying organisational arrangements in which electronic communication systems are used;
3. alternative design approaches for new communication technologies; and
4. work life in the new organisational form.

In building upon this classification, we describe factors relating to the organisation and suggest that some of the key challenges facing modern organisations are:

- the organisational structure within which CSCW may be used;
- specialisation of parts which are seen to require integrating mechanisms;
- co-ordination between the different parts and of content;
- work processes carried out through the use of specific knowledge and expertise; and
- learning seen as an adaptability to change and an ability to build up a collective reservoir of knowledge and skill.

For each of the challenges potential constraints and opportunities are summarised in Table 17.1, and illustrated using three cases.

In order to illustrate these challenges, three cases in which CSCW technologies are used are explored in the following sections and adaptive approaches for supporting groups are suggested.

17.3 A Large Multi-National Company

In a longitudinal study in a large multi-national company, a face-to-face GDSS (also known as a Group Support System, GSS) was used to address a number of problem solving situations often involving aspects of planning and total quality improvement. The use of the technology was initially assuring in that it was

Table 17.1. Social aspects of CSCW in organisations

Organisational challenges	Potential CSCW Constraints	Opportunities
Structure	The use of CSCW may bring additional complexity into the work environment.	Support teams with varying degrees of permanence facilitating teambuilding and networking processes.
Specialisation	Different communication protocols and "languages" of communication.	Integration of parts of the organisation.
Co-ordination	Heavy content structuring required in distributed different time sessions may be incompatible with organisational co-ordination strategy.	More information may be made available for co-ordinating parts but use should be complemented with conventions for interpersonal communication.
Work	Information accessibility varied. Ability to use the technology and adapt to it may be difficult.	Support distribution of work over space and time and facilitate sharing of skill and expertise
Learning	Organisational climate may stifle emergent ideas and prevent adaptability to changing circumstances and competitive position.	Support organisational learning through technological, work and social adaptation.

applied and extended to other parts of the organisation. Over the course of four years, the number of sites using the technology went from one to 6 to 26 and ultimately to in excess of 100. After that time, however, a steady decline in the number of active sites began and the technology did not reach the level of diffusion in the organisation of other technologies such as email.

A key challenge facing this organisation related to its structure. This structure was in the process of moving towards smaller autonomous working units. While the CSCW enabled a certain degree of co-ordination among teams with varying degrees of permanence, the very nature of movement towards smaller autonomous working units fragmented the diffusion process as initiated by the early adopter sites as other more pressing matters arose. The CSCW was not seen as a critical element of support. Efforts were made to regionalise operations such that co-ordination pressures were minimised, which ultimately reduced the importance of the CSCW. There was a particularly strong local culture and the CSCW did not enable integration among the specialised parts as this role was not perceived necessary.

Although there were work efficiencies demonstrated in the use of CSCW within the particular organisational units, there was little learning as the organisational climate tended to stifle emergent ideas and prevent adaptability to change; the application of CSCW reinforced these characteristics. Management put in place a protocol for CSCW use and rules of behaviour that resulted in freezing use of the technology. Freezing procedures and ways of doing things without encouraging organisational innovation led to a loss of champions and pockets of success. This and several sequential re-organisations across the

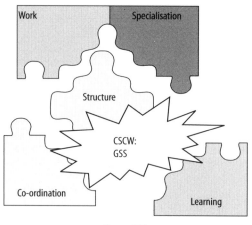

Figure 17.1

board led to a loss of key players, and their knowledge, to other companies. As little occurred in terms of learning either for the organisation as a whole or use of CSCW in particular, new application opportunities were not systematically investigated nor did they emerge.

17.4 An International Network of Organisations

This network of organisations consisted of people representing a set of international agencies who wanted to be able to exchange ideas and experiences on information technology projects in developing countries. The purpose of this network was to "allow informal dialogue to be extended in order to facilitate collaboration". It was agreed that "identified officials" from a diverse range of agencies, could share concerns, opportunities, and outline project proposals "off-the-record". Project information, ideas and experiences, joint funding initiatives, and publications were the main areas requiring consultation. The intention was to encourage brainstorming and an active exchange of ideas to ensure informed and effective collaboration in projects.

As the exchanged information was seen to be highly confidential, only selected individuals from member organisations were allowed to use the CSCW. Security was a prime consideration and was ensured through strict access privileges, encryption and log reports.

As the structure of this network relied on interaction among the members, co-ordination was the main challenge. The co-ordination effort was carried out by carefully structuring the content of meetings and discussions. This ensured that the meetings were productive; a participant noted as follows:

"Our experience with computer conferencing is that the more clearly defined the objectives of the exercise and the topic of the problem being discussed, the more likely something concrete can come out of it."

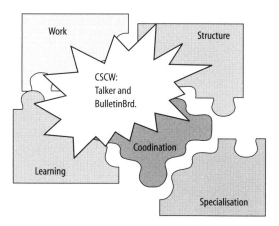

Figure 17.2

The synchronous meetings that took place were structured through an agenda decided in advance of the meetings by the participants themselves via email, phone and/or face to face contact. The asynchronous discussions were structured by topics which could be entered by the participants in their own time. The participants brought to the electronic space specialised roles and cultural sensitivities relating to their organisations and countries. These surfaced most during the synchronous meetings and integrating these specialisations involved a great deal of personal communication before, during, and after the meetings. Specific co-ordination roles also emerged within the meetings. These were those of: *chairperson* who was an authoritative senior member of staff who ensured that agenda items were discussed in sufficient detail, *facilitator* who assisted members in following the discussion, organising and voting on items, and *moderator* who provided participants with on-line assistance on how to use the technology and access the available tools.

The use of CSCW technology enabled a traditionally relaxed informal process to become more focused and task oriented. Within this work process no decisions were taken electronically or collaboration agreed upon in the synchronous meetings. This was mainly due to the fact that such decisions were traditionally taken informally, that the participants were still learning how to use the technology and that they were not altogether comfortable with using it. The CSCW was transforming a traditional informal process into an emerging formal inter-organisational setting but the technology itself was not flexible enough to support this change in work practices. The CSCW was used a few times and decommissioned after three years.

17.5 Linked Educational Teams

Professors at two universities brought together ten teams in a conscious effort to evaluate the impact of CSCW technology on global team interaction. Each of the ten teams comprised a total of six to eight participants. Half of the participants in each team was located in Hong Kong and the other half was located in the Netherlands. The Hong Kong participants were part-time graduate accounting students while the participants from the Netherlands were full-time senior undergraduate software engineering students. Both were working in a second language (English) and used a great deal of discipline specific terminology and were generally unfamiliar with each other's specialisation. The members at each location had not worked together before and had no prior experience in working in globally distributed contexts. The ten teams each had a unique topic to address but were given a common agenda and set of deadlines. The project began with a videoconference that explained the nature of the exercise and introduced team members to each other. The CSCW used comprised a set of different technologies, primarily a GSS complemented by NetMeeting videoconferencing used between the groups. Email was used within each group, and between the Hong Kong and Dutch members of the groups in an effort to sustain communication and co-ordination. No phone or face-to-face interaction was available and the GSS became a repository of the results of the interaction between teams. The teams interacted over a period of six weeks during which they gathered shared information, generated and selected research questions, and each team created a final joint report including analysis of issues from a global perspective. A number of insights emerged relative to organisational challenges.

The main organisational challenge in this case was that there was a great deal of specialisation within the teams. The CSCW enabled a forum through which the "language" of each sub-group was recorded. This meant that communication was interpreted as necessary to enable effective and efficient communication to be sustained. Through this process the teams learned how to apply the CSCW effectively to meet their needs. A considerable amount of cultural learning took place as team members brought their own disciplinary bias, working habits, and national culture into action with other team members.

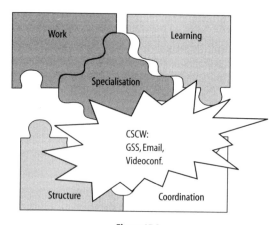

Figure 17.3

Structure was enabled through CSCW use that would otherwise have been extremely difficult to achieve. It enabled team members to focus their work as they were not familiar with the technology and group processes necessary to complete the task. There was little in the nature of emergent leadership among group members but the CSCW was central to supporting the teams over the course of the project. It facilitated team building.

Co-ordination was a constant challenge within the team projects. The participants agreed on the direction and division of labour within each of the phases of the project and periodically re-grouped in an effort to remove ambiguities and adjust their direction. The CSCW was especially effective in supporting distribution of work over space and time and facilitating sharing of skill and expertise.

17.6 Achieving Socio-Technical Fit in CSCW Groups

The above cases point to a number of social and technical issues relating to the need for better fit in the use of CSCW technologies to support groups. A particular application of structuration theory (Giddens, 1984) to computer mediated communication is offered by DeSanctis and Poole (1994). They propose a "Theory of Adaptive Structuration" which states that as group members use CSCW to complete a task, they are developing and applying rules and resources for the conduct of behaviour. The rules and resources of the group direct members as to which features of the technology they should appropriate and found that when individuals in a group interact using CSCW, each group produces and reproduces its own *structures-in-use*. This process, they claim, accounts for the continual changing nature of social structures involved in the use of systems to support groups.

If we apply this theory to the above cases we can identify the *mis-matches* between the social and technical forces. It appears that the groups at the multinational company did not appropriate the technology to suit their own ways of working. This may be due to (1) a lack of understanding of processes related to using the technology and/or the ways in which it could enhance their own working practices; and (2) the technology lacked the flexibility necessary for the groups to use it within their own work environments. CSCW was appropriated to a limited extent mainly because the technology represented an alien environment within which discussions that were normally informal, were formalised. On the other hand, CSCW was the only way in which the linked educational teams could communicate, meet and work together. The system enabled social processes between group participants to emerge and in turn enforced further appropriation of the CSCW technologies. As a mix of technologies were available to the participants of the linked educational teams, the group members had greater flexibility to use systems to support their work process.

These insights suggest that achieving fit between social and technical forces requires that groups appropriate CSCW technologies; they go through learning processes. This type of learning is technological, work and social adaptation when groups use these technologies.

17.6.1 Technological Adaptation

In the first stages of CSCW use, the groups described above were directed at learning how to use the technology and more importantly how to get around the numerous difficulties that it presented. Argyris (1980) suggests that experience with information technology leads to greater organisational learning through adjustment. Using his terminology this is single-loop learning: group members adjust their procedures according to changes in the environment bringing about a modification in their collective knowledge but not in their norms and values. In the groups using CSCW described, the technology became a means of attaining a joint objective and of carrying out an activity. The whole group had to be able to use the technology appropriately for the collaborative work to be worthwhile. If more flexible tools for problem solving and decision making had been available, the CSCW could have been adapted to a greater extent.

Therefore, technological adaptation should be supported through training and learning aids which allow group members to appropriate the technology to their own ways of communicating, interacting and working. With the increased involvement of end users in the feasibility and development stages, the popularity of prototyping methods has made it easier for rough and ready CSCW systems to be built and refined to suit the needs specialised user groups.

17.6.2 Work Adaptation

The use of CSCW brings about new ways of working and accomplishing tasks. This process of work adaptation comes into play when groups and individuals are involved in changing organisational patterns, including norms and values. This also involves a reassessment of how the groups see themselves and their role in the organisation or a set of organisations. In Argyris's (1980) terms this is double-loop learning. In addition, the way groups adapt to a work environment supported by CSCW enables certain types of behaviour. In this, learning modifies the way of working and the norms underlying the work practices.

In view of this dual effect, work adaptation requires two types of support. Supporting the work process itself requires a combination of information exchange mechanisms and a means of storing information for access at a later stage. Supporting the ways of working requires facilitation in order to enable more focused outcomes to be achieved. A recent trend in operational research has been a move away from mathematical techniques for improving the efficiency of operations to soft methods, focusing on problem solving and consensus building for policy making, e.g. Strategic Options Development and

Analysis (SODA), which is designed to help bring about consensus and commitment within a team (Eden, 1989).

Combined with other techniques and tools involving participation and collective decision making, the use of new technologies such as CSCW can bring about considerable improvements to the work process (Gibson, 1991; Wanniger and Dickson, 1992; Vreede, 1998)

> A common characteristic of a methodology that supports work adaptation is that it emphasises the development of decision making processes and is often instrumental in the reorganisation of work processes as a result of group work.

17.6.3 Social Adaptation

Electronic media enable a social system to evolve. The identity of the group takes shape according to the social norms that emerge on the electronic space giving rise to particular sets of rules and knowledge that the group members bring with them. These electronic social encounters with less frequent personal encounters, can be seen to result in what Giddens (1984) terms as, *combined human action*. This brings about patterns of interaction that then become established as standard practices. In the international network of organisations and linked educational teams, the CSCW served as a forum for the learning mechanisms that enabled collaboration, the exchange of information and access to resources. Argyris (1980) calls this duetro-learning, which is a continuous process of learning in which groups apply single-loop and double-loop learning interchangeably. This process gives rise to a new social environment. Within this emerging environment, social adaptation affects the way in which groups learn to use the technology, adapt it to their way of working and then adapt to an evolving and sometimes challenging environment of which the CSCW is a component.

Soft Systems Methodology (SSM) as developed by Checkland (1981a) may effectively support social adaptation as it enables group members to negotiate possible accommodation between the various, often complimentary but sometimes contradictory, world views. It invokes participation, information sharing and ultimately combined human action and may enhance social adaptation among groups using CSCW technologies. Lundquist and Huston (1990) have developed a methodology called Continuous Organic Development (CODE), which they anticipate will increase information literacy, enhance knowledge of organisational problems and the ability to manipulate information. CODE begins by applying SSM to build rich pictures describing real world action; it employs conceptual models of human activity systems relevant to the problem situation. The intention is to build on each individual's *weltanschauung* (world view) in order to orient group members to their organisation's knowledge base and will in the process learn about stores of information (social and designed), and how to access and utilise these. Members of organisations participate through CODE to build up their problem solving skills.

17.7 Summary, Lessons Learnt and Conclusion

This chapter has argued that in order to achieve socio-technical fit for computer supported co-operative work groups, certain organisational challenges need to be addressed and appropriately handled in the light of three processes of adaptation. Various approaches for supporting groups using CSCW technologies have been suggested within technological, work and social adaptation. However, experience suggests that in order to exploit the opportunities for supporting groups through CSCW to maximum advantage, it is necessary to be aware of the constraints. To conclude, the following table summarises lessons learnt from using CSCW technologies to support groups, and offers tips:

CSCW technology is still immature	Expectations introduced by unbridled technologist enthusiasm or vendor encouragement tend not to be met in the cold harsh light of reality. Truly integrated audio, video and data have yet to be achieved. CSCW tools require enhancement and, indeed, this is occurring, but the rate of change in CSCW technology is also very unsettling as organisations struggle to identify and implement applications.
Technology infrastructure is critical	CSCW technology is by definition collaborative and requires extended connectivity and telecommunications infrastructure to succeed. Unfortunately, remote connectivity is still primitive in many organisations and such technologies tend not to be easily integrated with other technologies and require technical as well as personnel support in order to be used effectively.
CSCW technology, by nature, requires change and champions are necessary	Although groups often rise to the occasion in spite of technological shortcomings, projects tend to be time intensive with elusive benefits, especially in early phases. Leadership makes a big difference. The technology also tends to extend out quickly beyond traditional organisational unit boundaries. Distributed parts of an organisation that may be trying CSCW need a champion that is high enough in the organisation and/or generally respected without being identified specifically with a particular organisational unit. Thus, champions need to have high visibility or authority in the organisation to effectively enable organisational fit to be achieved.

Old habits die hard	People accustomed to working with pencil and paper and attending meetings may resist the use of CSCW even though there are demonstrated benefits. Fledgling efforts at CSCW use may simply die away, especially in the absence of sustained encouragement for use. As such, efforts and effects may take a long time to bear fruit and be generally recognised. It is sometimes advisable to sit back and wait instead of pushing too quickly for acceptance and adoption. Adaptation works best if people have sufficient time to gradually integrate the technology into their own ways of working.
Old habits aren't necessarily bad habits.	Not all group dynamics and collaborative work may be supported by CSCW. It is particularly important that CSCW technology is not imposed on processes and ways of working that have no clear demonstrable benefit. To do so only heightens resistance and can lead to innovation diffusion failure. Respecting traditional habits and carefully choosing targets for application are paramount to success. Actively involving organisational members in selection activities helps to identify appropriate application opportunities.
Need attention to business process improvement.	Participation by a broad base of affected stakeholders is crucial to not only identify redundant ways of working but also to assure buy-in and assistance in creating new ways of working that bring together people and technology to improved effect. It is important to identify outdated assumptions and "think outside the box" when envisioning opportunities for application. Failure to do so can result in "paving the cowpath" in that CSCW technology is applied to processes and ways of work that are no longer functional.
Organisational change may stifle technological diffusion.	An assumption underlying the progression towards distributed teams and more decentralised decision making is that CSCW technology can help. But the opposite may be just as likely especially if organisational change, such as the move towards autonomous teams, is being made to relieve demands on co-ordination and integration of specialised parts.

The realisation that organisations are dynamic and people within them have to be trained, developed and made to share their experience, knowledge and skill has brought about a range of approaches that encourage group work within organisations and between organisations, increasingly in the form of collaborative projects. The range and choice of CSCW technologies that can be used effectively in bringing together the multiple contributions of a hetero-geneous group of individuals makes achieving organisational fit a continuing challenge. In addressing the organisational challenges and managing these according to approaches for adaptation described above, an organisation can provide reliable and flexible technological support that supplies the appropri-ate structure for the group to succeed. This can be quite a dynamic situation as groups proceed through phases of adaptation. CSCW technology must con-tinually evolve to meet these needs.

Acknowledgement

The authors would like to acknowledge Dr Gert-Jan de Vreede for his valuable critique and suggestions on this chapter.

Chapter **18**

CoLeARN: Collaborative Learning and Action Research Networkommunications

Annette Karseras

18.1 Introduction

My main intention in this chapter is to offer fresh insights into the way we understand "the socio-technical" by articulating some of the thinking and practice that went on around the initiation, implementation and development of CoLeARN.[1] My purpose is to relate episodes from the CoLeARN story in a grounded, context-centred way. This distinguishes it from many publications in this area, described by Rudy (1996, p. 198) as "unsatisfactory in being based upon unrealistic, laboratory-like simulations, and a positivist epistemology". CoLeARN was developed at SOLAR,[2] University College Northampton (UCN), UK.

As well as being based on actual events and processes, the emergence of CoLeARN is greatly influenced by the participative inquiry approaches and new methods of collaborative research being undertaken and developed as part of the broad agenda of SOLAR. Particular influences include the writing and work of Susan Weil[3] (1998; 1999), which is informed by literature and activities at the Centre for Systems Studies at Hull, the Centre for Action Research and Professional Practice at Bath, the Centre for Complexity and Management at Hertfordshire, and by the work of Donald Schön (1983), who had encouraged her decision to establish this centre.

Certainly during the initiation of CoLeARN, the approach used was a loosely formulated "meld" of influences that drew on ideas with a certain *déjà vu* quality; themes and issues that at the time of action I felt held a great deal of relevance for the type of work being undertaken at SOLAR, but which I have rarely

---

[1] CoLeARN stands for Collaborative Learning and Action Research Networkommunications and can be described as both a project and an approach to the integration of information and communications technology into social and organisational processes.

[2] SOLAR stands for Social and Organisational Learning and Re-animation. It is a postgraduate and post-experience centre concerned with social and organisational learning using participative research and collaborative inquiry approaches.

[3] Susan Weil is Professor of Social and Organisational Learning and Founder Director of SOLAR.

seen surfaced in literature related to others' approaches to socio-technical agendas. During the second and third years, many of these themes came to be explored in dialogue with centre associates such as Gareth Morgan,[4] Fritjof Capra,[5] Patricia Shaw and Ralph Stacey.[6] I was very conscious of the post-positivist paradigm which sought to account for subjective dynamics as well as objective phenomena occurring within spheres of action. I was also attentive to insights from the new sciences of complexity and chaos theory.

Writing this chapter has provided me with an opportunity to reflect and begin to post-rationalize the development of CoLeARN in ways that relate to information and communication technologies (ICT) and knowledge management agendas in ways that I hope will suggest new paths of possibility for future socio-technical endeavours. I should also like to encourage you to actively engage with this text in a way that has potential to stimulate an ongoing dialogue.[7]

> How do these experiences resonate or jar with your own working practices and informing discourses?

18.2 The Seedbed for CoLeARN

The seeds for CoLeARN were sown during SOLAR's establishment in 1996, and the development of a database to enable "off-site" communications amongst the people networks that were brought to the centre. From the start of this development, I was concerned that working relations between SOLAR and the management information systems (MIS) department at UCN should model the research methods and new approaches that were such distinctive features of the work that this centre had been set up to pursue.[8]

With the aim of "walking the talk" I set out to ensure that the congruence between espoused and actual practices of the centre could also be reflected in the functionality offered by the database *in use*. This entailed departing from the more traditional MIS approaches. For example, there were no initial meetings to formalise requirements, and no structured client specification for a technician to take away and work on.

---

[4] G. Morgan, SOLAR international open forum, Capital Conference Centre, London, 21–22 March 1997.

[5] F. Capra, SOLAR collaborative learning forum: Self-organising systems, University College Northampton, 29 May 1998.

[6] R. Stacey and P. Shaw, SOLAR international open forum, Capital Conference Centre, London, 10–11 September, 1997.

[7] annette.karseras@northampton.ac.uk

[8] Early aims of SOLAR included: Evolving new forms of thinking and practice about learning and change processes in complex social and organisational systems intended to generate social value. Contributing to the development of a research paradigm that stresses research with, not on people and research as, not about social change. Challenging individualistic, mechanistic, rationalistic/ instrumental and "quick fix" understandings of cultural change. Ensuring that the work of the centre remains connected to the actual dilemmas faced by people who are involved in stimulating and supporting social and organisational learning and change.

Instead, a significant proportion of the initial set up and design work was achieved through "live" dialogue at the SOLAR offices. The analyst programmer involved began to develop an understanding of the participative ventures and action research projects we were undertaking, as well as the quality and nature of the actual exchanges that were taking place. He became able to draw on, and feed, this qualitative understanding during our considerations about the specification and form of the database. Equally, working alongside him, I became more sensitive to the choices we had in modelling the data, about functions that we could automate, and to the "art" of queries. Increasingly, I became able to frame suggestions in ways that accounted for possibilities at a technical level.

Another significant factor influencing our approach during these early stages of developing a systems infrastructure for SOLAR was the very rapid growth and diversification of activities that were to be supported. It was critical, therefore, to remain responsive to changing priorities and activities whilst we were designing and implementing systems to support them. Often we encountered new problems that required us to adapt solutions as we were designing and implementing them in realtime, in response to context-centred (not postulated) needs. The approach that was emerging through our joint efforts not only permitted us to exchange explicit knowledge, but also allowed the seep of tacit knowledge. This kept us both attuned to each other's needs and ways of working, and attuned to the emerging requirements of this newly established research and development centre.

Our collaborative ways of working ensured the flexibility to adapt to, and interact with, the constantly changing and evolving sets of relationships and needs that underpinned the early activities of the centre. They were not predicated on the accuracy of a finite technical specification relating to a context identified as closed. Static.

> We were simultaneously learning from each other, learning our way around the database and learning about the environment in which we were working. Our work evolved as an adaptive, "sense and react" activity; not wholly pre-determined and never entirely predictable. Rather its evolution was charaterised by *co*-determining processes.

18.3 Electronic Communications and Participation

I hope this introduction to the CoLeARN story illustrates the effectiveness of participatory and collaborative approaches to systems design. Clearly the operational environment for CoLeARN is qualitatively different from settings in which socio-technical approaches have traditionally been used to encourage participation in the design, or re-design, of organisational structures and sub-systems, and their associated technical infrastructures (Mumford, 1997; Mirl, 1998). But my experiences of CoLeARN suggest that the "new socio-tech" must be more responsive to the challenges entailed by communication technologies. We are currently caught up in the transition from an electronic environment characterised by information processing, to one which increasingly features communication networks. Ample evidence of this shift is provided by the rapidly increasing numbers of organisations implementing intranets and groupware applications (Brinck, 1998; Grundin, 1998; Whitaker, 1997), and the growing amount of interest in the area of computer supported co-operative work (CSCW).

> In such a climate, I suggest that the socio-technical agenda must develop deeper understandings, not just of the way people can be included in choices about systems they use, and of which they are a part, but also about the way people engage with each other, the way they collaborate and work together, and how the new emphasis on electronic communication networks can both enhance and hinder their efforts in different ways, and at different stages.

18.4 Co-determination and Intentionality

As John Seely-Brown (1996–97) has noted, successful technologies should resonate with human agency instead of working against it, and in this way extend choices for future action. CoLeARN actively sets out to work with positive (rather than negative) agendas, to enhance opportunities to communicate, inquire, and collaborate (not to squeeze efficiency out of limited resources). My experiences of the new electronic climate suggest another subtle but powerful revision of our sense of participation, an accent which shifts us even further away from the mechanistic, staged, rigidity of excessive planning. This entails the socio-technical agenda developing a greater sensitivity to, and engagement with, the many self-organising processes at play in real world environments. It means working with these processes as they are evolving in ways that embrace the emerging dynamics entailed in co-determination (Varela et al, 1991). My CoLeARN experiences also indicate that socio-technical approaches might proceed with what Griffin, Shaw and Stacey (1997) describe as "intentionality" rather than "intention". Intentionality is a course of action precipitated by participation in networks of social relationships in such a way that action genuinely "attends from" a given historical and ethical context (in contrast to "intention" which perhaps implies the imposition of a pre-determined plan of action). This way of proceeding with people has relevance not just for systems design but also for the choices made about how and when we use technologies, and how they complement, support and extend from core communicative and collaborative work activities.

18.5 CoLeARN and SOLAR1

The socio-technical situation introduced earlier was a response to the need to enable "off-site" communications between SOLAR staff and the networks of people that shared our concerns. Twelve months on (in 1997), the acronym CoLeARN emerged as the title for an initiative aimed at enabling communications between members of "SOLAR1", the centre's first postgraduate cohort.[9] Near the end of its second year (in 1999) the SOLAR1 group comprised of nine senior professionals who combined part-time research towards a PhD with full-time professional practice. Participative and context-centred activity are critical themes for each of these individuals.

The idea of using network communications to support the SOLAR1 programme, and to enable collaboration between meetings, was introduced to the group early on. A series of one-to-one conversations included discussion on the use of email and the internet, online conferences and listserve discussion groups, internet relay chat (IRC), use of CD-ROMs and online databases, software for qualitative data analysis, bibliographic referencing systems, virtual reality, and video conferencing. As a result of these conversations a summary document was circulated outlining the group's facilities and expertise.[10] Further informal discussion of CoLeARN ensued as useful resources began to be swapped and know-how shared.

Towards the end of the first autumn term in 1997, presentations were scheduled on the area of each person's PhD proposal. Each presentation was followed by an opportunity for members of the group to feedback and engage with what had been said, drawing on points of convergence and divergence between proposals and opening questions to explore further. This early experience of "sharing" the focus of each other's research was important for developing the sense of collaboration that was key to the operation of the group as a learning cohort. The final presentation was the first opportunity to begin to draw together emerging but loosely formulated ideas about CoLeARN. The timing of this was intended to offer SOLAR1 members an opportunity to draw on the focus of their own and others' presentations, in order to provide a basis for collaboration enabled by network communications.

Conversations about CoLeARN continued informally during "on-site" sessions and, increasingly, email communications between sessions served to keep individuals in touch. However, the overriding priority for SOLAR1 members during the next few months was preparation of their research proposals for registration.[11] Effort and energies during the subsequent on-site sessions were focused around writing workshops and issues of quality and rigour in post-positivist action research. As a result, there was an overt lull in activities and dialogue related to CoLeARN. Feedback on this issue at a later date was to indicate that even though it was difficult to see what could have been

---

[9] The SOLAR PhD programme, validated by Leicester University, comprises monthly, two-day facilitated meetings and access to the centre's collaborative learning forums for the first two years and termly meetings with forum access for the remaining years.

[10] Transcripts of phone conversations, face-to-face meetings and email exchanges provided the basis for this summary document.

[11] At this time I was preparing a final submission for an online course in online education and training, Institute of Education.

omitted during this proposal writing period, benefit could have been derived from infusing CoLeARN more at this time. Working with multiple demands on session time is an ongoing tension for the group and will inevitably be something which is taken forward in the next cohort. At another level though, this lull provided an important opportunity for us to become more sensitive to individuals' concerns and to the dynamics between group members.

Once the majority of SOLAR1 members had their proposals underway, an opportunity arose for the first "round table" discussion about CoLeARN. There was no formalised agenda for this meeting. Rather the onus was on group members to surface ideas that they wanted to pursue. Amidst a flurry of Post-it notes and engaged chatter, we produced a pool of many innovative suggestions about how we might begin to explore an electronic "shared space" (Schrage, 1995) as an extension of our on-site collaborative arena.[12] The group also surfaced a range of reactions from enthusiasm to anxiety at the prospect of entering this electronic space; reactions that were to play themselves out in a variety of ways over the coming months.

It was not possible to pursue all of the suggestions immediately, and so the group elected to focus on current priorities. The development of a specialist resource base of references to relevant literature seemed to be by far the largest shared concern for SOLAR1 at this time. This was undoubtedly influenced by a conversation, immediately prior to the discussion, about the need to generate purchase recommendations for the library. This precursor perhaps elicited a more task orientated suggestion from the "round table" discussion than might otherwise have occurred. However, it provided a tangible purpose, one which was not imposed or pre-formulated, but which surfaced out of the group's own needs at that time in the context of their research. This purpose also provided an opportunity to "test the water".

> The group decided that the "Nursery Slopes" would be an appropriate title for this space, reflecting concerns for a gentle and easy introduction to this new electronic environment, and also reflecting the provisionality of the first excursion into a shared electronic space.

18.6 Knowledge in Post-positivist Research

I want to break from the CoLeARN story for a moment to offer an understanding of "knowledge" in post-positivist research, as this has a bearing on the way the next part of the story is interpreted. "Migratory", "codified" or "explicit" knowledge are all terms used to roughly describe knowledge that can be packaged and transmitted, dependent only upon the receiver's capability to extract it (von Krogh and Roos, 1996; Gibbons *et al.*, 1994). This "uncomplicated" knowledge transfer is well understood in the information processing literature. However, as von Krogh and Roos (1996) point out, the underlying assumptions

---

[12] Use of WebBoard (the conferencing system available to us through University College Northampton) was explored in conjunction with open access sites and passworded web pages.

propelling this kind of argument are relatively unsophisticated in terms of their understanding of "knowledge", which is rarely defined and often used inter-changeably with other concepts such as "information" and "data". Nonaka and Takeuchi (1995) take us further with their challenge to the Western emphasis on the "absolute, static and nonhuman nature of knowledge" (p. 58). They prefer to consider knowledge as a "dynamic human process" (p. 58), talking about the need to "turn our attention to dialogue as a means of social interaction, thus helping us to create new concepts" (p. 79).

> Knowlege is less about information (processing) and more about communication (networks); partly reflected perhaps by the shift in climate from IT to ICT.

But do Nonaka and Takeuchi go too far? The following comments suggest not. Gibbons *et al.* (1994) state that "Knowledge production is increasingly a socially distributed process" (p. 156) and that "its movement is constrained in a given network or set of social relations" (p. 24). Von Krogh and Roos (1996) also suggest that "knowledge comes into being when individuals share their experiences verbally" (p. 41), and Savage emphasises the need for dialogue amongst peers, workers and clients (1996, pp. 199, 205). All these descriptions reflect the post-positivist paradigm of knowledge generation within which SOLAR1 and CoLeARN are also operating.

As a participant at SOLAR1 meetings, I was becoming increasingly aware of the potency and generative nature of dialogue for developing new understand-ings and approaches to participative research, collaborative inquiry and critical reflection. We were all reading extensively but the way the members of the group were collectively making sense of this literature, interpreting it in dia-logue with each other, sharing and re-evaluating their own experiences, was the source of real value which was beginning to generate a very distinctive approach to research and knowledge generation.

18.7 The Collaborative Arena Extended: "On-site" and "Off-site" Dialogue

We rejoin the CoLeARN story at the point at which the group agreed to use a "shared electronic space" to pool suggestions for a specialist resource base. This initial task was broadly about *information sharing*, which seemed to be at odds with the take up of CoLeARN as an initiative to develop opportunities for *collaboration*. However, in hindsight we are able to identify a marked transitionary phase over the next couple of months of the group's work (Summer/Autumn 1998). Following a hands-on session introducing them to the software, a few SOLAR1 members did indeed begin to pool some references. But very swiftly, following the "Nursery Slopes" introduction, the shared space was used in a qualitatively different way; one that began to mirror the emphasis on dialogue that had been such a critical aspect of on-site meetings and which Gibbons *et al.* (1994), Nonaka and Takeuchi (1995), Savage (1996), von Krogh and Roos (1996), all figure as endemic to knowledge generation.

CoLeARN increasingly became infused into the working practices of the SOLAR1 group where a pattern of discussion prior to meeting on-site and subsequent reflection on sessions was becoming a regular feature. Guest contributors to on-site sessions were also invited to join in off-site conversations using CoLeARN. The ways in which the electronic space became inhabited extended from, and fed back into, the very particular ways of working and the social relationships that had developed, and were continuing to develop, during on-site collaboration. However, tensions began to surface, perhaps partly as a result of unequal off-site contributions by various members of the group. Was it perhaps the ability to "see" exchanges taking place through this text-based medium that heightened an awareness of who was (and was not) contributing, and of the quality and substance of those contributions? Was the use of WebBoard a reflection of a particular stage of interaction within the group or did it serve to promote and influence the group's interaction? To what extent were these codetermining processes?

18.8 Group Purpose: The "Abbey Agreement"

Process issues had always been a strong theme in SOLAR1's work. However around this time SOLAR1 began to focus in a very directed way on their own group working. What were the pushes and pulls within the group? Where were the dins and silences? How could the group challenge itself about where dialogue didn't lead? These kinds of questions resulted in the "Abbey Agreement",[13] which contained suggestions about the ways group members wanted to see their collaborative potential taken forward during the second year of the SOLAR PhD programme. The Abbey Agreement was framed as a live "inquiry", as a source of reflection and discussion, and for indicating direction as the year proceeded. In other words, and as one person put it on the day, the hope was to keep the Abbey Agreement, "fluid but firm enough to bump into"! The Abbey Agreement was written up and posted to the shared space. The following excerpt from one communication refers to it, and suggests the real importance of this inquiry for SOLAR1:

> "I think we could spend more time on the Abbey Agreement as a way of exploring collaboration, data mapping etc. We generated this at the last session but haven't really taken it any further – I think we could lose some learning here if we just skip over it – Would support the comments made in TD's email and feel there are a number of unresolved agenda's/tensions at play about our collaboration – Think we need to surface and work with these live before we engage with one another's research."

---

[13] The Abbey Agreement was inspired by the then recent Good Friday Agreement and named after The Abbey – the location at which the meeting was held.

Discussion of the Abbey Agreement was taken forward not just into the following session but also through the next few months and into the new year (1999). SOLAR1 members continued to revisit and revise the document. They used it to explore and inquire into the issues it raised, not just for their own group purpose but also to discuss the processes entailed in formulating it. Some used the learning derived from these processes to inform the social relationships and interactions they were building with co-inquirers in their individual research projects.

18.9 Facilitating Network Communications

Initial use of the WebBoard had assumed, to an extent, a consensus view underwritten by a mandate of inclusiveness in which there was an expectation that everyone's opinions would be pooled, that everyone would just "pitch in" as they did, during on-site sessions. We can only guess what effect making this assumption explicit would have had at the time it was framing perceptions. Following the initial work on the Abbey Agreement, there was evidence of a further transitionary phase in the way the group was relating through network communications. During one on-site discussion, it became increasingly clear that several people had begun to identify with a facilitation role as a positive shift away from the consensus approach. Rather than all members of the group overseeing and "hearing" all discussions in a shared space (WebBoard), one or two people became assigned to channel individual email and phone communications with the purpose of checking which of the items agreed out of previous on-site meetings were still "up front" and relevant for everyone who would be attending the subsequent on-site session. The broad purpose of communications was similar to previous "between session" communications – if more clearly articulated. However, the process by which this was achieved shifted from collaborative to more one-to-one and co-operative communications.

There was broad agreement on the appropriateness of this model, qualified by the observation that the nature of facilitation would not entail exactly the same process each time, as each person had their own style of exploring, setting up and communicating with other people. There did remain some ambivalence over whether it was desirable to "overhear" responses others were making about session planning and reflection. What effect had this had on the group? How much did this actually contribute (perhaps even subliminally) to a shared sense of identity? To development as a learning cohort? To knowledge generation and exchange?

Certain pragmatic considerations also surrounded suggestions for this model of facilitation. One person indicated how everyone was very much "on the edge" in terms of managing work and PhD commitments, and that it was not always possible to become embroiled in "between session" discussions or, realistically, to make them a priority.

How much did the Abbey Agreement also have to do with this shift? Did working through some of the unresolved agendas and tensions mentioned above contribute to the adoption of this facilitator model? How much was this a matter of familiarity – inevitable with the passage of time? How much of trust? How much was it the result of critical reflection and refinement of existing strategies? Did the remit of CoLeARN – a collaborative inquiry in itself – influence or permit the possibility of enacting this shift?

Discussion about these and other questions go on. The transitions and changes in SOLAR1 members' use of network communications, and the ways in which CoLeARN is infused in the PhD programme are likely to go through several more phases as scheduled on-site meetings become less frequent over the next couple of years.

18.10 Points for Ongoing Learning

The chance to initiate and implement CoLeARN has been a challenging and rewarding experience, not least because we have been able to work with positive agendas that seek to incorporate and enhance human agency rather than to remove it. I hope that the grounded account I have given of the early development of CoLeARN demonstrates congruence between espoused and actual practice, and that it adequately relays some of the qualities that I consider to be so important in a socio-technical approach. I have endeavoured to include the ebbs and flows, the "ups and downs" of this process, as part and parcel of an emergent journey. It is from these contrasting experiences that perhaps the most significant points of learning can be taken forward.

> In particular I hope that our work over the last couple of years offers insights into:
> - the value of developing an awareness of self-organising processes in collaborative activities by working with and out of a group's experience;
> - ways of remaining responsive to these processes as they are evolving, moving with unanticipated needs and situations as well as those that can be planned for;
> - the kinds of choices we make about how and when we use technologies, and how they best complement, support and extend from core communicative, cooperative and collaborative work activities;
> - the importance of generative dialogue, and related to this, post-positivist understandings of knowledge generation.

As I have indicated in this chapter, I firmly believe that the "new socio-tech" will benefit from extending its reach in ways that account for the shift from an information centred (IT) climate to one increasingly characterised by communication networks (ICT). This is important at local spheres of action, and also at organisational levels. It is by understanding the different ways individuals and groups engage with each other – directly and through the use of technology – that the systemic implications of these local spheres of action for organisational considerations can be better understood.

Chapter **19**

Stop Information Technology from Undermining Group Autonomy!

Markku I. Nurminen and Antti K. Tuomisto

19.1 Introduction

Socio-technical approaches search for optimal solutions for social and technical systems with the help of an organisational autonomous group. The attraction of such groups is not based on higher job satisfaction alone. Autonomous groups also encapsulate the control of disturbances to be treated locally. It is important to realise that responsibility and autonomy are two sides of the same coin. However, the bridge between the group autonomy and the information system (IS) to be designed does not exist in current Information System Design (ISD) methodologies. Therefore ISs often weaken or even violate this autonomy. The system may unnecessarily prescribe a certain way of performing tasks in terms of the sequence of the tasks or division of labour. It may allow detailed surveillance even when its object belongs to the area of group privacy as part of the autonomy. The deficiencies confronted in the group's autonomy reflect problems in the group's responsibility.

In this chapter we demonstrate that the unintended violations against group autonomy can be overcome by applying the social interpretation of information technology (IT). In order to do this, we proceed by formulating the constituent characteristics of the autonomous group and by giving corresponding characteristics for the application of IT. In our contribution we define the concept Autonomous Group's Information System (AGIS) in the spirit of socio-technical tradition. The definition is illustrated with one case study, and the application potential of the novel concept is discussed.

19.2 Socio-Technical Approaches

When the socio-technical approaches were introduced in the 1940s by the Tavistock Institute in London, they were a manifestation of two missions of great importance. First, the significance of the social system, that is, people in work organisations, was recognised and acknowledged. Secondly, the dissimilarity between the social

> Open systems are self-regulating, flexible and adaptable (Buchanan and Huczynski, 1985).

system and the technical system was emphasised. These two principles led to the conclusion that the two systems had to be designed separately, because they follow different types of rules. Such design should take place in parallel because the two systems are mutually dependent, and this leads to the concept of "open sociotechnical system" (Trist and Bamworth, 1951).

The success of these two principles has been demonstrated in various ways. For example, a manager with leadership type management approach has a competitive advantage over a colleague without it (Navarro, 1994). Multi-professional teams are established to take responsibility over complicated business processes (Lipnack and Stamps, 1997). In knowledge management it is realised that knowledge resides within people (Sanchez and Heene, 1997).

Practically all socio-technical projects have included autonomous groups as a part of the social system in the joint design (Hackman, 1981; Mumford, 1983a; Trist, 1981). This means, in fact, the construction of a collective subject, that is, an organisational work group as defined by Hackman (1990). Autonomy, on the other hand, expands the unit of analysis towards job enrichment techniques described by Buchanan (1979).

The autonomy of the group is always relative (Gulowsen, 1972; Susman, 1976). While some of the recent approaches to groupware and computer-supported co-operative work (CSCW) emphasise the group's internal affairs to the extent that the group's environment almost disappears from sight, the autonomous group of the socio-technical approach is always a part of a larger organisation with well-defined boundaries and deliverables.

The autonomous group typically has the right to decide, at least to some extent, about its working procedures and division of labour. Thus it reduces the need for hierarchical control by encapsulating the most exceptional situations, often called variances, to be treated within the group instead of sending the question to higher levels of organisation (Mumford, 1983a). Such an encapsulation has proved attractive for other approaches to organisation of work, and this property is seen as important particularly in turbulent environments (Galbraith, 1973). In addition to its flexibility and uncertainty management, an autonomous group can efficiently use the usual ways of end-users to cope with computerised ISs within their action domain (Gasser, 1986; Suchman 1987).

The socio-technical development of a work organisation also offers a platform for the participation of workers. If the members of the future group are also genuine actors in the design of the work of the group, the name autonomous group is not an exaggeration. For example, methodologies like ETHICS (Mumford, 1995a) and Multiview (Avison and Wood-Harper, 1990) emphasise the importance of user participation in the development process. The users are far better perceived, if they are conceived of as an autonomous group rather than related to as end users that participate. The participative approach will lead to the enforcement of accountability and responsibility, which require appropriate support from computer-based ISs (Kirveennummi and Tuomisto, 1997; 1998).

Finally, we present the nine socio-technical principles for good design that were developed by a group from the Tavistock Institute of Human Relations in

London (Mumford, 1987, pp. 69–70). These principles will be included in the framework of AGIS.

1. The principle of compatibility. The process of design must be compatible with its objectives. In order to create a participative social system it must be created participatively.

2. The principle of minimal critical specification. "No more shall be specified than is absolutely essential" and only what is essential needs to be identified. This leaves a considerable amount of discretion to a work group.

3. The sociotechnical criterion. Variances must be controlled as close to their point of origin as possible.

4. The multi-function principle. Individuals and groups should have a range of tasks.

5. The principle of boundary location. Boundaries must be chosen with care and they require management.

6. The principle of information flow. Information systems should be designed so that information goes directly to the place where the required action is taken. This will normally be the work group.

7. The principle of support congruence. Systems of social support should reinforce the required behaviour (e.g. group work should have group payment).

8. The principle of design and human values. Organisational design should provide a high quality of working life, such as a demanding and varying job, social support, learning area for decision making etc.

9. The principle of incompletion. Design is an interactive and continuous process.

19.3 IT in Socio-Technical Approaches

Information technology is probably the most influential technology of today. It is therefore natural that IT has been subject to many approaches, many of which can even be regarded as ISD methodologies. For example Structured Systems Analysis and Design (SSADM), Yourdon Systems Method (YSM), Merise and others (e.g. Avison and Fitzgerald, 1995) have made a strong contribution to the design of the complex work systems from an IT perspective. These methodologies include methods for the design and implementation of the computer-based ISs with an emphasis on information requirement analysis, yet they lack concepts to deal with the actual work and social systems. On the other hand, for example, ETHICS and Multiview (e.g. Avison and Fitzgerald, 1995) seem to be short on the physical design and implementation of the computer-based ISs. The strength of socio-technical methodologies is their emphasis on the social systems, particularly in the autonomous groups.

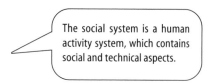

The social system is a human activity system, which contains social and technical aspects.

One cautious conclusion could be that these are not fully-fledged ISD methodologies, since they concentrate on either the technical or social system. An IS can be interpreted according to Checkland and Holwell (1998) as a system that serves the social system.

In order to create a computer-based IS that supports an organisational human activity system, we will regard the system to be served as an autonomous group, where both systems and their relationship are crucial. Thus, while most socio-technical methodologies are strong in the definition of information requirements derived from genuinely socio-technical factors such as variances and their control, they are practically empty when the design should proceed to system architecture and databases.

The rudimentary collection of technically-oriented development socio-technical methods may be seen as a symptom of the lack or at least insufficient articulation of, the relationship between the social and technical systems. When the information needs are specified, no further analysis or design is regarded as necessary. Now the relationship between the IS which serves and the human activity system to be served becomes essential. In our view, an IS comes extremely close to the work situation, and the joint design of the two systems should be integrated very tightly (Hellman, 1989; Nurminen, 1988; 1991). Otherwise there is the danger that those parts of the computer systems which have not been designed explicitly with the work situation in mind, bring forth unexpected effects which are not often positive. The following case study demonstrates the working of an organisational autonomous group, its IS requirements and the dangers included in current IS practices.

19.4 Case in Point

The example is the inventory of a food-processing industry. First, we describe the organisational context of the inventory and the work activity within the inventory. Then we outline how IT can be used to support that activity. The focus is on the autonomous group. However, the group does not work appropriately unless its individual members act in a co-ordinated way.

When the production department workers in the packing department had finished their work and were able to deliver the new products to the inventory, they performed a transaction on the integrated material control system. This transaction had three outcomes for each pallet of products:

- it was a report of finished work;

- it transferred the responsibility for the products to the inventory; and
- it recorded the pallet in stock at hand.

This inventory address was printed and attached to the pallet.

These three aspects were integrated to a single transaction because when this system was designed twenty years ago the number of terminals was restricted. This integration, however, undermined group autonomy. The bulk inventory was made responsible for goods which they had not yet received. Sometimes, indeed, it happened that a number of the pallets was shipped directly to a waiting truck, and those products never arrived at the bulk storage. Such exceptions caused much confusion. The cause for this undermining is that the locus of the transaction was wrong because the bulk-men, as a party to this transaction, were ignored.

In dozens of empirical studies (e.g. Heikkilä, Nurminen, Reijonen and Tuomisto, 1995; Kesti, Kirveennummi and Tuomisto, 1995; Nurminen, Kesti and Reijonen, 1994) we have met similar undermining of group autonomy. The system may unnecessarily prescribe a certain way of performing tasks in terms of the sequence of the tasks or the division of labour. It may allow detailed surveillance of action or situation even if these should belong to the area of group privacy as part of the autonomy. Another dilemma is found in the biased notion of responsibility, as was the case in the accountability for the products in the inventory.

How is such undermining possible? Obstacles must rather be examples of the frequently discussed "unintended consequences" of the introduction of IT. Rather, the whole autonomy issue probably simply never crossed their minds. In what follows, we introduce a theoretical framework which helps make sense of this kind of jeopardisation of group autonomy.

19.5 Autonomy of the Technical System

Computer-based ISs are generally understood as technical constructs (Checkland and Holwell, 1998). This implies that the users are unable to generate a social interpretation of the systems they use. For example, they think that they receive data from the system or record information on the system even in the case of systems with shared databases with multiple users. The social interpretation of this structure suggests a group's communication system. Messages are transmitted, often with a delay, and integrated with other messages from input users to output users. This communication network is typically imperceivable to the users, although for example some CSCW (e.g. Bannon and Schmidt, 1989) and groupware (e.g. Ellis, Gibbs and Rein, 1991) approaches intend to explicitly model the communication and co-ordination patterns.

The imperceptability among users is no surprise. This bias is strengthened by means of many ISD methodologies. For example, according to our observations the application

> Designers are likely to conceive ISs as technical, i.e. non-social artefacts.

of CASE-tools can lead to systems which give the impression that the work of the user is to update the databases. Yet we know that such a narrow definition is not the same as getting the work done properly.

In our opinion, use and also development of ISs should not be separated conceptually nor practically from the human activity that they are supposed to support. The social interpretation of IT is a means of avoiding such separation.

19.6 Boundary in Terms of Resources

The boundary may be defined as a contract between the group and the management and it consists of static and dynamic parts.

In the static part the group's actors and resources are defined. It is declared who belongs to the group. The work space, tools and instruments are listed. The contract also specifies the rules of "the work game". For example, how the group can get a new worker or get rid of one, what are the general principles of personnel policy to be followed, etc. The control of resources implies accountability which has to be agreed upon. For example cleaning, repairing and maintenance are not unambiguous duties without an agreement.

Any details of this contract may be recorded in the ISs. For example, salaries paid to the group's members are channelled to the organisation's payroll system. In the inventory the storing space and forklift trucks are the group's resources. Yet we must remember that the more detailed the contract is, the less space there is left to autonomy (Principle 2). Therefore, when the rules of the static part of the boundary are determined, the participative approach must be undertaken (Principle 1).

19.7 Boundary in Terms of Task Performance

The autonomous group can be seen as a single individual from the organisation's viewpoint. The group is represented as a unit and all contracts are entered into with this collective subject. The detailed division of work and working methods are typically left to be solved within the autonomy. The relative autonomy demands that the group also adequately informs its superiors of the internal issues such as the organisation of work. This might be justified, because the management must ascertain that the local working routines of the group do not undermine the company's quality certificate, for example.

In the dynamic view of the boundary we follow the group performing its tasks at an aggregate level as if it would be one individual. The group has a generic description of its tasks. This description is useful when the group evaluates an incoming task: does this belong to us or not? At the instance level, each task has a specification of the expected outcome such as a blueprint or a more standardised work description.

The outcome of the group may be regarded as a result of a process, which is often a part of a larger process, both the group and the management have to be aware which cases are started but not yet finished. It is also relevant to know how much is done and when the completion can be expected. This kind of follow-up cannot be very detailed without jeopardising the autonomy. Starting and terminating transactions have to be recorded as part of this track-keeping. Adequate controls as to the quality and quantity of work objects have to be performed in order to maintain the accountability of the group.

The management has to deal with the external parties and internal self-management (Principle 5). The static boundary sets up the procedures between the group and the rest of the organisation including the external management. The internal self-management is about daily work activities, issues of auto-nomy (e.g. long-term development) and management of the boundary transac-tions. The boundary issues are always related to relative autonomy and self-management. The dynamic view of boundary management reminds us of the shared concern for information and material flow over the border, and the management of integrated activities within the given autonomy. Autonomy relates to the activities in the IS that are accountable for:

- tasks and sub-tasks and their expected outcomes;
- management of the stages of the task chain;
- inspection of the status of the tasks, etc.

The aim is to give flexible computer-based IS support for performance tracking and evaluation to the group as well to the management. The related roles of responsibility and accountability are also presented in the AGIS. They ascer-tain the appropriate working practices to the management.

19.8 Inside the Boundary

Inside the boundary the group uses its discretion and autonomy to deal with everyday variances and challenging tasks. The internal activities of a group have gained much interest in IT studies which include support for communication, control, co-ordination and collaboration activities. These general groupware, CSCW and DSS-flavoured issues are now spiced up with the socio-technical principles of minimal criteria specification (Principle 2), local variance control (Principle 3), multi-function (Principle 4), information management (Principle 6) and support congruence (Principle 7). Now when the groups are conceived as autonomous, open and social systems, the needs for IS support are expanded. There are no longer merely data objects or data processing events, rather, all activities are linked to purposeful action performed by the group.

Internal behaviour describes the work objects and their manipulation, tools and objects of co-ordination, responsibility areas *per se*. In addi-tion, the relationships between these and the self-management activities including tracking and

> The group itself has to know what its members are doing, what the group is supposed to do and how the group manages the daily activities.

evaluation activities are described. Also some level of group identity support can be given, e.g. maintenance of group norms and metrics, social history, who talks to whom, social network, etc. In terms of Ellis and Wainer (1994) these are respectively the ontological model, the co-ordination model, and the user-interface model. The ontological model is a description of the objects and the operations on these objects that are available to users. The co-ordination model is a description of the dynamic aspects of the system, that is the control and data flows. Finally, the user-interface model is a description of the interface between the system and the users, and amongst the users.

Due to the self-management aspect, these activities require the tracking and evaluation functions required by the internal and external needs. Part of the self-regulation, self-governance and independence-related data are for group members only. Part of the self-management data relates to dynamic or static boundary contracts, and thus it is a concern of external management too.

The IS support of the group's internal activities is based on the previous groupware model. However, now the group is implicitly a work group with relative autonomy in an organisational setting. The responsibility part of autonomy requires appropriate care-taking of resources, equipment, inventory space, etc. These tasks are embedded into ISs to support the group's internal activities and to ensure through effective reporting facilities the management of high quality work procedures.

The autonomy perspective supports the flexible division of work inside the group and to grasp the IS requirements for this we need another example. The inventory actually has two autonomous groups: a large warehouse, called bulk, and a smaller area for delivery purposes, called buffer. The emphasis of the task structure in the buffer is in delivery in contrast to the bulk's storing function. Another difference is that the buffer men have more differentiated roles. When a buffer man in a chaser role has collected the entire order, a senior worker comes, checks and records the correctness of the delivery.

Another interesting feature is in the organisation of the chasing tasks where it had proved practical to allocate one order for one person. The allocation of another person to the same order had not given a double efficiency. Thus each chaser is performing his own project. Two co-ordination tasks emerge:

- the distribution of orders among the chasers and
- the planning of the collection of one order.

The collection of orders must be managed by the group and it is obvious that some kind of explicit co-ordination will improve both the efficiency of the group's work and the quality of customer service. Too much opportunism is not good for team spirit either. On the other hand, a dream (or a nightmare) would be a computerised control system, which in detail tells which and where is the next item to be chased, when the chaser has promptly reported the previous one. A sufficient degree of co-ordination could perhaps be achieved by means of a simple reservation system. Each chaser declares his plan and reserves certain identified pallets. For conflicting reservations there could be a CSCW application for negotiating (e.g. in a network of wirelessly-coupled work stations mounted in the forklift trucks.) A non-computerised alternative to this could be a voice-based co-ordination system, in which the chasers declare their territories reserved by shouting loudly.

There is another role in the buffer inventory. This role is supposed to maintain a reasonable inventory level by ordering and transferring goods from the bulk whenever the stock at hand in the buffer is too low. The inventory filling should be merged with other activities. This inventory-filling role could also anticipate the deliveries by having access to future orders for the next day. Of course these internal activities must satisfy the contracts made about transactions.

We observed above that the IS of an autonomous group can also include subsystems of individual scale for co-ordinating between the role instances. Typically there is also a collective system, which fits in with the boundary of group responsibility. The personal system units are its subsystems. The system boundaries may be dynamic: a certain subsystem may belong to a certain occupant of the appropriate role only temporarily. This was the case in chasing the goods of one order. This order and the goods reserved for it belong to the particular chaser's system as long as the chasing has been finished.

19.9 Lessons Learned

Next we summarise the observations made from the inventory case in Table 19.1. The aim is to demonstrate how autonomy and AGIS can help to ensure high quality of group work and computerised ISs. AGIS helps to prevail the key features of the group in an IS design and development and form an inseparable whole of the group's work.

Our understanding of the reason for this kind of undermining is that the IS needs of the autonomous group have never been collected together and regarded as an inherent part of the group autonomy. In order to give conceptual support to such a tight connection we introduce the concept of AGIS. It is a fully-fledged "local" IS with all the functions of storing and processing. These correspond to the internal activities of the group. Thus, AGIS has a clearly defined boundary, both static and dynamic. This suggestion extends the group's responsibility to cover also the data and processes of the AGIS.

The framework of the AGIS is built on inseparability, responsibility, accountability and sociotechnical principles. These help to present and correct the violations against the group's autonomy. The autonomy of the group is enhanced by the static and dynamic perspective on the border, and the internal activities of the group. Together with the role concept these three components are the key elements of the AGIS.

19.10 Conclusions

The aim of this study is to demonstrate how IT can be merged into an autonomous group's action as an inseparable part. In doing this we utilised the

Table 19.1. The cases of undermined autonomy in the inventory group

Undermined autonomy	Lesson
The bulk inventory was made responsible for goods which they had not yet received.	Unintended violation against the dynamic border.
The determination of the shelf position was done by the production workers, even if this self-evidently belongs to the domain of group autonomy.	Unintended violation against the static border.
The bulk-men did not have the opportunity to change the procedure of allocation towards more optimal allocation strategy with respect to their experience and knowledge.	Violation of the inside autonomy (for technical reasons).
The autonomy issue is not on the agenda during IS design and development.	The social interpretation of IT is not allowed to escape from this issue.
The follow-up of the group's activity cannot be very detailed without jeopardising the autonomy.	Make the group's autonomy and its IT-autonomy correspond to each other.
Before accepting the orders, the sales personnel must check whether the required amount of the product in question can be delivered on the day requested. Inventory provides that information.	Horizontal collaboration over the boundary.
The buffer men have more differentiated roles.	The group has a need to design its internal division of work in the long term and situationally. Its IS has to support this.

tension between group autonomy and integrated system architectures. These architectures often violate the group autonomy, according to our empirical findings. We took each obstacle identified and sought an alternative design in order to meet the requirements of the group better. This is what we call social interpretation of the structure and function of the system (Hellman, 1989; Nurminen, 1991). The conclusion of this arrangement is that if some action can be defined inside the area of the group's autonomy, then the corresponding IT must be within the AGIS. Otherwise IT will undermine group autonomy.

This study has presented a preliminary definition of an AGIS to enforce the inseparability. The background for such a system lies heavily in socio-technical approaches.

The main components of AGIS are:

- a static and dynamic perspective on the border, and
- internal activities of the group.

These are subject to group autonomy in a socio-technical perspective. The future study will contain a more detailed analysis of the border and internal support. It is believed that an autonomous group's border, dynamic features, internal performance, group identity and self-management will have a tremendous impact on computer-based IS requirements. The unintended consequences of IT on work can be reduced so that IS will no longer hinder work. Another research question will then be to support group work effectively.

The ninth principle of socio-technical design says that "design is an interactive and continuous process". We believe that the evolutionary approach will provide an AGIS a prospective future in terms of high quality working life and effective IS development in an organisational setting (Principles 8 and 9).

Chapter **20**

A Socio-Technical Approach to Social Learning Analysis in the Australian Defence Force

Leoni Warne

20.1 Introduction

Information systems (IS) researchers and practitioners have been concerned about the low success rates of projects for almost three decades. While the definitions and the exact rate of success may remain debatable, too many delivered systems fail to meet users' expectations, are "shelved" or are "bypassed" by clients.

Although technical deficiencies are sometimes the reasons for the suboptimal use of systems, there has been an increasing emphasis on investigating the social and organisational factors (the social aspects of socio-technical design) that may produce more successful systems (Butterfield and Pendegraft, 1996; Davenport, 1994b; DeLone and McLean, 1992).

This chapter describes a pilot study for a research project being conducted by the Australian Defence Science and Technology Organisation. This study investigates the social aspects of learning in military command situations, so that better technical systems may be developed to support this work.

20.1.1 Socio-Technical Systems

Much has been written about how best to minimise any misunderstanding or conflict between the potential users of a system and those developing the system (Amoako-Gyampah and White, 1993; Cavaye, 1995). Mumford's ETHICS (Effective Technical and Human Implementation of Computer-based Systems) method seeks to achieve a better balance between technology and people in the design and development of "socio-technical" systems through participation (Mumford, 1984).

This approach is still very much technology driven. Increasingly, researchers are seeking ways to address this imbalance.

Beyer and Holtzblatt (1995) advocate using the apprenticeship model as a base. Here the client is the expert (master) of the

> While the importance of optimising both the social and technical aspects is clearly acknowledged, in practice it is often the technical system that is optimised, and the social system that is adapted to suit it.

219

work and how to do it, and he or she teaches the developer (apprentice) by talking about what they are doing as they are doing it. This "apprenticeship" leads to a participatory approach to the development, and a partnership between the clients and the developers. The focus is "user-driven" design. The social aspects of the design are better understood and the technical system can be guided by the social system. This is also the focus of the research study described in this chapter.

20.1.2 The Defence Science and Technology Organisation C3 Research Centre

The Defence Science and Technology Organisation (DSTO) is part of the Australian Defence Organisation (ADO) which comprises the Australian Defence Force (ADF) and the Department of Defence. The DSTO's objective is to give professional and impartial advice on the application of science and technology that is best suited to Australia's defence and security needs (Andriole and Halpin, 1991).

The DSTO C3 Research Centre, within the Information Technology Division, is involved in a range of separate, but related, research and development projects under the Takari Program. This program addresses one of the greatest military challenges: collecting raw information, converting it into useable knowledge, and making it available to every commander who needs it, at the right time, in the right quantity and in the right format (Department of Defence, 1998). The process, and means, by which commanders decide to achieve strategic, operational and tactical objectives is called command, control and communications (C3). Communication systems are the means by which decisions are made and executed, and are therefore an integral part of supporting the command and control process (Andriole and Halpin, 1991).

20.1.3 The Social Learning Architectures Research Study

Although the latest computer technology is freely available to ADF personnel, and large supporting command systems are frequently specified and built, the major individual use made of IS technology in the ADF appears to be for messaging and word processing using laptop computers. Large systems are not always useful because the way work is done has changed since they were specified and built several years earlier. The Social Learning Architectures Task is an attempt to circumvent this problem by understanding and modelling the successful social learning patterns that underpin collaborative command and control work. For the purposes of this task, social learning is defined to include: the procedures by which knowledge and practice are transmitted across posting cycles, across different work situations and across time.

> The basic premise for the Social Learning Architectures Research Study is that, since most work occurs in a social setting, systems that are designed on the basis of an understanding of the social and organisational environment will be more successful.
>
> It is an attempt to move away from specifying systems for information processes to a better understanding of how people work, and how they learn and how systems can be built to support this.
>
> Rather than attempting to mould work habits to fit a technical system, it will be possible to configure a system to suit social systems and work habits.

It is hoped that a further outcome of the study will be the facilitation of a "learning organisation" within the ADF, so that people can continually expand their ability to create positive organisational outcomes, where innovation is nurtured, and where learning is a continuous process (Senge, 1992). If the personnel in ADF command posts can learn faster and better than their opponents, they will have a powerful and sustainable advantage over their enemy.

20.2 The Pilot Study

The pilot study was conducted over a six month period in 1998. The purpose of the pilot study was twofold: to see if it was feasible to observe, understand and document social learning processes, particularly in command and control situations; and to trial the use of ethnographic techniques for this purpose.

20.2.1 The Setting

The setting chosen for the pilot study was a Wing Command of the Royal Australian Air Force (RAAF), Strike Reconnaissance Group (SRG) consisting of two squadrons, each with their own Commanding Officer. The primary mission of SRG is to conduct strike missions using F111 aircraft. The F111 requires a pilot and a navigator drawn from the "aircrew world". Members of the "aircrew world" are posted to flying positions or ground jobs. The strike aircrew community is periodically refreshed by posting in new members every six months (O'Neill, 1998).

The pilot study investigated the "aircrew world", the Squadron Headquarters and the Wing Headquarters. Five field trips were made over a six month period: four to the Wing Headquarters (HQ) at the Strike Reconnaissance Group at Amberley Air Base in Queensland, and one to Darwin. In Darwin, the Wing being studied was joined by members of other Wing headquarters, to form 95Wing HQ, an artificial organisation specifically formed to play "the enemy" in a mock war simulation exercise.

20.2.2 Ethnography

Ethnography is not a new research methodology, it has been standard practice in anthropology for decades. Ethnographers try to immerse themselves in the situation they are researching, in an attempt to gradually see and understand the key concepts that influence the setting being studied, rather than attempting to test hypotheses. So far ethnographic techniques have been used most successfully in IS research to learn how technology is used *in situ* (Preece et al, 1994). But observations have tended to be task-focused rather than attempting to understand the whole activity of work over a period of time, as in this pilot study.

20.2.3 Discussion of the Ethnographic Methodology Used

Over the study period, the composition of the observation teams varied. The ethnographic study began with a team of four researchers: three computer scientists and one social scientist. It ended with: two computer scientists, one social scientist and one researcher from an IS/organisational studies background.

We first met the staff in the Headquarters being studied, and explained the purpose of the study. Then field trips were organised, so that the research team could spend several days at a time observing the work taking place in different settings within the Wing HQ, using directed questioning to clarify any issues that were confusing or unclear. Great care was taken to remain as unobtrusive as possible during these field trips. Observations were written up in field notes, individually. These field notes were then circulated to all study team members and discussed at team meetings.

The field notes of different ethnographers revealed interesting contrasts in what each had observed. Some ethnographers were information focused, identifying what was articulated in conversations, what artifacts were used, and the contents of these artifacts. Other ethnographers focused on the interactions that occurred between people, the body language, the relationships, and how these relationships affected the discourse. Without attempting to make any conclusions, it is also interesting to note that the information-oriented ethnographers were from a computer science or engineering background, while the interaction-oriented ethnographers were from a social sciences or IS background (Agostino, Gori and Warne, 1999).

Team meetings were held after each field trip to identify and consolidate the findings and to identify key social learning issues. Negotiations needed to bridge: the different backgrounds of each team member, their different experiences in the setting, the different meanings people assigned to what they saw, the different language people used, and the different issues that they perceived to have arisen from the work.

The different perspectives of the team members enriched the data, and the minutes of the team meetings became the objective record of the data analysis and the study findings. The team found ethnography a suitable and successful methodology for the purpose of this study.

20.3 Social Learning in the Wing HQ: A Discussion of Findings

It was valuable for the research team to have the opportunity to compare the social learning structures that were primarily associated with peace time (as observed at Amberley); with those associated with war time (as observed at the military exercise at Darwin), and consider whether there were differences between the two situations.

The findings of the pilot study reflected the richness of the disciplines involved in the study. In several instances, individual team members observed behaviour or situations that were illustrative of theories within their own discipline. These theories then had to be explained to other team members, and assimilated by the team as a whole, before being accepted as legitimate findings.

20.3.1 Peace Time

In 1998, the work of a Wing HQ at SRG was "air tasking", "project management", and "document management". At the Squadron HQ level work involved the maintaining and building of flying skills (O'Neill, 1998).

Aircrew Categorisation

The aircrew categorisation scheme is the primary means for maintaining practice and learning in the aircrew world. It controls and monitors the three components of aircrew competency: how to fly (or navigate) and operate the F111; rules and guidance; and tactics.

New members into the SRG aircrew community are regarded as non-operational with no understanding of any of the three knowledge bases until they successfully complete the F111 training. They are then posted to the squadrons at the lowest operational level where they learn how to use the F111 in combat. They move up through the different levels of the aircrew categorisation scheme acquiring knowledge about the tactics, rules and guidance for being a "wingman" in a formation, leading an F111 formation and, eventually, leading a combat package that contains different types of aircraft performing different roles: aircrew at the highest level of the categorisation scheme are quite rare. The learning processes for progressing through the aircrew categorisation scheme involve a combination of bookwork and practical experience in the form of flying (O'Neill, 1998).

The categorisation scheme is based on formal, organisational learning supplemented by social learning constructs. A key learning process takes place at the debriefings held after every flight. Using videotapes, photos and "mudmaps" (hand-drawn diagrams) showing engagements at different times the debriefing process examines all aspects of the mission: the planning process, the way each aircrew member performed their job, interactions between pilot and navigator, interactions between aircraft, and the execution of the objective. This forum provides an opportunity to learn from the experience of others.

Currency

Individual knowledge is seen to be dynamic in the aircrew world due to the continual evolution of the knowledge in the three knowledge structures. Aircrew must fly regularly to maintain currency and retain their categorisation, otherwise they are downgraded.

Aircrew returning to flying after a ground job are often at the lowest level of aircrew categorisation. However, they progress through the levels quicker than a newcomer because they only need to update their baseline knowledge.

Senior officers will often be rated at lower levels of the categorisation scheme as increasing organisational responsibilities lead to a reduction of flying time. Consequently, senior officers regularly need to consult junior officers for current information when making decisions. This includes the quite common situation where the senior officer has served in the junior officer's position at an earlier point in their career. Whilst the position may be the same, the practice and associated information has changed (O'Neill, 1998).

Legitimate Peripheral Participation

When aircrew are not flying, they perform a range of secondary duties in the Squadron HQ. These include producing the flying programme and maintaining aircrew categorisation statistics. Secondary duties are rotated every six months.

When assigned secondary duty work the incoming aircrew member is simply given the "gen" (a folder of current issues and contact numbers) and is expected to be productive immediately. Aircrew are prepared for these secondary duties because they interact with each of the secondary duty roles on a regular basis when flying missions. For instance, aircrew interact with the person performing the flying programme role to find out when they will be flying over the weeks, which aircraft they will be flying that day, and the purpose of the flight. Over time, the aircrew members will have opportunities to witness how those performing the secondary duty roles deal with problematic situations.

Learning about the work of others through peripheral interaction is termed legitimate peripheral participation (Lave and Wenger, 1991). Through this process, an individual is assumed to have developed basic knowledge about all routine work. The "gen" folder is one mechanism for expanding this information by providing the informal social network (the contact numbers) by which work gets done, as well as the set of current issues. Another way this information is acquired is by listening to stories told by other people who have had relevant experiences in a secondary role (O'Neill, 1998). In this way, aircrew have the opportunity to understand and assimilate the duties of a secondary role, before they are required to take the role on themselves.

Impact of Individual Career Paths

The aircrew world and Squadron HQ can draw on a pool of trained people, and therefore assume that a newcomer has basic knowledge. The Squadron HQ, therefore, accesses a pool that has been "trained" through the process of legitimate peripheral participation with the secondary roles, as well as by more formal means.

The Wing HQ does not have access to a pool of people who understand the Wing Headquarters' work environment. Whilst aircrew have day-to-day interactions with the Squadron HQ, their interactions with the Wing Headquarters are far less frequent, reducing the opportunities for learning by legitimate peripheral participation or by listening to the stories of the experienced.

Allocating tasks to each role within the Wing HQ is at least partially dependent upon an individual's previous experience. For non-aircrew members, the ideal career path involves being trained in a discipline (e.g. logistics), serving at a Squadron HQ, being posted elsewhere, then being posted into the Wing HQ. The benefit of this career path is that it enables an individual to develop competency in a functional area; gain knowledge of SRG through a posting at the Squadron HQ; and learn through legitimate peripheral participation how another person handles the role in the Wing HQ (O'Neill, 1998).

One of the Commanders interviewed by the research team suggested that individuals who have followed this career path are productive at the Wing HQ within a month of starting work there. Furthermore, the Commander believed that individuals who have not followed this career path, in particular those who have not served at the Squadron HQ before serving at the Wing HQ, are often struggling six months into their posting at the Wing HQ. Preliminary observations seem to support this anecdotal evidence, suggesting that legitimate peripheral participation, early in a career, can facilitate learning at later postings, in related work areas.

20.3.2 War Time

For two weeks, the Wing HQ joined with personnel from other Wings to become 95Wing, or the enemy "Orange Air", for a mock war exercise conducted out of the Air Force Base at Darwin. The Officer Commanding 95Wing and his staff came from the Wing HQ at Amberley, and all had worked together as a team previously. The settings for most of the observations made of this "war" were the Operations Room and the Briefing Room at 95Wing HQ.

The Orange Air Operations Room was where air-tasking orders were constructed, where the Officer Commanding (OC) exercised command and where he dealt with crises and contingencies. There was a table in the Operations Room where laptop computers were available for the creation of documents, folders contained different types of information, and telephones were available. The table was used as a central location for checking on requirements and conducting muted conversations and telephone calls. Members of Orange Air would frequently wander in to talk to people at the table about the work that was going on (Agostino, Gori and Warne, 1999). Also in the Operations Room, was a paper map of the "war zone". The map was annotated with plastic overlays, so that missions could be planned visually and changes could be immediately visible. Several people were tasked with keeping this map, and related notices, up to date. Small groups would constantly form around the map, as people gathered for the information required to plan the air tasking orders and missions. This arrangement was extraordinarily successful, as the table and map became a focus for both formal learning and informal social learning about the "war" and the missions.

The Briefing Room was used in a number of different ways. It was the venue for formal mission briefs and debriefs. The debriefings proceeded much as they had in the Squadrons at Amberley, with special emphasis on lessons learned. The Briefing Room was also an arena for semi-formal planning, and it provided a meeting place for people to discuss things informally, especially before and after briefs (Agostino, Gori and Warne, 1999).

The work of 95Wing HQ involved aligning activity systems to perform an afternoon and evening mission every day. To drive this alignment, a tight timeline was used to establish a rhythm of work to which all players needed to conform in order for missions to be successfully conducted. Some problems occurred early in the exercise as there was a mismatch in expectations between the Operations Room and other areas which were tasked with keeping the Operations Room up to date. Initially, there was no shared understanding of the importance of the timeline as a driving force for the work. However, as all sections of 95Wing aligned themselves with the timeline, the missions began to run more smoothly, and the stress level in the Operations Room began to decrease.

There was considerable emphasis on the learning opportunities provided by the exercise, and lessons learned were both formal and informal points of discussion after every mission cycle. It became clear that personnel who had been on previous, similar exercises managed to fit into the routine and rhythm of the work far more quickly than those who had not had some experience with this type of military exercise. One of the proposed outcomes of this military exercise was a CD-ROM with a summary of lessons learned to inform and assist the personnel involved in the next exercise.

On a number of occasions the real world encroached on the mock war, and the Command Staff needed to juggle their real world obligations with those of the exercise, having to "live in two worlds" at the same time (Agostino, Gori and Warne, 1999).

20.3.3 War and Peace

> However, it is clear that some social learning structures can remain invisible, becoming observable only when they fail or when an exception is noted.

Many of the social learning structures became most apparent in times of stress, or when they failed to work effectively. Although some issues became more visible under "war conditions", all of the identified structures (individual expertise, currency, legitimate peripheral participation, career paths, team work, shared understanding) seem to underpin social learning equally in both peace and war. One such exception occurred during the military exercise in Darwin.

It was apparent that all the roles in the 95Wing HQ were very busy, working towards the strict deadlines of the timeline. However, the two people performing the Mission Director role seemed to have time to engage in other activities such as liaising in planning for future exercises, and maintaining standard operating procedures. A discussion with a senior officer about the Mission Director role revealed that the shape of the work at the Wing HQ had changed in the past two years, from air tasking to mission tasking. This reshaping was due to the perceived need to facilitate interoperability with other forces in the future. To advance this need, new concepts and practices were being phased in. Consequently the Mission Director role is gradually being re-shaped from administration to mission planning and execution (Agostino, Gori and Warne, 1999). In this way, another catalyst for social learning became apparent to the team – the need to adapt to a changing work environment.

> Understanding the workplace interactions and social learning also requires insight into dimensions of power within organisations, because power is central to what becomes knowledge.

An understanding of Foucault's (1983) notion of power illuminates some of the interactions observed at SRG. For example, the data gathered confirms that rank and hierarchy do not dominate power relations: currency rather than rank is the dominant force. It is too simplistic to say that power and rank are inextricably linked. In fact, power and power relations at SRG are not set according to the hierarchy of the military, but rather by an individual's knowledge of a multiplicity of manoeuvres, tactics, techniques and other functions. During the military exercise in Darwin, the Officer Commanding 95Wing clearly demonstrated his authority on a number of occasions, but while his authority stems from his rank, it also comes from the knowledge and expertise that he has developed over the years. In this way, he has legitimate power and theoretically has the right to impose certain kinds of directives and decisions regardless of the wishes of those under him. However, in spite of this legitimate authority, he shows respect for the expertise of the staff he commands; he acknowledges the authority of others and listens to their expert knowledge and advice. In terms of social learning and knowledge transfer it is clear that even those of junior ranks are not powerless, but are also central to the transmission and future investment in the learning that occurs around, in and through them (Agostino, Gori and Warne, 1999). This was an interesting finding as it diverged from the prevailing view that information is equated with power and importance in many organisations, and that holders of that information frequently resist the sharing, or devolution, of that responsibility (Davenport, Eccles and Prusak, 1992).

20.4 Conclusion

Both formal and informal social learning structures were identified during the pilot study. Individual mastery, according to Senge (1992) forms one of the disciplines of a learning organisation and this was seen to be well supported in the pilot study setting. Some problems were noted in the area of building a shared vision, and, during the exercise, it became clear how a breakdown in shared understanding can cause immediate problems in an operational setting.

> Issues of individual expertise, currency, legitimate peripheral participation, career paths and experience, team work, shared understanding, shared vision, the changing work environment, power and authority all appear to be components of the social learning architecture in a command and control organisation.

It is not yet clear what the relative importance of each of these elements is, or indeed, if they apply beyond the setting of the pilot study. However, it is already possible to speculate that the technical support for the informal social learning structures identified should come from group decision support systems, intelligent software agents and team based system architectures.

At the final brief to the Commander of SRG, the multi-layered findings were presented and validated. Some of the pilot study's findings were not a surprise, but others were, and are to be further examined by SRG Command Staff. The pilot study has been seen to be successful from the military's perspective, the DSTO's perspective, and the research team's perspective. Concepts of social learning in the workplace, and the utility of ethnographic techniques for studying these concepts, have been validated. As a result, the ethnographic research will continue in a new setting.

The success of the ethnographic methodology for this research suggests there may be a much wider role for this form of information gathering: it may be the best way to fully understand and analyse social systems in a work setting, and the best way to ensure successful optimisation of both the social and technical aspects of a computing systems development.

Ethnographic information gathering:

- involves immersion in the setting being observed;
- is time and resource intensive;
- is facilitated by working in teams;
- is facilitated by a multidisciplinary approach;
- results in rich, multi-layered pictures of the social systems being analysed;
- gives researchers/analysts a deeper understanding of the social aspects of socio-technical systems.

It is too early to conclude that the social learning architecture to be developed from this study will definitely lead to better systems specifications for more usable and enduring systems. However, this task will certainly lead to an enhanced understanding of the social structures that most successfully support people working, learning and collaborating in command and control in the ADF.

Lessons learned from the pilot study

- Social learning is a complex, multi-layered social system.
- Social systems are as complex as technical systems.
- The informal aspects of social learning are as important, if not more so, than the formal, organised aspects of organisational learning.
- Informal aspects of social learning are not yet supported by technical systems.
- Social structures become more visible when they fail, or when an exception is noted.
- Ethnography is a very useful methodology for understanding and analysing the social aspects of socio-technical systems.

Acknowledgments

The author wishes to acknowledge the vital contribution made to this work by Dr John O'Neill, the originator and first task manager of this research study, and by Dr Jennie Clothier, whose vision made it possible. Thanks are also due to team members Katerina Agostino, Ronnie Gori, Paul Prekop and Malathi Carthigaser, and to all the RAAF personnel who participated in the study.

Chapter 21

Technology, Organisation and Qualifications in Software Development

Stefan Berndes and Uwe Lünstroth

21.1 Introduction

This chapter is about the effects of technological and organisational change on the qualifications of software developers. Software development is characterised by the high qualifications of the software developers and the rapid changing technological conditions. Several case studies are presented that show negative and positive examples with regard to sociotechnical principles. The application of the sociotechnical approach on knowledge work is encouraged by the work of Taylor and Felten (1993). As the qualitative case studies will show, software development is an outstanding example in this field of knowledge work.

The principles of sociotechnical design lead the process of joint optimisation of technological and social aspects in organisational design. Here, these principles are applied to identify conditions in software development that promote or hinder the development of qualifications of software engineers (see Table 21.1).

The case studies came from software development companies in Germany during the INVAS[1] project. This project, which is financed by the German Ministry of Science and Education (BMBF), originally focussed on the older software engineer and the effects that might appear in software developing companies as consequences of the demographic change in the industrial countries in the next few decades.

The questions were:

1. what causes can be found to hinder the older engineer participating in innovative work; and

2. under which conditions should it be possible to retrain these people.

It soon appeared that these problems and possible solutions merely depend on strategies and conditions within software developing companies and a solution should be found independently from general demographic problems within the

---

[1] INVAS = Innovationen bei veraenderten Altersstrukturen 'innovation in times of changing demographic structures'.

230

Table 21.1. Sociotechnical design principles (adapted from Cherns, 1987)

Principle	
1. Compatibility	Organisational changes should not only be directed to goals but should try to reach them within the process of change.
2. Minimum critical specification	"Specify as little as possible, and identify only what is essential and critical to the organisation's success" (Albach, 1993).
3. Variance control	"Variances not removed or eliminated through technology should be controlled by the organisation closest to their point or origin. Key variances should not be allowed to cross unit operations" (Berndes and Luenstroth, 1998).
4. Boundary location	"Boundaries should not be drawn that inhibit the sharing or flow of information, knowledge, and skills" (Lehr, 1992).
5. Information flow	"Information should go first to the point of action" (Littig, 1997). "The key to effective information flow is to design systems with the involvement and participation of the team using the data" (Behrens, 1993).
6. Power and authority	"Those who need equipment, materials, or other resources to carry out their responsibilities should have access to them and authority to command them. In return, they accept responsibility for them and for their prudent and economical use" (Weisbecker, Frings and Supe, 1997).
7. Multifunctional/multi-skill	Takes into account the changes on labour skills and is of special importance in the area of highly qualified software developers.
8. Support congruence	"Management philosophy should be consistent and that management's actions should be consistent with its expressed philosophy" (Humphrey, 1996).
9. Design and human value	This principle states that an objective of organisational design should be to provide a high quality of work.
10. Bridging the transition	Keeping the balance of pushing forward without invoking adverse stress needs to be consciously and continuously reviewed
11. Incompletion – build in continuous improvement	The new paradigm is that of an organisation flexibly adapting to its environment.

labour market during the next decades (Berndes and Lünstroth, 1998). A simple categorisation of software companies will be introduced.

21.2 Interdependence of Technology, Organisation and Qualifications

Software engineers with high qualifications are in danger of their qualifications degrading within the process of technological and organisational changes. This could happen if they are not able to fit into life-long learning and regular retraining in this rapidly developing field of computer science. We try to show that problems with older software engineers are caused in part by disregarding sociotechnical principles.

21.2.1 Case Study A: Older Software Developers are Caught in a Niche

Case study A describes the conditions which may lead to degradation. In Table 21.2, one can follow the parallel development of technology and the qualifications of employees in software development. It represents the company history of a large insurance company. There are more than 100 workers in software development today, with an average age of 38 years.

Most of the software used here is not very complicated but it has to handle a large amount of data for financial transactions. There are well-established security standards not only for data exchange but also for the software development process. The tools and middleware have standard forms which are regulated and controlled by a special department. There are high standards in documentation and a program module repository was installed a long time ago. The original program, to which the changes are applied, may have a core program existing from the 1960s.

Developers are often highly specialised in the programs with which they have worked since they came to the company. They have never changed department, trained on other programming languages, have not worked on or even thought about new paradigms in software or hardware. As long as these workers are needed in their special fields of work, their qualifications are needed and useful. Problems arise in times of technological and organisational change.

Larger organisational changes are often accompanied by changes in software standards, and under such circumstances parts of the older programming department, or even the whole department in case of changes to another software concept, might be made obsolete. This change in needed qualifications is endangered because the software engineers are often only used to a very specialised field of software development and fixed to an older software or hardware paradigm (such as procedural programming or mainframe architecture). They have not been trained on a wider spectrum of computer science and have often lost the ability to learn a new paradigm.

From the sociotechnical there was little time for possibilities in self-development along with the changing technology and new paradigms and concepts in software programming and hardware design.

21.3 Keeping Up with the Demands for New Qualifications

21.3.1 Case Study B: Knowing the Demand for Continual Learning

Table 21.3 shows a large company that develops software for complex technical products with currently about 100 software engineers (average age of about

Table 21.2. Case study A as an example of the company type "software development for commercial business with customers inside the company" (as studied in a large company in banking and insurance business)

Time	1950s	1960s	1970s	1980s	1990s	2000 and thereafter
Characteristic hardware and software structures	Hollerith division	Change from tube computers to electronic computers		Beginning of the 1980s: Network computers Middle of the 1980s: First personal computers	Middle of the 1990s: Beginning of the installation of client–server applications	In preparation: Enhancement of internet and intranet applications
Employees and qualification	One team of programmers within the computation centre of the company (for example, mathematicians)		Expansion of the workforce in software engineering with employment of craftsmen and teachers		Beginning of increasing demand for computer scientists in commercial business (banks, insurance companies)	

Table 21.3. Case study B as an example of the company type "software development for technical products" (as studied in a large company)

Time	1960s	1970s	1980s	1990s	2000 and thereafter
Characteristic hardware and software structures	Hardware division, paper card computing	A software division in addition to the hardware division was built; assembler programming language	A division for development of a complex technological product was built; UNIX operating system	Foundation of organisational structures for production of reusable software; on the other hand standard software was bought for display purposes; programming language C++	Tendency to give whole problem solutions to the customer; network structures with interconnection between different products and operator places
Employees and qualification		International experts in computer science as employees in software development	Employees for the newly founded division with university degrees (more engineers, physicists and mathematicians than computer scientists)	Rapid growth of employee stock, many trained workers without a university degree (technician, "Fachinformatiker")	Tendency to have more employees with a diploma in computer science

35 years, a third are over 40 years old). In the 1980s the technological dimension of the product was dominating so that most of the employees came from engineering, physics and mathematics rather than from computer science. Tendencies towards higher standardisation and a growing demand for networking, to enable connection of different products, forced the company to have experts in such computer science aspects. In the 1990s, the qualification standards in software development for technical products shifted towards skilled people with degrees in computer science.

As qualification standards increase, there is a parallel tendency to have less qualified workers in software development. The management has thought of making the workers assist the experts who have a degree in computer science. These workers are either former technicians of the company and trained in a year long course in special topics of hardware elements and programming languages, or young workers on a training programme (lasting three years) in different parts of computer work and software development. These workers do not have a university degree and are often trained specially on certain technological topics or tasks such as documentation and software testing.

Senior software engineers can work with younger engineers with fresh knowledge from university, but this is not always possible owing to problems in project management which lead to time pressure. The older and younger software engineers fit into one team because their qualifications lie in the same field but on different levels of experience. These different levels complement one another. They are directed to the same technological product, to the same hardware and software technology and each side can learn from the other and is willing to do so.

Sociotechnical principles are followed, allowing a team collaboration between younger and older software developers, self-development in changing tasks and continuous learning both, within the team and on abilities which will be useful for the development of the future product.

21.4 Difficulties in Introducing an Organisational Change

21.4.1 Case Study C: Changing Software Development from Production for Internal to External Customers

Case study C focuses on older software developers in the situation of changing business strategy. In the branch of software development the term "older" is attributed to the professional coming from university after a time period of about a decade, in which his university working knowledge is getting nearly worthless due to rapid technological change. The case shows older engineers who had not been given a chance to keep up with the changes by continually learning and adapting to the new technological background.

Several hundred software developers, many of them with the status of a freelancer but closely bound to activities in this company, are working in the subsidiary of a large company. Former departments that were working with older systems and software (IBM mainframe, Cobol as programming language) differ significantly in age structure from the competence centres, which are working on new applications (client–server architecture, C++ as a programming language, internet applications). Although there is no difference in the average age, which is about 35 years, in the older systems group there are far more older software developers. A third are older than 45 years, had a former education in the financial business area and were trained only for a year for the job in software development. A second third are around 35 years old and with higher qualifications, mostly a degree in computer science, and the last third is about 25 years old. So the older systems group has the same average age as the group for new applications but without the homogeneous age and qualification structure (graduates in computer science) of the latter group.

The experience of the older software developers is valuable because modelling business processes is not only a task of knowing technology but mainly of programming useful functions for the customer. Problems arise with flexibility and motivation, which are necessary to actively support the technological and organisational changes. For support of older systems fewer developers will be needed, but abilities to communicate with external customers, to think in business terms rather than in technological terms and the will to cope with the growing knowledge about new technology are demanded.

Continuous learning has to be achieved to prevent the dequalification process. Self-development and qualifications should have been planned beforehand. Self-development is a task for negotiations and arrangements between company and software engineer on career visions, future career possibilities and the financing of qualification programs.

21.4.2 Case Study D: Changing Skills from Technology to Customer Service

Case study D is an example of drastic changes in business orientation from very specialised programming to customer consultancy with few tasks in programming.

A software development company with several hundred software developers was bought by a consortium of large companies in the IT field. Seeing a high demand in service activities on business and management standard software, the bought company was supposed to switch from technology to customer service activities. As a large number of the former software engineers had a long specialisation experience (average age of 42 years), they did not have a wider range of knowledge in computer science and the activities in learning were only in fields of software engineering that were part of the narrow specialisation.

This situation is a bad starting point to make such an ambitious change from technology to service. Needless to say, the attempt to retrain these people with skills useful in customer contact and communication was not a great success. Lack of motivation, being unused to training and no wider scope than the special technology issues hindered suitable thinking in business terms. As the literature about adult education (Lehr, 1992) shows, these circumstances are bad preconditions for learning success.

21.5 Perspectives of Fostering Continuous Learning

Case studies E and F give an insight into positive examples of anticipating sociotechnical principles to foster the qualification process through continuous learning (E) and through a career perspective (F) which looks one decade ahead.

21.5.1 Case Study E: Qualification Efforts and Job Rotation

This case is an example of company activities, following sociotechnical principles on qualifications with its measures in training and job rotation. The increased amount of training of experienced older software engineers with a degree in computer science shows positive economic effects in this large company with worldwide competition in the technical product field.

Competition has resulted in drastic reductions in development time (from a few years to several months) and tighter financial restrictions. The case study was carried out in a team with about 50 software engineers. These highly qualified developers in the customer-oriented software development and application are between 35–38 years old on average. The average experience in this company branch is about 10 years. The main issue is not to do with age or years of experience. The main point is that they may have first been taught another software or hardware paradigm in their university courses other than the one on which they are now working.

The former software development department has made an organisational change from a functional to a complete project organisation type in recent years. This was accompanied by 20 working days per year for training issues. Superiors of this company say that for effective qualifications, twice that amount of time is necessary. It was recently decided to share the time needed for qualification purposes on a one-to-one basis between company and software engineer. The effects of the qualification process and learning in the company are strengthened by job rotation. Eighty per cent of the software developers now have different activities compared to only two years ago. These training effects led to more efficiency in decreasing defects and testing components, as well as the work of interconnection between the software and the technical product.

21.5.2 Case Study F: Career Development in Young Software Companies

The efforts on qualifications within software development are not only valuable in the perspective of rapid changing technology but also in a career perspective. An extraordinary example is given in this case study. It shows opportunities for software engineer careers, which are made possible through continuous qualification efforts and the vision for career opportunities in this small software company.

About 50 software engineers with an average age of 31 years are working on databases, special technical applications, systems integration and client–server applications.

Many older developers at the age of mid-to-late thirties of the subsidiary have now got tasks in which their experience is demanded. They have been leaders of projects and then began to develop qualifications to do tasks with an increased share of management activities. Developers, about 35 years old and with 6–9 years' experience in this company, are now responsible for technical sales, presales and consulting or directing documentation projects. This is done without losing contact with current knowledge and technological tendencies such as internet, email applications and WAN.

The aim is to develop the skills and interests of the engineer as well as to have advances in keeping up with the demands of the customer who is interested in useful functions more than in technology.

21.6 Generalisation of Results and Summary

Two company types can be found with regard to organisational effects on the ability of the software developer, to make changes in qualifications:

1. a company type which is based in commercial business (software for insurance and bank businesses or for other service industries and standard software services); and
2. another company type which produces software for technical products (in fields varying from medical services to the air and space industry to machine tool production).

In companies which develop software for technical products the situation is different because technical knowledge about the product is demanded more than about commercial and financial processes. The high complexity of the used technology in software development afforded knowledge of the central processing units and basic hardware processes. This situation has led to the employment of more qualified software engineers, either with knowledge of the technical process and product for which the software was developed (case study B) or with knowledge of computer science (case studies E and F). So these companies gave work to engineers with extra skills in software engineering or to computer science engineers who often were rare experts of their special field.

In the companies which build software for technical products there is no organisational obstacle to life-long learning of software engineers. They are going with newly built teams from product to product (case study B), being qualified in training on the job and special courses with strong connections to the next steps in technology (case study E), and they are getting both experience and new technological knowledge in a wider field of software issues (case study F). They get the ability to judge the value of new technological developments in hardware and software because they have experience about the costs and benefits for the customers. They can judge about acceptable and unacceptable usage of new inventions in their field of application.

In comparison with the commercial type of business software company, these experienced software developers often have a better starting point, having been educated at university, having an engineering degree and better organisational circumstances within a team structure with changing products more often than one time in a decade. If the software engineer can cope with qualification changes in the software technological field these conditions ensure that he will not be dequalified.

In these cases different organisational responses to the rapid technological development evolve and tend to either go along sociotechnical principles or tend to ignore them. Each case study was analysed according to the sociotechnical principles. Table 21.4 gives the results in generalised terms.

Following sociotechnical principles leads to a fostering of self-development and a perspective on life-long learning, which enables the developer to have useful qualifications, either for future tasks in his current company or regarding the future labour market. Ignoring such principles leads to qualifications in narrow specialised fields without a vision for future developments. For a majority of older software developers this leads to the degradation of their qualifications in times of organisational and business field changes when new qualifications are demanded in a very short time.

To a high degree, the software developing companies in the sample of the INVAS case studies in different branches of software development show a

Table 21.4. Do software developing companies obey sociotechnical principles?

Sociotechnical design principle	Company type	
	Software for commercial business (Cases A, C and D)	Software for technical products (Cases B, E and F)
1. Compatibility	No	No
2. Minimum critical specification	No	Yes
3. Variance control	Yes	No
4. Boundary location	No	Yes
5. Information flow	No	No
6. Power and authority	No	No
7. Multifunctional/multi-skill	No	Yes
8. Support congruence	No	Yes
9. Design and human value	No	No
10. Bridging the transition	No	Yes
11. Incompletion – build in continuous improvement	No	Yes

general point of deficiency in personnel management: not all developers can participate equally.

The ignorance of the personnel management to principle 1, "Compatibility", (see Table 21.5) can be seen by two objectives:

- There is no long-term planning of fields of activity for enhancement of qualifications. Usually the engineer will have a meeting only once a year with his superior to agree on future task objectives and on training measures.

Table 21.5. Sociotechnical principles

- *Compatibility* (Principle 1): It is necessary to develop long term perspectives for the career of the software engineer with the planning of secondary qualifications or retraining and planning of the career itself (setting milestones for possible work areas and for qualifications within the company). To achieve this, sociotechnical principles have to be applied, to enable self-development, continuous learning and a learning perspective in team collaboration and shared access to information.

- *Minimum critical specification* (Principle 2) demands the opportunity for the software engineer to look for appropriate retraining measures and also demands financial aid from the company for this purpose. This will primarily be relevant for near future activities, by making changes in tasks and later on (in the "senior phase", beginning at an age of about 40 years) of jobs that make use of the experience of the older software engineers. These jobs may contain elements of coaching, innovation planning or customer consultant service.

- *Variance control* (Principle 3) demands acceptance of every software engineer as a lay-quality manager in the sense of improving the project management through techniques of self-guidance which includes judgement of time needed for certain software development tasks. Reducing time stress in the software projects to enable a better planning of measures for retraining. It is the enhancement of the quality of the software development process due to a certification process.

- *Boundary location* (Principle 4): The task is to help avoiding the development of strong boundaries (niches) that foster dequalification processes.

- *Information flow* (Principle 5), which has to be applied on information about possible qualification measures of sources external and internal to the company.

- *Power and authority* (Principle 6) is seen with respect to consulting tasks of personnel and qualification management. A special issue is to enable the software developer to stay in contact with changing fundamental software and hardware concepts and paradigms. Enhancement of qualification in abstract or general software-related fields could be made possible by university sabbaticals. This should be in time periods shorter than major changes in technological concepts and paradigms, for example every six years.

- *Multifunctional/multi-skills* (Principle 7), which may lead to measures for enhancing possibilities of job rotation and others to develop multi-skill qualifications.

- *Design and human values* (Principle 9) should have to foster self-development. It is the task of the personnel and qualification management to back up the visions and ideas of the software engineer. They must think about the further perspective, maybe one decade ahead, when another change in technology and associated organisational changes becomes unavoidable. It is of advantage for both the software engineer and the company.

- *Incompletion* (Principle 11): Taylor and Felten (1993) describe Principle 11 as demanding structural mechanisms for continually dealing with change on all levels. The specific level here in consideration is continuous learning and qualification of the software engineer.

- The personnel management, while used to young software developers and their creative work in innovative processes, are not acquainted with older developers and their possible problems of career development.

These findings suggest an initiative to foster a perspective on the development of qualifications and life-long learning in software engineering. The management responsible for qualifications and career development (Behrens, 1993) has to change its primary view towards the sociotechnical principles. Sociotechnical principles lead the way to measures, which enable qualification and requalification processes, and this is a way to overcome the degradation effects to the qualifications of the software developers.

The proposed principle "development of qualifications" states:

> The software developer who is getting older, should be able to work in software engineering in the company he is currently working with, through his whole career, or to have qualifications that are in demand in the current labour market.

References

Ackoff, R. (1967) Management Misinformation Systems. *Management Science* 14(4): 147–156.

Agostino, K., Gori, R. and Warne, L. (1999) *The Enterprise Social Learning Task: Context, and Conclusions from the Pilot Study.* DSTO, Department of Defence.

Ahuja, M. and Carley, K. (1998) Network Structure in Virtual Organisations. *Journal of Computer-Mediated Communications* V3: 4. Also to appear in *Organizational Science.*

Albach, H. (1993) Culture and Technological Innovation. *Akadamie der Wissenschaften zu berlin, Forschungsbericht* 9. Berlin: Walter de Gruyter.

Alexander, C., Ishikawa, S. and Silverstein, M. (1977) *A Pattern Language: Towns, Buildings, Construction.* New York: Oxford University Press, 1977.

Amelsvoort, P.J.L.M. van (1992) Het vergroten van de bestuurbaarheid van productie-organisaties (Increasing the Controllability of Production Organisations). Eindhoven: Technische Universiteit, PhD thesis (in Dutch).

Amelsvoort, P.J.L.M. van (1996) Het programmeren en regisseren van veranderingsprocessen. Vormgeven aan complexe veranderingsprocessen van organisatievernieuwing (Planning and Directing Change Processes: Designing Complex Change Processes of Organisational Renewal). Vlijmen: ST-groep (in Dutch).

Amelsvoort, P.J.L.M. van and Scholtes, G.H. (1993) Zelfsturende teams: Ontwerpen, invoeren en begeleiden (Self-managed Teams: Design, Implementation and Support). Oss: ST-groep (in Dutch).

Amoako-Gyampah, K. and White, K.B. (1993) User Involvement and User Satisfaction: An Exploratory Contingency Model. *Information and Management* 25: 1–10.

Andriole, S.J. and Halpin, S.M. (1991) *Information Technology for Command and Control: Methods and Tools for Systems Development and Evaluation.* New York: IEEE.

Angell, I.O. (1990) Systems Thinking about Information Systems and Strategies. *Journal of Information Technology* 5(3): 168–74.

Argyris, C. (1980) T-Groups for Organisational Effectiveness. *Harvard Business Review* 58: 115–125.

Argyris, C. (1998) Empowerment: The Emperor's New Clothes. *Harvard Business Review* 76(3): 98–105.

Argyris, C. and Schön, D.A. (1978) Organisational Learning: A Theory of Action Perspective. Reading, MA: Addison-Wesley.

Argyris, C. and Schön, D.A. (1996) *Organisational Learning II.* New York: Addison Wesley.

Avgerou, C., Cornford, T. and Poulymenakou, A. (1995) The Challenge of BPR to the Information Systems Profession. *New Technology, Work and Employment.* 10(2):132–141.

Avison, D.E. and Fitzgerald, G. (1988) *Information Systems Development Methodologies, Techniques and Tools.* London: Blackwell.

Avison, D.E. and Fitzgerald, G. (1995) *Information Systems Development: Methodologies, Techniques and Tools.* 2nd edition. London: McGraw-Hill.

Avison, D.E. and Wood-Harper, A.T. (1990) *Multiview: An Exploration in Information Systems Development.* Oxford: Blackwell Scientific Publications.

Avison, D.E. and Wood-Harper, A.T. (1991) Conclusions from Action Research: The Multiview Experience. In M.C. Jackson (ed.) *Systems Thinking in Europe.* New York: Plenum.

Baecker, R., Grudin, J., Buxton, W. and Greenberg, S. (eds) (1995) *Readings in Human-Computer Interaction, Toward the Year 2000.* New York: Morgan-Kaufman.

Bailey, R. (1995) Performance vs. Preference. *Proceedings of the Human Factors Society, HFES,* New York: 316–320.

Bank, J. (1992) *The Essence of Total Quality Management.* New York: Prentice Hall.

Bannon, L. and Schmidt, K. (1989) CSCW: Four Characters in Search of a Context. In. *Proceedings of the First European Conference on Computer Supported Cooperative Work,* London. EC-CSCW '89: 358–372.

Bansler, J. and Haun, E. (1991) The Nature of Software Work. In V. Besselaar, A. Clement and P. Jarvinen (eds) *Information System Work and Organizational Design.* North Holland, Amsterdam.

Barry, B. (1989) Information Technology and Organizational Development. In R. Woodman, and W. Pasmore (eds.) *Organizational Change and Development.* JAI Press: 213–231.

Barua, A., Lee, C.H. and Whinston, A. (1996) The Calculus of Reengineering. *Information Systems Research* 7: 409–428.

Baskerville, R. and Smithson, S. 1995) Information Technology and New Organizational Forms: Choosing Chaos over Panaceas. *European Journal of Information Systems* 4: 66–73.

Bayer, H., Gropius, I. and Gropius, W. (eds) (1975) *Bauhaus 1919-1928.* New York: The Museum of Modern Art.

Beaumont, H. (1993) Martin Buber's I-Thou and Fragile Self-Organisation: Contributions to Gestalt Couples Therapy. *The British Gestalt Journal* 2: 85–95.

Beekun, R. (1989) Assessing the Effectiveness of Sociotechnical Interventions: Antidote or Fad. *Human Relations* 42: 877–897.

Behrens, J. (1993) Laufbahngestaltung für Service-Ingenieure im Außendienst von Computerfirmen. In H.J. Bullinger, V. Volkholz, K. Betzl, A. Köchling and W. Risch (ed.) *Alter und Erwerbsarbeit der Zukunft.* Berlin: Springer: 227–232.

Benjamin, R. and Blunt, J. (1992) Critical IT Issues: The Next Ten Years. *Sloan Management Review* Summer: 7–19.

Berndes, S. and Lünstroth, U. (eds) (1998) Erfahrung als Voraussetzung für zukunftsfähige Software-Entwicklung am Standort Deutschland. Cottbus: Eigenverlag (Lehrstuhl Technikphilosphie, PT – 02/1998).

Beyer, H.R. and Holtzblatt, K. (1995) Apprenticing with the Customer. *Communications of the ACM* 38: 45–52.

Bikson, T.K. and Eveland, J.D. (1996) Groupware Implementation: Reinvention in the Sociotechnical Frame. *Proceedingsof the CSCW '96,* Cambridge, MA: ACM Press: 428–437.

Bion, W.R. (1961) *Experiences in Groups.* London: Tavistock.

Bjerknes, G. and Bratteteig, T. (995) User Participation and Democracy: A Discussion of Scandinavian Research on System Development. *Scandinavian Journal of Information Systems* 7(1): 73–98.

Bjørn-Andersen, N. and Chatfield, A. (1996) Using IT for Creating the 21st Century Organization. Invited plenary presentation at the Fifth International Conference on Information Systems Development, Gdansk, September.

Bleakley, F. (1993) Many Companies Try Management Fads, Only to See Them Flop. *Wall Street Journal* 6 July: A1.

Boehm, B. (1988) A Spiral Model of Software Development and Enhancement. *IEEE Computer* 21(2): 61–72.

Bohl D. (1997) Saturn Corp – A Different Kind of Pay. *Compensation and Benefits Review* 29: 51–56.

Bostrom, R. (1980) *A Socio-Technical Perspective on MIS Implementation.* Colorado Springs, CO: ORSA/TIMS.

Bostrom, R.P. and Heinen, J.S. (1977a) MIS Problems and Failures: A Socio-Technical Perspective. Part I: The Causes. *Management Information Systems Quarterly* 2: 17–32.

Bostrom, R.P. and Heinen, J.S. (1977b) MIS Problems and Failures: A Socio-Technical Perspective. Part II: The Application of Socio-Technical Theory. *Management Information Systems Quarterly* December.

Boulding, K.E. (1989) Towards a Theory of Vulnerability. *Journal of Applied Systems Analysis* 16: 1–17.

Bowers, J. (1995) Making it Work: A Field Study of a CSCW Network. *The Information Society* 11:189–207.

Brass, D. (1985) Technology and Structuring of Jobs: Employee Satisfaction, Performance, and Influence. *Administrative Science Quarterly* 29: 518–539.

Bridges, W. (1991) *Managing Transitions: Making the Most of Change.* Reading, MA: Addison-Wesley.

Brinck, T. (1998) *CSCW and Groupware.* http://www.crew.umich.edu/~brink/cscw.htm

British Computer Society (1997) Examination Syllabus, Swindon.

Brooks, F.P. Jr. (1996) The Computer Scientist as Toolsmith II, *Communication ACM* **39**(3): 61–68.

Buchanan, D. (1979) *The Development of Job Design Theories and Techniques.* Westmead: Saxon House.

Buchanan, D.A. and Huczynski, A.A. (1985) *Organizational Behavior: An Introductory Text.* London: Prentice-Hall.

Burkhardt, M. and Brass, D. (1990) Changing Patterns or Patterns of Change: The Effects of a Change in Technology on Social Network Structure and Power. *Administrative Science Quarterly* **35**: 104–127.

Burrell, G. and Morgan, G. (1979) Sociological Paradigms and Organisational Analysis. London: Heinemann.

Butterfield, J. and Pendegraft, N. (1996) Cultural Analysis in IS Planning and Management. *Journal of Systems Management* **47**: 14–17.

Capra, F. (1996) The Web of Life: A New Synthesis of Mind and Matter. London: Flamingo.

Caroll, J. (1974) Breakout from the Crystal Palace. London: Routledge & Kegan Paul.

Cavaye, A.L.M. (1995) User Participation in System Development Revisited. *Information and Management* **28**: 311–323.

Checkland P.B. (1981a) *Systems Thinking, Systems Practice.* Chichester: Wiley.

Checkland P.B. (1981b) Rethinking a Systems Approach. *Journal of Applied Systems Analysis* **8**(3): 3–14.

Checkland, P.B. and Holwell, S. (1998) *Information, Systems and Information Systems: Making Sense of the Field.* Chichester: Wiley.

Checkland, P.B. and Scholes, J. (1990) *Soft Systems Methodology in Action.* Chichester: Wiley.

Cherns, A. (1976) The Principles of Socio-technical Design. *Human Relations* **9**(8): 783–792.

Cherns, A. (1987) Principles of Socio-technical Design Revisited. *Human Relations* **40**(3): 153–162.

Ciborra, C.U. (ed.) (1996) *Groupware and Teamwork: Invisible Aid or Technical Hindrance.* Chichester: Wiley.

Clarke, S.A. (1997) Critical Complementarism and Information Systems: A Total Systems Approach to Computer-based Information Systems Strategy and Development. PhD thesis, University of Brunel, Uxbridge, UK.

Clarke, S.A., Lehaney B. and Martin, S. (1998) A Theoretical Framework for Facilitating Methodological Choice. *Systemic Practice and Action Research* **11**(3): 295–318.

Clegg, C., Waterson, P. and Carey, N. (1994) Computer Supported Collaborative Working: Lessons from Elsewhere. *Journal of Information Technology* **9**(2): 85–98.

Clement, A. (1994) Computing at Work: Empowering Action by "Low-Level Users". *Communications of the ACM* **31**(1): 53–63.

Cohen, B. and Zhou, X. (1991) Status Processes in Enduring Work Groups, *American Sociological Review* **56**: 179–188.

Crossan, M.M., Lane, H.W., White, R.E. and Klus, L. (1996) The Improvising Organisation: Where Planning Meets Opportunity. *Organisational Dynamics* Spring: 20–35.

Dasgupta, S. (1991) The Structure of Design Processes. *Advances in Computers* **26**: 1–67.

Davenport, T.H. (1994a) *Process Innovation: Reengineering Work through Information Technology.* Boston: Harvard Business School Press.

Davenport, T.H. (1994b) Saving IT's Soul: Human-Centered Information Management. *Harvard Business Review* **72**: 119–131.

Davenport, T.H., Eccles, R.G. and Prusak, L. (1992) Information Politics. *Sloan Management Review* **34**: 53–65.

Davenport, T.H. and Short, J.E. (1990) The New Industrial Engineering: Information Technology and Business Process Redesign. *Sloan Management Review* Summer **31**(4): 11–27.

Davenport, T.H. and Stoddard, D.B. (1994) Reengineering: Business Change of Mythic Proportions? *Management Information Systems Quarterly* June: 121–127.

Davis, F.D. (1993) User Acceptance of Information Technology: Systems Characteristics, User Perceptions and Behavioral Impacts. *International Journal of Man-Machine Studies* **38**(3): 475–487.

DeLone, W.H. and McLean, E.R. (1992) Information Systems Success: The Quest for the Dependent Variable. *Information Systems Research* **3**: 60–95.

DeSanctis, G. and Scott Poole, M. (1994) Capturing the Complexity in Advanced Technology Use: Adaptive Structuration Theory. *Organization Science* 5(2): 121–147.

Denning, P.J. (1991) Technology or Management? (editorial) *Communication ACM* 4(3): 11–12.

Department of Defence (1998) The Defence Science and Technology Organisation. Updated: 18 September 1998, <http://www.dsto.defence.gov.au> (20 November 1998).

Dillon, A. and Morris, M. (1996) User Acceptance of New Information Technology – Theories and Models. In M. Williams (ed.) *Annual Review of Information Science and Technology* 31: 3–32. Medford, NJ: Information Today.

Drucker, P. (1988) The Coming of the New Organization. *Harvard Business Review* Jan-Feb: 45–53.

Duffy, M. (1993) London's Embarrassing Mistake. *Wall Street and Technology Journal.*

Earl, M.J. and Skryme, D. (1992) Hybrid Managers: What Do We Know about Them? *Journal of Information Systems* 2: 169–187.

Eason, K. (1988) *Information Technology and Organisational Change.* London: Taylor and Francis.

Eckhouse, J. (1999) Bond the New and the Old. *Informationweek* 716 11 January: 108–109.

Eden, C. (1989) Using Cognitive Mapping for Strategic Options Development and Analysis. In J. Rosenhead (ed.) *Rational Analysis for a Problematic World.* Chichester:Wiley: 21–70.

Edstrom, A. (1977) User Influence and the Success of IS Projects: A Contingency Approach. *Human Relations* 30(7): 589–607.

Ehn, P. (1988) *Work Oriented Design of Computer Artefacts.* Stockholm: Arbetslivscentrum.

Eijnatten, F.M. van (1993) *The Paradigm that Changed the Workplace.* Stockholm/Assen: Arbetslivscentrum/Van Gorcum.

Eijnatten, F.M. van and Fitzgerald, L.A. (1998) Designing the Chaordic Enterprise: 21st Century Organisational Architectures that Drive Systemic Self-Transcendence. Paper presented at the 14th EGOS colloquium, Maastricht, 9–11 July 1998.

Eisenhardt, K. (1989) Building Theories from Case Study Research. *Academy Management Review* 14(4): 532–550.

Ellis, C.A., Gibbs, S.J. and Rein, G.L. (1991) Groupware. Some Issues and Experiences. *Communication of the ACM* 34(1): 38–58.

Ellis, C.A. and Wainer, J. (1994) A Conceptual Model of Groupware. In *Proceedings of the Conference on Computer Supported Cooperative Work.* Chapel Hill, NC: 79–88.

Emery, F. (1995) Participative Design: Effective, Flexible and Successful, Now! *Journal for Quality and Participation* 18(1): 6–9.

Emery, F.E. and Emery, M. (1975) Guts and guidelines for raising the quality of working life. In D. Gunzbwg (ed.) *Bringing work to life: The Australian Experience.* Melbourne: Cheshire Publications/Productivity Promotion Council of Australia: 28–54.

Emery, F.E and Trist, E.L. (1961) Socio Technical Systems. In C.W. Churchman and M. Verhulst (eds) *Management Science, Models and Techniques.* Volume 2. Pergammon: 83–97.

Espejo, R. and Harnden, R. (eds) (1987) *The Viable Systems Model: Interpretations and Applications of Stafford Beer's VSM.* Chichester: Wiley.

Feeny, D.F., Earl, M.J. and Edwards, B. (1996) Organizational Arrangements for IS: Roles of Users and Specialists. In M.J. Earl (ed.) *Information Management: The Organisational Dimension.* New York: Oxford University Press: 232–233.

Feeny, D.F. and Willcocks, L.P. (1998) Core IS Capabilities for Exploiting Information Technology. *Sloan Management Review,* Spring: 9–22.

Fielden, K. (1995) A Systemic View of Mediation. Presented at the Australian Systems Conference, 26–26 September, Edith Cowan University, Perth, Australia.

Fisher, J. (1998) Defining the Role of a Technical Communicator in the Development of Information Systems. *IEEE Transactions on Professional Communication* 41(3): 186–199.

Fitzgerald, G. (1990) Achieving Flexible Information Systems: The Case for Improved Analysis. *Journal of Information Technology* 5(1): 5–11.

Fitzgerald, L.A. (1996) *Organisations and Other Things Fractal. A Primer on Chaos for Agents of Change.* Denver, CO: The Consultancy.

Fitzgerald, L.A. (1997) What in the World is the Matter with Systems Thinking? A Critique of Modern Systems Theory and the Practice of "Systems Thinking" it Informs. In Chase (ed.) *Readings of the STS Roundtable, Seattle,Washington: October 21–24.* Northwood, NH: The STS Roundtabl: 41–48.

Fitzgerald, L.A. and Eijnatten, F.M. van (1998) Letting Go for Control: The Art of Managing in the Chaordic Enterprise. *International Journal of Business Transformation* 1(4): 261–270.

Flood, R.L. (1990) *Liberating Systems Theory*. New York: Plenum.

Flood, R.L. (1995) Total Systems Intervention (TSI): A Reconstitution. *Journal of the Operational Research Society* 46: 174–191.

Foucault, M. (1983) The Subject and Power. In H. Dreyfus and P. Rabinow (eds) *Michel Foucault, Beyond Structuralism and Hermeneutics*. Chicago: Chicago University Press.

Freeman, P. (1980) The Central Role of Design in Software Engineering: Implications for Research. In H. Freeman and P.M. Lewis (eds) *Software Engineering*. New York: Academic Press.

Friedman, M. (1992) *Dialogue and the Human Image: Beyond Humanistic Psychology*. Thousand Oaks, CA: Sage Publications.

Friedman, A.L. and Cornford, D.C. Computer Systems Development: History, Organisation and Implementation. Chichester: Wiley.

Fulk, J. and DeSanctis, G. (1995) Electronic Communication for Changing Organisational Forms. *Organization Science.* 6(4): 337–349.

Galbraith, J. (1973) *Designing Complex Organizations*. Reading, MA: Addison-Wesley.

Galbraith. J.R. (1977) *Designing Complex Organisations*. Reading, MA: Addison-Wesley.

Galston, W.A. (1991) *Good, Virtue and Diversity in the Liberal State*. Cambridge: Cambridge University Press.

Gamma, E., Helm, R., Johnson, R. and Vlissides, J. (1995) *Design Patterns: Elements of Reusable Object-oriented Software*. Reading, MA: Addison-Wesley.

Garson, G.D. (1995) *Computer Technology and Social Issues*. New York, USA: Idea Group Publishing.

Garvin, D. (1984) What does 'Product Quality' really mean? *Sloan Management Review* Fall: 25–39.

Gash, D. and Orlikowski, W.J. (1991) Changing Frames: Understanding Technological Change in Organizations. *Academy of Management Proceedings*, 51st Annual Meeting, Miami Beach, FL: 189–193.

Gasser, L. (1986) Integration of Computing and Routine Work. *ACM Transactions on Office Information Systems* 4(3): 205–225.

Geber, B. (1992) Saturn's Grand Experiment. *Training* 29(6): 27–35.

Gelertner, D. (1998) *The Aesthetics of Computing*. London: Weidenfeld & Nicoloson.

Gibbons, Limoges, C., Nowotny, H., Schwarizman, S., Trow, M., Scott, P. (1994) *The New Production of Knowledge*. London: Sage.

Gibson, D.V. (1991) Executive GDSS: Behaviourial Considerations at Individual, Organisational, and Environmental Levels of Analysis. *Journal of Organizational Computing* 1(3):303–322.

Giddens, A. (1984)*The Constitution of Society*. Cambridge: Polity.

Gill, K.S. (1991) Summary of Human-centred Systems Research in Europe (Part 1). *Systemist* 13(1): 7–27.

Gingras, L. and McLean, E.R. (1979) A Study of Users and Designers of Information Systems, *IS working paper 2-79*, Graduate School of Management, UCLA.

Gleick, J. (1987) *Chaos: Making a New Science*. New York: Viking.

Gould, C. (1988) *Rethinking democracy*. Cambridge: Cambridge University Press.

Gouldner, A.W. (1976) *The Dialectic of Ideology and Technology*. London: Macmillan.

Greenbaum, J. and Kyng, M. (1991) Design at Work: Cooperative Design of Computer Systems. Hillsdale, NJ: Lawrence Erlbaum.

Griffin, J.D. (1998) *Dealing with the Paradox of Culture in Management Theory*. PhD thesis, University of Hertfordshire.

Griffin, D., Shaw, P. and Stacey, R. (1997) Knowing and Acting Ethically in Conditions of Uncertainty: A Complexity Perspective. In *Proceedings of the Uncertainty, Knowledge and Skill Conference*, Hasselt, Belgium, 6–8 November.

Grindley, K. (1991) Managing IT at Board Level: The Hidden Agenda Exposed. London: Price Waterhouse, Pitman.

Grover, V., Jeong, S.R., Kettinger, W.J. and Teng, J.T.C. (1995) The Implementation of Business Process Reengineering. *Journal of Management Information Systems* 12(1): 109–144.

Grundin, J. (1998) CSCW: History and Focus. http://www.ics.uci.edu/~grundin/

Gulowsen J. (1972) A Measure of Work-Group Autonomy. In L.E. Davis and J.C. Taylor (eds) *Design of Jobs*. Harmondsworth: Penguin Books: 206–218.

Haak, A.T. (1994) Dutch Sociotechnical Design in Practice: An Empirical Study of the Concept of the Whole Task Group. Assen: Van Gorcum, PhD thesis, University of Groningen.

Habermas, J. and Luhmann, N. (1971) Theorie der Gesellschaft oder Social-Technologie – Was leistet Systemforschung? (Societal Theory or Social Technology – What Accomplishes Systems Research?). Frankfurt am Main: Suhrkampf (in German).

Hackman, J.R. (1981) Sociotechnical Systems Theory: A Commentary. In A.H. van de Ven and W.F. Joyce (eds) *Perspectives on Organization Design and Behavior*. New York: Wiley.

Hackman J.R. (1990) *Groups that Work (and Those that Don't)*. San Francisco: Jossey-Bass.

Hackman, J.R. and Wageman, R. (1995) Total Quality Management: Empirical, Conceptual, and Practical Issues. *Administrative Science Quarterly* 40(2): 309–343.

Hall, G., Rosenthal, J. and Wade, J. (1993) How to Make Reengineering Really Work. *Harvard Business Review* 71(6): 119–131.

Hammer, M. (1996) *Beyond Reengineering*. New York: HarperBusiness.

Hammer, M. and Champy, J. (1993) *Reengineering the Corporation: A Manifesto for Business Revolution*. New York: HarperBusiness.

Hanna, D.P. (1988) Designing Organisations for High Performance. Reading, MA: Addison-Wesley.

Hannon, P.D. and Atherton, A.M. (1997a) The Practice of Building Strategic Awareness Capability in Entrepreneurial Small Firms. In E. Lefebvre and R. Cooper (eds) *Proceedings of the Hasselt Conference on Uncertainty, Knowledge and Skill*, Diepenbeek: Limburg University / Keele University, 7–8 November.

Hannon, P.D. and Atherton, A.M. (1997b) Small Firm Success and the Art of Orienteering: The Value of Plans, Planning, and Strategic Awareness in the Competitive Small Firm. In: E. Lefebvre and R. Cooper (eds) *Proceedings of the Hasselt Conference on Uncertainty, Knowledge and Skill*. Diepenbeek: Limburg University / Keele University, 7–8 November.

Hansen, J.L. and Christensen, P.A. (1995) *Invisible Patterns: Ecology and Wisdom in Business and Profit*. USA: Qorum Books.

Hartwick, J. and Barki, H. (1994) Explaining the Role of User Participation in Information System Use. *Management Science* 40(4): 440–465.

Hayes, F. (1997) Beyond Users: Why one Project Failed. *Computerworld* 31(32): 103.

Heikkilä, J., Nurminen, M.I., Reijonen, P. and Tuomisto A. (1995) Evaluation of the Deployment of a Customer Database System: A Case Study. Unpublished research report, University of Turku (in Finnish).

Hellman, R. (1989) *Approaches to User-Centered Information Systems*. Turku University, Turku, Finland.

Herbst, P. (1974) *Socio-technical Design*. London: Tavistock Publications.

Herzberg, F. (1968) One More Time: How Do you Motivate Employees? *Harvard Business Review* January-February: 53–62.

Hiltz, S.R. and Turoff, M. (1992) Virtual Meetings: Computer Conferencing and Distributed Group Support. In R.P. Bostrom, R.T. Watson and S. Kinney (eds) *Computer Augmented Teamwork*. Van Nostrand Reinhold: 67–85.

Hirschheim, R.A. (1985) *Office Automation: A Social and Organisational Perspective*. IS Wiley Series in Information Systems.

Hirschheim, R. and Klein, H.K. (1989) Four Paradigms of Information Systems Development. *Communications of the ACM* 32(10): 1199–1216.

Hirschheim, R. and Klein, H. (1994) Realizing Emancipatory Principles in Information Systems Development: The Case for ETHICs. *Management Information Systems Quarterly* 18(1): 85–105.

Hitchins, D.K. and Shrivenham, R. (1991) A Unified Systems Hypothesis. In M.C. Jackson (ed.) *Systems Thinking in Europe*. New York: Plenum: 207–214.

Hoffman, T. (1998) Winning Weapons. *Computerworld*, Premier 100 Supplement, 16 November: 17–20.

Holti, R. and Sutton, D.C. (1992) Towards a Definition of "the" Socio-technical Approach, [WWW document] URL: http://www.comlab.ox.ac.uk/oucl/users/john.nicholls/sts.html

Hoogerwerf, E.C. (1998) Opnieuw leren organiseren: Sociotechniek in actietheoretisch perspectief. (Once More, Learning to Organise: Sociotechnical Systems Design in an Action-Theoretical Perspective). Nijmegen: Katholieke Universiteit, PhD thesis (in Dutch).

Hopkins, J.B. (1997) Twenty Five Years before the Class: A Personal Reflection on Changing Times in UK Higher Education. Unpublished paper from an ongoing doctoral project, Open University.

Hopkins, J.B. (1998) Unpublished papers from an ongoing doctoral project, Open University.

Humphrey, W.S. (1996) *Introduction to the Personal Software Process*SM. Reading, MA: Addison-Wesley.

Introna, L.D. (1997) *Management, Information and Power*. London: Macmillan.

Jackson, M.C. (1990) Beyond a System of Systems Methodologies. *Journal of the Operational Research Society* **41**(8): 657–668.

Jackson, M.C. and Keys, P. Towards a System of Systems Methodologies. *Journal of the Operational Research Society* **35**(6): 473–486.

James, L. and Jones, A. (1976) Organizational Structure: A Review of Structural Dimensions and their Conceptual Relationship with Individual Attitudes and Behavior. *Organizational Behavior and Human Performance* **16**: 74–113.

Jones, J.C. (1980) *Design Methods: Seeds of Human Futures*. 2nd edition. Chichester: Wiley Interscience.

Jones, M. (1994) Don't Emancipate, Exaggerate: Rhetoric, Reality and Reengineering. In R. Baskerville et al. (eds) *Transforming Organizations with Information Technology*. IFIP Transactions. North-Holland, Elsevier Science: 357–377.

Karseras, A. (1996) Collaborative Learning and Action Research Networkommunications. Unpublished paper submitted to the Institute of Education for Postgraduate Certificate in Online Education and Training.

Kauffman, S. (1995) *At Home in the Universe: The Search for the Laws of Complexity*. London: Viking.

Kavanagh, J. (1998) IT Departments Don't Learn the Art of Teamwork, *The Times* (Inter//face//), 2 December.

Kelada J.N. (1996) *Integrating Reengineering with Total Quality*. Milwaukee, WI: ASQC Quality Press.

Kensing, F. and Munk-Madsen, A. (1993) PD: Structure in the Toolbox. *Communications of the ACM* **36**(4): 78–85.

Kensing, F., Simonsen, J. and Bødker, K. (1998) MUST: A Method for Participatory Design. *Human-Computer Interaction* **13**:167–198.

Kesti, J., Kirveennummi, M. and Tuomisto, A. (1995) Evaluation of the Deployment of a University Library Acquisition System: A Case Study. Unpublished research report, University of Turku, (in Finnish).

King, J. (1995) High Level Requirements Analysis: The Design and Development of Information Systems in Complex Institutional Settings. Invited keynote presentation at the First IFIP 8.6 Working Conference on Diffusion and Adoption of Information Technology, Oslo.

Kirveennummi, M. and Tuomisto, A. (1997) From Participation in ISD to Improvements in Organization. In Design of Computing Systems: Cognitive Considerations, Proceedings of the 7th International Conference on Human-Computer Interaction, HCI International '97: 817–820.

Kirveennummi, M. and Tuomisto, A. (1998) Effective Participation in Information Systems Development: The Work Portfolio Approach. In Proceedings of the 6th European Conference on Information Systems, ECIS '98, Aix-en-Provence, France: 31–43.

Klein, H.K. and Hirschheim, R. (1993) 'An Application of Neohumanist Principles in Information Systems Development', in *Human, Organisational and Social Dimensions of Information Systems Development*, eds Avison, D., Kendall, J.E. and DeGross, J.I. A-24: 263–280.

Koestler, A. (1967) *The Ghost in the Machine*. London: Hutchinson.

Krackhardt, D. (1994) Graph Theoretical Dimensions of Informal Organizations. In K. Carley and M. Prietula (eds) *Computational Organization Theory*, Hillsdale, NJ: Lawrence Erlbaum.

Krogt, F.J. van der (1995) Leren in netwerken: Veelzijdig organiseren van leernetwerken met het oog op humaniteit en arbeidsrelevantie (Learning in Networks: The Many-Faceted Job of Organising Learning Networks in Order to Achieve Humanity and Work Relevance). Utrecht: Lemma (in Dutch).

Land, F.F. and Hirschheim, R.A. (1983) Participative Systems Design: Rationale, Tools and Techniques. *Journal of Applied Systems Analysis* **10**: 91–107.

Landauer, T. (1995) *The Trouble with Computers*. Cambridge, MA: MIT Press.

LaPlante, A. (1994) No Doubt about IT. *Computerworld* **28**(33): 79–86.

Lave, J. and Wenger, E. (1991) *Situated Learning: Legitimate Peripheral Participation*. Cambridge: Cambridge University Press.

Leavitt, H. (1958) *Managerial Psychology*. Chicago: University of Chicago Press.

Lee, M.S., Trauth, E.M. and Farwell, D. (1995) Critical Skills and Knowledge Requirements of IS Professionals: A Joint Academic/Industry Investigation. *Management Information Systems Quarterly* September: 313–337.

Lehaney, B. and Clarke, S.A. (1997) Critical Approaches to Information Systems Development: Some Practical Implications. In F.A. Stowell et al. (eds) *Systems for Sustainability: People, Organizations, and Environments*. New York: Plenum: 333–338.

Lehr, U. *Psychologie des Alterns*. Heidelberg Wiesbaden: Quelle und Meyer.

Leonard-Barton, D. (1988) Implementation as Mutual Adaptation of Technology and Organization. *Research Policy* **17**: 251–267.

Lipnack, J. and Stamps, J. (1997) *Virtual Teams. Reaching across Space, Time, and Organizations with Technology*. New York: John Wiley & Sons.

Littig, P. (1997) Lernende Organisation in der Praxis – Erste Ergebnisse aus der Studie "Das Lernende Unternehmen. In U. Witthaus and W. Wittwer (eds) *Vision einer lernenden Organisation. Herausforderung für die betriebliche Bildung*. Bielefeld: Bertelsmann: 53–68.

Lockett, M. (1989) *The Factors behind Successful IT Innovation*. Oxford: Oxford Institute of Information Management and Templeton College: 6.

Lorenz, E.N. (1963) Deterministic Nonperiodic Flow. *Journal of the Atmospheric Sciences* **20**(2): 130–141.

Luhmann, N. (1984) *Soziale Systeme: Grundriss ener allgemeinen Theorie* (Social Systems: Foundations for a General Theory). Frankfurt am Main: Suhrkamp (in German).

Lundquist, E.T. and Huston, M.M. (1990) Information-Rich Environments for Continuous Organic Development in Organisations: Research in Progress. *Journal of Applied Systems Analysis* **17**: 79–87.

Lyytinen, K. and Hirschheim, R. (1987) Information Systems Failures: A Survey and Classification of the Empirical Literature. In *Oxford Surveys in Information Technology*. Oxford: Oxford University Press: 257–309.

MacCarthy, F. (1994) *William Morris: A Life for Our Time*. London: Faber & Faber.

McCarthy, J. (1994) The State-of-the-art of CSCW: CSCW Systems, Cooperative Work and Organisation. *Journal of Information Technology* **9**(2): 73–83.

McConnell, D. (1994) *Implementing Computer Supported Cooperative Learning*. Kogan Page.

McKeen, J.D., Guimaraes, T. and Wetherbe, J.C. (1994) The Relationship Between User Participation and User Satisfaction: An Investigation of Four Contingency Factors. *Management Information Systems Quarterly* **18**(4): 427–451.

Main, T. (1985) Some Psychodynamics of Large Groups. In A.D. Colman and M.H. Geller (eds) *Group Relations Reader 2*. A.K.Rice Institute Series.

Manganelli, R.L. and Klein, M.M. (1994) *The Reengineering Handbook. A Step-by-Step Guide to Business Transformation*. New York: American Management Association (Amacom).

Markides, C. (1998) Strategic Innovation in Established Companies. *Sloan Management Review* Spring: 31–42.

Maslow, A.H. (1943) A Theory of Human Motivation. *Psychological Review* **50**: 370–396.

Merry, U. (1995) *Coping with Uncertainty: Insights from the New Sciences of Chaos, Self-Organisation and Complexity*. New York: Praeger.

Midgley, G. (1995a) What is this Thing Called Critical Systems Thinking. In K. Ellis et al. (eds) *Critical Issues in Systems Theory and Practice*. New York: Plenum: 61–71.

Midgley, G. (1995b) Mixing Methods: Developing Systemic Intervention. Hull University Research Memorandum, No. 9.

Milgrom, P., Roberts, J. (1990) The Economics of Modern Manufacturing: Technology, Strategy, and Organization. *The American Economic Review* **80**: 511–528.

Miller, E.J. (ed.) (1999) *The Tavistock Institute Contribution to Job and Organisational Design*, Dartmouth (forthcoming).

Mirl, E. (1998) Managing Change in a Socio-technical Environment. http://www.nemonline.org/mirl/ec/change.htm

Mollon, P. (1994) *The Fragile Self: The Structure of Narcissistic Disturbance and its Therapy*. Jason Aronson Inc.

Morgan, G. (1977) *Images of Organisation*. 2nd edition. London: Sage.

Morgan, G. (1986) *Images of Organization*. New York: Sage.

Mumford, E. (1983a) *Designing Human Systems, The ETHICS Approach*. Manchester: Manchester Business School.

Mumford, E. (1983b) *Designing Participatively*. Manchester: Manchester Business School,.

Mumford, E. (1984) *Designing Human Systems for New Technology: The ETHICS Method*. Manchester: Manchester Business School.

Mumford, E. (1985) Defining System Requirements to Meet Business Needs: A Case Study Example. *The Computer Journal* 28(2): 97–104.

Mumford, E. (1987) Sociotechnical Systems Design; Evolving Theory and Practice. In G. Bjerknes, P. Ehn and M. Kyng (eds) *Computers and Democracy: A Scandinavian Challenge*. Aldershot: Avebury:59–76.

Mumford, E. (1993) *Designing Human Systems for Health Care: The ETHICS Method*. Rotterdam: 4C Corporation.

Mumford, E. (1995a) *Effective Systems Design and Requirements Analysis – The ETHICS Approach*. London: MacMillan Press.

Mumford E. (1995b) Book Review of Hammer, M. and Champy J. "Reengineering the Corporation: A Manifesto for Business Revolution". *European Journal of Information Systems* 4:116–120.

Mumford, E. (1996) *Systems Design: Ethical Tools for Ethical Change*. Basingstoke: Macmillan.

Mumford, E. (1997) The Reality of Participative Systems Design: Contributing to Stability in a Rocking Boat. *Information Systems Journal* 7: 309–322.

Mumford, E. and Macdonald, B. (1989) Xsel's Progress: The Continuing Story of an Expert System. Chichester: Wiley.

Mumford, E. and Sutton, D.C. (1991) The Computer Bulletin, *The British Computer Society* IV(3), 6 August:12–15.

Mumford, E. and Weir, M. (1979) *Computer Systems in Work Design: The ETHICS Approach*. London: Associated Business Press; New York: Wiley.

Munkvold, B.E. (1998) Implementation of Information Technology for Supporting Collaboration in Distributed Organizations. Dr.ing. thesis 1988:40, The Norwegian University of Science and Technology, Trondheim.

Navarro, J.J. (1994) Computer Supported Self-Managing Teams. *Journal of Organizational Computing* 4(3): 317–342.

Nielsen, J. (1993) *Usability Engineering*. Cambridge, MA: Academic Press.

Nonaka, I. and Takeuchi, H. (1995) *The Knowledge-Creating Company: How Japanese Companies Create the Dynamics of Innovation*. Oxford: Oxford University Press.

Norman, D.A. (1998) *The Invisible Computer: Why Good Products Can Fail, the Personal Computer is so Complex, and Information Appliances are the Answer*. Cambridge, MA: MIT Press.

Nurminen, M.I. (1988) *People or Computers: Three Ways of Looking at Information Systems*. Lund: Studentlitteratur & Chartwell Bratts.

Nurminen, M.I. (1991) Information Systems in Transaction Networks. In P. van den Besselaar, A. Clement and P. Järvinen (eds) *Information System, Work and Organization Design*. Amsterdam: North-Holland: 3–21.

Nurminen, M.I., Kesti, J. and Reijonen P. (1994) Evaluation of the Deployment of a Purchasing System: A Case Study. Unpublished research report, University of Turku (in Finnish).

O'Neill, J. (1998) Social Learning: Preliminary Findings of a Pilot Study (DSTO-CR-0098), DSTO, Department of Defence.

Oliga, J.C. (1991) Methodological Foundations of Systems Methodologies. In R.L. Flood and M.C. Jackson (eds) *Critical Systems Thinking: Directed Readings*. Chichester: Wiley: 159–184.

Oravec, J.A. (1996) *Virtual Individuals, Virtual Groups: Human Dimensions of GroupWare and Computer Networking*. Cambridge: Cambridge University Press.

Orkikowski, W.J. (1996) Evolving with Notes: Organizational Change around Groupware Technology. In C.U. Ciborra (ed.) *Groupware and Teamwork: Invisible Aid or Technical Hindrance*. Chichester: Wiley: 23–60.

Page, D., Williams, P. and Boyd, D. (1993) *Report of the Public Enquiry into the London Ambulance Service*. London: HMSO.

Pasmore, W.A. (1988) *Designing Effective Organizations: The Sociotechnical Systems Perspective*. New York: John Wiley & Sons.

Pasmore, W., Francis, C., Haldeman, J. and Shani, A. (1982) Sociotechnical Systems: A North American Reflection on Empirical Studies of the Seventies. *Human Relations* 35: 1179–1204.

Pava, C. (1986) Redesigning Sociotechnical Systems Design: Concepts and Methods for the 1990s. *Journal of Applied Behavioral Science* 22: 201–221.

Perls, F.S., Hefferline, R.F. and Goodman, P. (1972) *Gestalt Therapy*. Souvenir Press Ltd.

Perrow, C. (1983) The Short and Glorious History of Organizational Theory. In J.R. Hackman, E. Lawler and L. Porter (eds) *Perspectives on Behavior in Organizations*. New York: McGraw-Hill: 90–97.

Perry, B. (1984) Enfield: A High Performance Work System. Bedford, MA: Digital.

Pevsner, N. (1991) *Pioneers of Modern Design: From William Morris to Walter Gropius* (first published in 1936 under the heading *Pioneers of the Modern Movement*). Harmondsworth: Penguin Books.

Piaget, J. (1952) *The Child's Concept of Number*. London: Routledge & Kegan Paul.

Poell, R.F. and Krogt, F.J. van der (1997) Organising Work-Related Learning Projects. *International Journal of Training and Development* 1(3): 181–190.

Polster, E. and Polster, M. (1973) *Gestalt Therapy Integrated*. New York: Vintage Books.

Poster, M. (1990) *The Mode of Information*. London: Polity Press.

Potter, J. and Wetherell, M. (1994) Discourse and Social Psychology: Beyond Attitudes and Behaviour. London: Sage.

Prather, C.W. (1996) How's Your Climate for Innovation. *R & D Innovator* May 1996. http://www.thinking.net/CRPage1.html

Preece, J., Rogers, Y., Sharp, H., Benyon, D., Holland, S. and Carey, T. (1994) *Human-Computer Interaction*. Wokingham: Addison-Wesley. Qualitative Research: http://www.auckland.ac.nz/msis/isworld.

Raghavan, S., Zelesnik, G. and Ford, G. (1994)*Lecture Notes on Requirements Elicitation*, (Doc. No. CMU/SEI-95-EM-10) Carnegie Mellon University.

Remenyi, D. (1997) Risk and the Management of Information Systems. *Management Accounting – London* 75(2): 54.

Rittel, H.W. and Webber, M. (1973) Dilemmas in a General Theory of Planning. *Policy Sciences* 4: 155–169.

Rogers, E.M. (1995) *Diffusion of Innovations*. 4th edition. New York: The Free Press.

Ross, D. (1991) *The Origins of American Social Science*. Cambridge: Cambridge University Press.

Rudy, I. (1996) A Critical Review of Research on Electronic Mail. *European Journal of Information Systems* 4(4): 198–213.

Sackman, H. (1974) Computers and Social Options. In E. Mumford and H. Sackman (eds) Human Choice and Computers. Amsterdam: North-Holland.

Sanchez, R. and Heene, A. (1997) *Strategic Learning and Knowledge Management: The Strategic Management Series*. Chichester: Wiley.

Saunders, C., Robey, D. and Vaverek, K. (1994) The Persistence of Status Differentials in Computer Conferencing. *Human Communication Review* 20(4): 443–472.

Savage, C.M. (1996) 5th Generation Management: Co-creating through Virtual Enterprising, Dynamic Teaming, and Knowledge Networking. Revised edition. Newton: Butterworth Heinemann.

Scarbrough, H. and Manton, S. (1997) *BPRC Focus Group: The Relevance and Contribution of Socio Technical Systems*. http://bprc.warwick.ac.uk/focus4.html

Schein, E. (1994) Innovative Cultures and Organizations. In T.J. Allen and M.S. Scott Morton (eds) Information Technology and the Corporation of the 1990s. New York: Oxford University Press: 125–146.

Schön, D.A. (1983) *The Reflective Practitioner: How Professionals Think in Action*. New York: Basic Books.

Schrage, M. (1995) *No More Teams*. New York: Doubleday.

Schuler, D. (1994) Community Networks: Building a Participatory Medium. *Communications of the ACM*. **37**(1):39–51.

Scott, J. (1991) *Social Network Analysis*. Thousand Oaks, CA: Sage Publications.

Scott-Morton, M.S. (ed.) (1991) *The Corporation of the 1990s: Information Technology and Organizational Transformation*. New York: Oxford University Press.

Seely-Brown, J. (1996–97) The Human Factor. *Information Strategy* December–January.

Senge, P.M. (1992) *The Fifth Discipline: The Art and Practice of the Learning Organization*. Sydney: Random House.

Shaw, P. (1997) Intervening in the Shadow Systems of Organisations: Consulting from a Complexity Perspective. *Journal of Organizational Change Management* **10**(3): 235–250.

Simon, H.A. (1973) The Structure of Ill-Structured Problems. *Artificial Intelligence* **4**: 181–200.

Sitter, L.U. de. (1993) A Sociotechnical Perspective. In F.M. van Eijnatten (ed.) *The Paradigm that Changed the Workplace*. Stockholm/Assen: Arbetslivscentrum/Van Gorcum: 158–184.

Sitter, L.U. de, Hertog, J.F. den and Dankbaar, B. (1997) From Complex Organisations with Simple Jobs to Simple Organisations with Complex Jobs. *Human Relations* **50**(5): 497–534.

Solomon, C. (1991) Behind the Wheel at Saturn. *Personnel Journal* **70**(6): 72–74.

Sproull, L. and Kiesler, S. (1986) Reducing Social Context Cues: Electronic Mail in Organizational Communication. *Management Science* **32**(11): 1492–1512.

Sproull, L. and Kiesler, S. (1991) *Connections, New Ways of Working in the Networked Organisation*. Cambridge, MA: MIT Press.

Stacey, R.D. (1996) *Complexity and Creativity in Organisations*. San Francisco: Berrett-Koehler.

Stacey, R.D. (1993) *Strategic Management and Organisational Dynamics*. London: Pitman.

Stacey, R.D. (1997) *Complexity and Creativity in Organisation*. London: McGraw-Hill.

Stowell, F.A. and West, D. (1991) Client Participation in Information Systems Design. In M.C. Jackson (ed.) *Systems Thinking in Europe*. New York: Plenum.

Suchman, L.A. (1987) *Plans and Situated Actions: The Problem of Human–Machine Communication*. Cambridge: Cambridge University Press.

Susman G.I. (1976) *Autonomy at Work. A Sociotechnical Analysis of Participative Management*. New York: Praeger Publishers.

Sutton, D.C. and Sutton, M.M. (1990) Wheels within Wheels: A Development of Traditional Socio-technical Thinking. *Management Education and Development* **21**(2): 122–132.

Taylor, J.C. and Felten, F.F. (1993) *Performance by Design: Sociotechnical Systems in North America*. Englewood Cliffs, NJ: Prentice-Hall.

Thompson, P. (1991) *The Work of William Morris*. Oxford: Oxford University Press.

Tichy, N. and Fombrun, C. (1978) Network Analysis in Organizational Settings. *Research Paper* 102A, New York, Columbia University, Graduate School of Business.

Toffler, A. (1980) *The Third Wave*. London: Collins.

Tomsho, R. (1994) How Greyhound Lines Re-engineered Itself Right into a Deep Hole. *Wall Street Journal* 20 October: A1.

Torkzadeh, G. and Doll, W.J. (1993) The Place and Value of Documentation in End User Computing. *Information and Management* **24**: 147–158.

Trist, E.L. (1981) The Socio-Technical Perspective. The Evolution of Sociotechnical Systems as a Conceptual framework and as an Action Research Program. In A. van de Ven and W.F. Joyce (eds) *Perspectives on Organization Design and Behavior*. New York: John Wiley & Sons: 49–75.

Trist, E.L. (1993) A Socio-Technical Critique of Scientific Management. In E. Trist, and H. Murray (eds) *The Social Engagement of Social Science: A Tavistock Anthology*. Volume 2: *The Socio-Technical Perspective*. Philadelphia: University of Pennsylvania Press: 580–598.

Trist, E.L. and Bamforth, K.W. (1951) Some Social and Psychological Consequences of the Long Wall Method of Coal-Getting. *Human Relations* **4**(1): 6–24 and 37–38.

Trist, E.L., Higgin, G., Murray, H. and Pollock, A.B. (1963) *Organisational Choice*. London: Tavistock.

Trist, E.L. and Murray, H. (1993) *The Social Engagement of Social Science: A Tavistock Anthology*. Volume 2. *The Socio-Technical Perspective*. Philadelphia: University of Pennsylvania Press: 294–302

Tushman, M. (1977) Special Boundary Roles in the Innovation Process. *Administrative Science Quarterly* **22**: 587–605.

Varela, F., Thompson, E. and Rosch, E. (1991) *The Embodied Mind*. Cambridge, MA: MIT Press.

Von Hellens, L.A. (1995) Quality Management Systems in Australian Software Houses: Some Problems of Sustaining Creativity in the Software Process. *Australian Journal of Information Systems* September: 14–24.

Von Hellens, L.A. (1997) Information Systems Quality versus Software Quality: A Discussion from a Managerial, an Organisational and an Engineering Viewpoint. *Information and Software Technology* 39: 801–808.

von Krogh, G. and Roos, J. (eds) (1996) *Managing Knowledge: Perspectives on Cooperation and Competition.* London: Sage.

Vreede, G.J. (1998) Collaborative Business Engineering with Animated Electronic Meetings. *Journal of Management Information Systems* 14(3): 141–164.

Wah, L. (1998) The Risky Business of Managing IT Risks. *Management Review* 87(5): 6.

Walsham, G. (1993) *Interpreting Information in Organisations.* Chichester: Wiley.

Wanninger, L.A. and Dickson, G.W. (1992) Phased Systems Design, Development, and Implementation: Process and Technology. In K.E. Kendal (ed.) *The Impact of Computer Supported Technologies.* Amsterdam: Elsevier.

Watzlawick, P. (1989) *Muenchhausen's haren en Wittgenstein's ladder: uit de greep van de werkelijkheid* (Muenchhausen's hairs and Wittgenstein's ladder: Out of the Grip of Reality). Deventer: Van Logchum Slaterus (in Dutch).

Weil, M. (1998) More Important than Ever. *Manufacturing Systems* October: A1–A12.

Weil, S. (1998) Rhetorics and Realities in Public Service Organizations: Systemic Practice and Organizational Learning as Critically Reflexive Action Research (CRAR). *Systemic Practice and Action Research* 11(1): 37–62.

Weil, S. (1999) Recreating Universities for "Beyond the Stable State": From "Dearingesque" Systematic Control to Post-Dearing Systemic Learning and Inquiry. *Journal of Systems Research and Behavioural Science* 16(2).

Weisbecker, A., Frings, S. and Supe, G.S. (1997) PROMPT – Organisationsgestaltung und Methoden für menschengerechte Software-Entwicklungsprozesse. In Fraunhofer-Institut für Arbeitswirtschaft und Organisation (ed.) *Software-Technologien in der Praxis.* Stuttgart: 1–24.

Weitzman, E.A. and Miles, M.B. (1995) *Computer Programs for Qualitative Data Analysis.* Thousand Oaks: Sage.

Wetherbe, J.C. and Vitalari, N.P. (1994) Systems Analysis and Design: Best Practices. St Paul, MN: West.

Whitaker, R. (1997) Computer Supported Cooperative Work (CSCW) and Groupware: Overview, Definitions and Distinctions. http://www.informatik.umu.se/~rwhit/cscw.htm

Wilson, P. (1991) Computer Supported Cooperative Work (CSCW): Origins, Concepts and Research Initiatives. *Computer Networks and ISDN Systems* 23: 91–95.

Winfield, I. (1991) *Organisations and Information Technology: Systems, Power and Job Design.* London: Blackwell Scientific Publications.

Winograd, T. (1989) Letter to editor. *Communication ACM* 32(12): 1412–1413.

Winograd, T. and Flores, F. (1988) Understanding Computers and Cognition: A New Foundation for Design. Norwood, NJ: Ablex Corporation.

Woodward, K. (1980) *The Myths of Information technology and Post-Industrial Culture.* Cambridge: Cambridge University Press.

Wynne, B. (1991) May Sheep Safely Graze? A Reflexive View of the Expert-Lay Knowledge Divide. In S. Lash, B. Szerszynski and B. Wynne (eds) *Risk, Environment and Modernity.* London: Sage.

Yontef, G.M. *Awareness, Dialogue and Process: Essays on Gestalt Therapy.* The Gestalt Journal Press Inc.

Zack, M. and McKinney, J. (1995) Social Context and Interaction in Ongoing Computer-Supported Management Groups. *Organization Science* 6(4): 394–422.

Zee, H.J.M. van der (1995) Het ontwikkelen van een theorie voor de praktijk. (Developing a Theory for Practice). *Opleiding en Ontwikkeling* 5: 49–56 (in Dutch).

Zmud, R.W. and Cox, J.F. (1979) The Implementation Process: A Change Approach. *Management Information Systems Quarterly* 3(2): 35–43.

Zuboff, S. (1988) *In the Age of the Smart Machine.* New York: Heinemann.

Index

255